WITHDRAWN
UTSA Libraries

International Political Economy Series

Series Editor: Timothy M. Shaw, Visiting Professor, University of Massachusetts, Boston, USA and Emeritus Professor, University of London, UK

Titles include:

Leslie Elliott Armijo (*editor*)
FINANCIAL GLOBALIZATION AND DEMOCRACY IN EMERGING MARKETS

Robert Boardman
THE POLITICAL ECONOMY OF NATURE
Environmental Debates and the Social Sciences

Jörn Brömmelhörster and Wolf-Christian Paes (*editors*)
THE MILITARY AS AN ECONOMIC ACTOR
Soldiers in Business

Stuart S. Brown (*editor*)
TRANSNATIONAL TRANSFERS AND GLOBAL DEVELOPMENT

Gerard Clarke and Michael Jennings (*editor*)
DEVELOPMENT, CIVIL SOCIETY AND FAITH-BASED ORGANIZATIONS
Bridging the Sacred and the Secular

Gordon Crawford
FOREIGN AID AND POLITICAL REFORM
A Comparative Analysis of Democracy Assistance and Political Conditionality

Fred P. Gale
THE TROPICAL TIMBER TRADE REGIME

Meric S. Gertler and David A. Wolfe
INNOVATION AND SOCIAL LEARNING
Institutional Adaptation in an Era of Technological Change

Anne Marie Goetz and Rob Jenkins
REINVENTING ACCOUNTABILITY
Making Democracy Work for the Poor

Andrea Goldstein
MULTINATIONAL COMPANIES FROM EMERGING ECONOMIES
Composition, Conceptualization and Direction in the Global Economy

Mary Ann Haley
FREEDOM AND FINANCE
Democratization and Institutional Investors in Developing Countries

Iain Hardie
FINANCIALIZATION AND GOVERNMENT BORROWING CAPACITY IN EMERGING MARKETS

Keith M. Henderson and O. P. Dwivedi (*editors*)
BUREAUCRACY AND THE ALTERNATIVES IN WORLD PERSPECTIVES

Jomo K.S. and Shyamala Nagaraj (*editors*)
GLOBALIZATION VERSUS DEVELOPMENT

Angela W. Little
LABOURING TO LEARN
Towards a Political Economy of Plantations, People and Educationin Sri Lanka

José Carlos Marques, and Peter Utting (*editors*)
BUSINESS, POLITICS AND PUBLIC POLICY
Implications for Inclusive Development

S. Javed Maswood
THE SOUTH IN INTERNATIONAL ECONOMIC REGIMES
Whose Globalization?

John Minns
THE POLITICS OF DEVELOPMENTALISM
The Midas States of Mexico, South Korea and Taiwan

Philip Nel
THE POLITICS OF ECONOMIC INEQUALITY IN DEVELOPING COUNTRIES

Pia Riggirozzi
ADVANCING GOVERNANCE IN THE SOUTH
What are the Roles for International Financial Institutions in Developing States?

Lars Rudebeck, Olle Törnquist and Virgilio Rojas (*editors*)
DEMOCRATIZATION IN THE THIRD WORLD
Concrete Cases in Comparative and Theoretical Perspective

Eunice N. Sahle
WORLD ORDERS, DEVELOPMENT AND TRANSFORMATION

Suzana Sawyer and Edmund Terence Gomez (*editors*)
THE POLITICS OF RESOURCE EXTRACTION
Indigenous Peoples, Multinational Corporations and the State

Benu Schneider (*editor*)
THE ROAD TO INTERNATIONAL FINANCIAL STABILITY
Are Key Financial Standards the Answer?

Matthew A. Schnurr and Larry A. Swatuk (*editors*)
NATURAL RESOURCES AND SOCIAL CONFLICT
Towards Critical Environmental Security

Adam Sneyd
GOVERNING COTTON
Globalization and Poverty in Africa

Howard Stein (*editor*)
ASIAN INDUSTRIALIZATION AND AFRICA
Studies in Policy Alternatives to Structural Adjustment

Peter Utting, Shahra Razavi and Rebecca Varghese Buchholz (*editors*)
THE GLOBAL CRISIS AND TRANSFORMATIVE SOCIAL CHANGE

William Vlcek
OFFSHORE FINANCE AND SMALL STATES
Sovereignty, Size and Money

International Political Economy Series

Series Standing Order ISBN 978-0-333-71708-0 hardcover
Series Standing Order ISBN 978-0-333-71110-1 paperback
(*outside North America only*)

You can receive future titles in this series as they are published by placing a standing order. Please contact your bookseller or, in case of difficulty, write to us at the address below with your name and address, the title of the series and one of the ISBNs quoted above.

Customer Services Department, Macmillan Distribution Ltd, Houndmills, Basingstoke, Hampshire RG21 6XS, En

Natural Resources and Social Conflict

Towards Critical Environmental Security

Edited by

Matthew A. Schnurr
Assistant Professor, Department of International Development, Dalhousie University, Canada

and

Larry A. Swatuk
Associate Professor and Director, International Development Programme, School of Environment, Enterprise and Development (SEED), University of Waterloo, Canada

Introduction, selection and editorial matter © Matthew A. Schnurr and Larry A. Swatuk 2012
Individual chapters © contributors 2012

All rights reserved. No reproduction, copy or transmission of this publication may be made without written permission.

No portion of this publication may be reproduced, copied or transmitted save with written permission or in accordance with the provisions of the Copyright, Designs and Patents Act 1988, or under the terms of any licence permitting limited copying issued by the Copyright Licensing Agency, Saffron House, 6–10 Kirby Street, London EC1N 8TS.

Any person who does any unauthorized act in relation to this publication may be liable to criminal prosecution and civil claims for damages.

The authors have asserted their rights to be identified as the authors of this work in accordance with the Copyright, Designs and Patents Act 1988.

First published 2012 by
PALGRAVE MACMILLAN

Palgrave Macmillan in the UK is an imprint of Macmillan Publishers Limited, registered in England, company number 785998, of Houndmills, Basingstoke, Hampshire RG21 6XS.

Palgrave Macmillan in the US is a division of St Martin's Press LLC,
175 Fifth Avenue, New York, NY 10010.

Palgrave Macmillan is the global academic imprint of the above companies and has companies and representatives throughout the world.

Palgrave® and Macmillan® are registered trademarks in the United States, the United Kingdom, Europe and other countries.

ISBN 978–0–230–29783–8

This book is printed on paper suitable for recycling and made from fully managed and sustained forest sources. Logging, pulping and manufacturing processes are expected to conform to the environmental regulations of the country of origin.

A catalogue record for this book is available from the British Library.

A catalog record for this book is available from the Library of Congress.

10 9 8 7 6 5 4 3 2 1
21 20 19 18 17 16 15 14 13 12

Printed and bound in the United States of America
by Edwards Brothers Malloy

Contents

List of Tables and Figures	vii
Preface	viii
Notes on Contributors	x
List of Acronyms	xiv

1	Towards Critical Environmental Security *Matthew A. Schnurr and Larry A. Swatuk*	1
2	What Are We Really Looking For? From Eco-Violence to Environmental Injustice *Peter Stoett*	15
3	Climatic Security and the Tipping Point Conception of the Earth System *Chris Russill*	33
4	Insecurities of Non-Dominance: Re-Theorizing Human Security and Environmental Change in Developed States *Wilfrid Greaves*	63
5	Water and Security in Africa: State-Centric Narratives, Human Insecurities *Larry A. Swatuk*	83
6	Avoiding the Resource Curse in Ghana: Assessing the Options *Peter Arthur*	108
7	Sexual Violence, Coltan and the Democratic Republic of Congo *Shelly Whitman*	128
8	Official Secrets and Popular Delusions: Security at the End of the Fossil Fuel Age? *Shane Mulligan*	152
9	Securing Alberta's Tar Sands: Resistance and Criminalization on a New Energy Frontier *Philippe Le Billon and Angela Carter*	170

| 10 | The State-Corporate Nexus: Trading Social Benefits for Environmental Costs and Localized Vulnerability
Chris Arsenault | 193 |
| 11 | Bodies on the Line: The In/Security of Everyday Life in Aamjiwnaang
Sarah Marie Wiebe | 215 |

Afterword: Ecoviolence, Security, Geopolitics 237
Simon Dalby

Index 244

List of Tables and Figures

Tables

5.1 Selected data on Nile Basin states highlighting HDI, population structure, access to water and sanitation — 96

5.2 Selected data on Nile Basin states highlighting GDP, project agricultural output and cities — 97

Figures

5.1 Poor, rural populations remain at a disadvantage in accessing clean drinking water — 91

8.1 World crude oil production – EIA — 154

9.1 Major US and world media reports on tar sands and environmental issues — 179

Preface

This collection of essays emerged out of an international conference entitled 'Environmental Violence and Conflict: Implications for Global Security', which took place in Halifax, Nova Scotia, in February 2010. This conference brought together a wide array of scholars, policymakers and activists to evaluate the role of the non-human environment in precipitating and perpetuating violence. The meeting was made possible by a grant from the Canadian Department of National Defense (DND) under its Security and Defence Forum Special Project Fund. One of the key aims of the conference was to foster deeper engagement between the security and environmental communities, whose expertise are too often isolated from each other. We also hoped to promote dialogue and understanding among key analysts and actors in order to better position states, communities, non-governmental and inter-governmental organisations to confront emerging threats to environmental security.

What emerged out of this conference was a deep critique of the dominant, state-centric discourse regarding the place of 'the environment' in security studies. Perhaps this was to be expected, given the widely shared philosophical viewpoints of the people attending the meeting. However, many of the participants were unknown or only partly known to each other, working separately on diverse issues of environmental (in)security, and the too-often negative impacts of state-centric approaches to 'securing' the environment, but held together by a common interest in the scholarship of Simon Dalby and others writing from the perspective of critical political ecology. The meeting was characterized by a series of '*Ah ha!*' moments, where the not-so-obvious connections between, for example, peak-oil 'denialists', coltan resource mafias and the health of Canadian Aboriginal peoples were made plain. For us, both organizers and participants, these were exciting entry points to investigate how issues of security reflect broader patterns of political struggle and social control. As the editors, we have tried to distil these findings down to their essence while preserving the breadth and diversity of the individual case studies. We hope that, at minimum, this collection helps further discussion and encourage sustained research regarding the role and place of 'critical environmental security'.

As the editors, we wish to thank a number of people who helped us bring this collection to publication. The staff and faculty of Dalhousie's

Centre for Foreign Policy Studies and the Department of International Development Studies were instrumental in making the workshop a success: many thanks to Shannon Langton, Shelly Whitman and David Black for all their hard work. We also wish to thank all those who participated in the Halifax workshop; we hope that we have captured some of the liveliness of that meeting in this collection. Corrine Cash, Ann Griffiths and Mohsin Farooque provided important editorial assistance. IPE Series Editor, Timothy Shaw, and Palgrave Macmillan Senior Commissioning Editor, Christina M. Brian, provided helpful advice and encouragement throughout the publishing process. Anonymous reviewers provided important insights and critiques as the project moved from rough draft to final product. Larry Swatuk would like to thank his wife, Corrine Cash, for her steadfast support. Never once has she questioned his sanity – at least not to his face. Matthew Schnurr thanks his spouse, Natalie Rosen, for her constant encouragement. Together they would like to dedicate this work to Louis Isaac Schnurr, in the hope that these discussions about environmental security will lead toward a more equitable and sustainable future for his generation.

Notes on Contributors

Chris Arsenault is a journalist with Al Jazeera English based in Doha, Qatar and author of the book *Blowback: A Canadian History of Agent Orange and the War at Home*.

Peter Arthur is Associate Professor of Political Science and International Development Studies at Dalhousie University, Canada. He received his Ph.D. in Political Science in 2001 from Queen's University, Canada. His research interests include issues relating to the contribution of small-scale enterprises in development, electoral politics in Ghana, capacity development and post-conflict reconstruction, and the promotion of good governance in Africa. His work has been published in a number of edited volumes and journals, including *Africa Today*, *African Studies Review*, *Commonwealth and Comparative Politics* and *Journal of Contemporary African Studies*.

Angela Carter is Assistant Professor of Political Science and Environmental Studies at Memorial University of Newfoundland's Grenfell Campus, where she has played a lead role in establishing the Environmental Policy Institute and Master of Arts in Environmental Policy programme. She holds an M.A. (Carleton), M.A. (Cornell) and a Ph.D. (Cornell). Carter researches comparative environmental policy regimes surrounding oil developments in key Canadian and American cases. She is currently a collaborator on a Social Sciences and Humanities Research Council Strategic Research Grant, 'The Environmental Assessment Processes of Canadian "Frontier" Oil and Gas', with principal investigator Dr Gail Fraser and Dr Anna Zalik.

Simon Dalby is Professor of Geography, Environmental Studies and Political Economy at Carleton University. Professor Dalby's research work concerns critical geopolitics, environmental security and political ecology and how these matters link up with discussions of empire, the war on terror and contemporary modes of metropolitan insecurity. He is co-editor of *Rethinking Geopolitics* (Routledge, 1998), *The Geopolitics Reader* (Routledge, 1998, 2006) and the scholarly journal *Geopolitics*, and author of *Environmental Security* (University of Minnesota Press, 2002) and *Security and Environmental Change* (Polity, 2009).

Wilfrid Greaves is a Ph.D. candidate at the Munk School of Global Affairs and the Department of Political Science at the University of Toronto, where his research examines security, resource development and environmental change in the Canadian and circumpolar Arctic regions. An SSHRC Doctoral Fellow, his work has been published in *The Journal of Military and Strategic Studies*, *The Pearson Papers* and *International Journal* (forthcoming in 2012). A graduate of the University of Calgary and Bishop's University, his other research interests include security theory, Canadian foreign policy, multilateral peacebuilding, and the international mission in Afghanistan.

Philippe Le Billon is Associate Professor at the University of British Columbia with the Department of Geography and the Liu Institute for Global Issues. He has published widely on the links between natural resources and armed conflicts, but also on the political economy of war and corruption. He is the author of *Wars of Plunder: Conflicts Profits and the Politics of Resources* (Hurst/Columbia UP, 2012), *Fuelling War: Natural Resources and Armed Conflicts* (IISS/Routledge, 2005) and is the editor of *The Geopolitics of Resource Wars* (Cass, 2005). His current research focuses on extractive sector governance and geographies of violence.

Shane Mulligan completed his doctorate at Cambridge University, UK, in 2004, and finished a SSHRC Postdoctoral Fellowship at the University of Waterloo in 2010. He spent several of the intervening years studying energy, and especially fossil fuel depletion, through the lens of international relations. He now works as a consultant with renewable energy co-operatives in the Waterloo Region, while striving to develop realistic expectations and relevant skills for an energy-poor future.

Chris Russill is Associate Professor in the School of Journalism and Communication at Carleton University, Ottawa, Canada. He completed his Ph.D. in communication at Penn State, and his M.A. and B.A. at York University. His research focuses on global environmental communication and the emerging media infrastructure for observing and modelling the earth. He has written widely on climate change communication with special attention to the examples of Al Gore, Stephen Schneider, James Hansen, 350, The Weather Channel, Heidi Cullen, the UN and advocates for applying open-source principles to climate change science.

Matthew A. Schnurr is Assistant Professor in the department of International Development Studies at Dalhousie University, Halifax, Canada. He completed his Ph.D. in Geography at the University of British

xii Notes on Contributors

Columbia, his M.A. in Geography at the School of Oriental and African Studies, London, and his B.Sc. in Biology at Queen's University, Kingston. He is an environmental geographer with research interests in environment and development, agricultural biotechnology, political ecology and environmental history, with a geographic focus on eastern and southern Africa. His work appears in a number of journals, including *Review of African Political Economy*, *Journal of Southern African Studies*, and *Journal of Historical Geography*.

Larry A. Swatuk is Associate Professor and Director of the International Development programme in the School of Environment, Enterprise and Development (SEED) at the University of Waterloo, Canada. Dr Swatuk has been a visiting professor or research fellow at Rhodes University, University of Western Cape, National University of Lesotho and the African Centre for Development and Strategic Studies in Nigeria. For about two decades he has investigated and written about the potential for natural resources to act as catalysts for cooperative behaviour among states and communities.Among his recent publications are the co-edited collection (with Lars Wirkus) *Transboundary Water Governance in Southern Africa: Examining Underexplored Dimensions* (Nomos Press, 2009), and a conflict resolution training manual written for Cap-Net, the UNDP-supported Capacity Building Network for Integrated Water Resources Management (available free online at www.cap-net.org).

Peter Stoett is Professor of Global Politics at the Department of Political Science, Concordia University. His main areas of expertise include international relations and law, global environmental politics, human rights and Canadian foreign policy. In 2012 he will sit as the Fulbright Visiting Research Chair in Canadian-American Relations at the Woodrow Wilson Center in Washington. Professor Stoett has conducted research in Europe (including the Balkans), eastern, southern and western Africa, Central America, and Asia. He is the author/editor of seven books, including (with Christopher Gore) *Environmental Challenges and Opportunities: Local-Global Perspectives on Canadian Issues* (Edmond Montgomery, 2009), (with Eric Laferriere) *International Ecopolitical Theory: Critical Reflections* (UBC Press, 2006) and (with Allen Sens) *Global Politics: Origins, Currents, and Directions,* Fourth Edition (Toronto: ITP Nelson, 2010).

Shelly Whitman is Deputy Director for the Centre for Foreign Policy Studies, Dalhousie University, and Project Director of the Child Soldiers Initiative. In addition, she lectures in Political Science and International Development Studies. From 2000 to 2002, she was Head of Research for the Inter-Congolese Dialogue. From 2002 to 2007, she was Lecturer in Political Science at the University of Botswana. Dr Whitman also was a Research Consultant at UNICEF Headquarters in New York. She worked directly for Ambassador Stephen Lewis on the OAU Panel to investigate the Rwanda Genocide, and has worked on projects related to small arms and light weapons, gender and security.

Sarah Marie Wiebe is a Ph.D. candidate in Canadian politics and public policy at the School of Political Studies, University of Ottawa. Her dissertation, titled *Place Politics: Ecological Citizenship in Canada's Chemical Valley*, explores the ecological politics of citizen engagement in this region of south-western Ontario. The dissertation examines conceptions of the relationship between bodies, land and the environment, with a particular focus on the impact of pollution on a First Nations Community, the Aamjiwnaang First Nation. Her work examines the role of 'place' in Canadian public health policy. In addition to her ongoing research, she is the Graduate Student Representative for the Canadian Political Science Association.

List of Acronyms

3G	Third Generation Mobile Telecommunications
ACIA	Arctic Climate Impact Assessment
AMCOW	African Ministers' Council on Water
APO	After Peak Oil
BC	British Columbia
BP	British Petroleum
BPO	Before Peak Oil
CBC	Canadian Broadcasting Corporation
CCS	Carbon Capture and Storage
CDC	Centers for Disease Control and Prevention
CEMA	Cumulative Environmental Management Association
CEO	Chief Executive Officer
CEPAC	*Communaute des Eglises de Pentecote en Afrique Centrale*
CEQ	Council of Environmental Quality
CFA	Cooperative Framework Agreement
CHS	Commission on Human Security
CIA	Central Intelligence Agency
CNDP	*Congres National pour le Defense de les Peuples*
CNOOC	China National Offshore Oil Corporation
COP	Conference of the Parties
CSIS	Canadian Security Intelligence Service
CSOs	Civil Society Organizations
DDT	Dichlorodiphenyltrichloroethane
DFAIT	Department of Foreign Affairs and International Trade (Canada)
DOD	Department of Defense
DRC	Democratic Republic of the Congo
DTCB	Diamond Trading Company Botswana
DTI	Department of Trade and Industry
EDC	Endocrine Disrupting Chemicals
EEZ	Exclusive Economic Zone
EIA	Energy Information Administration
EISA	Energy Independence and Security Act (US)
EITI	Extractive Industries Transparency Initiative
ENGOs	Environmental Non-Governmental Organisations
ENSO	El Nino Southern Oscillation

EU	European Union
FAO	Food and Agricultural Organisation
FARDC	*Forces Armées de la Republique Démocratique du Congo*
FBI	Federal Bureau of Investigation (US)
FCPA	Foreign Corrupt Practices Act
FDLR	*Forces Democratique pour la Liberation du Rwanda*
FEMA	Federal Emergency Management Agency
G8	Group of Eight Highly-Industrialized Countries
GAO	Government Accountability Office
GDP	Gross Domestic Product
GHG	Greenhouse Gases
GIS	Global Imaging System
GNP	Gross National Product
GNPC	Ghana National Petroleum Corporation
GPRA	Ghana Petroleum Regulatory Authority
GSM	Global System for Mobile Telecommunications
HDI	Human Development Index
HIV/AIDS	Human Immunodeficiency Virus/Acquired Immunodeficiency Syndrome
ICC	International Criminal Court
ICISS	International Commission on Intervention and State Sovereignty
ICO2N	Integrated Carbon Dioxide Network
IEA	International Energy Agency
ILO	International Labour Organization
IMF	International Monetary Fund
INSET	Integrated National Security Enforcement Team
IPCC	Intergovernmental Panel on Climate Change
IPCS	International Programme on Chemical Safety
IR	International Relations
IWRM	Integrated Water Resources Management
LCD	Liquid Crystal Display
MAB	Mediation and Arbitration Board
MDGs	Millennium Development Goals
MNCs	Multinational Corporations
MOE	Ministry of the Environment (Canada)
MONUC	United Nations Organization Mission in the Democratic Republic of the Congo
MONUSCO	United Nations Organization Stabilization Mission in the Democratic Republic of the Congo
NAFTA	North American Free Trade Agreement

NBI	Nile Basin Initiative
NDC	National Democratic Congress (Ghana)
NDP	New Democratic Party
NEB	National Energy Board (Canada)
NEPAD	New Partnership for Africa's Development
NGO	Non-Governmental Organisation
Nile-COM	Council of Ministers of Water Affairs of the Nile Basin
NPP	New Patriotic Party (Ghana)
NRDC	Natural Resources Defense Council
OECD	Organisation of Economic Cooperation and Development
OEPA	Ontario Environmental Protection Agency
OGC	Oil and Gas Commission
OGCA	Oil and Gas Commission Act (British Columbia)
OPEC	Organisation of Petroleum Exporting Countries
PARECO	Coalition of Congolese Patriotic Resistance
PCB	Polychlorinated Biphenyl
PDAs	Personal Digital Assistants
PHAC	Public Health Agency of Canada
POPs	Persistent Organic Pollutants
RBC	Royal Bank of Canada
RCMP	Royal Canadian Mounted Police
RET	Radical Environmental Targeting
SADC	Southern African Development Community
SAGD	Steam Assisted Gravity Drainage
SAPs	Structural Adjustment Programmes
SOMIGL	Société Minère des Grands Lacs
SSA	Sub-Saharan Africa
SSHRC	Social Sciences and Humanities Research Council (Canada)
STOP	Stop Tar Sands Operations Permanently
US	United States
UK	United Kingdom
UN	United Nations
UNDP	United Nations Development Programme
UNEP	United Nations Environment Programme
UNODC	United Nations Office on Drugs and Crime
WEO	World Energy Outlook
WHO	World Health Organization
WLAP	Ministry of Water Land and Air Protection (British Columbia)
WSSD	World Summit on Sustainable Development

1
Towards Critical Environmental Security

Matthew A. Schnurr and Larry A. Swatuk

Introduction

The year 2012 marks the twentieth anniversary of the United Nations Conference on Environment and Development (commonly called the Earth Summit) held at Rio de Janeiro, and the tenth anniversary since Rio's follow-up meeting at Johannesburg, the World Summit on Sustainable Development (WSSD). Much of our thinking about 'the environment' has been transformed since Rio, but much too has remained unchanged. As 'the world' gears up for Rio +20, this introductory essay begins with a brief reflection on what has changed and what has stayed the same within the intersections of environment and security over the past 20 years. Our focus then shifts to the directions we would like to see both the analysis and practice of 'environmental security' move in the immediate term – that is, a move towards critical environmental security.

An old world order: Environment and security since Rio

The term 'environmental security', which refers to the complex relationships between environmental change and violent conflict, first gained prominence in both scholarly and policy circles in the year 1990, triggered by significant events in both international security and global environmental politics (Matthew et al., 2010: 11). The fall of the Berlin Wall and the end of apartheid in South Africa overthrew long-standing understandings of national security, while the lead-up to the first Earth Summit in Rio provided an opportunity to operationalize the transformative notion of sustainable development, coined in the 1987 World Commission on Environment and Development's report *Our Common*

Future. This confluence of events led many scholars and policy experts to begin questioning the links between global security and environmental politics, with a particular focus on the environmental causes of violent conflict.

Early research in this area, such as that by the Canadian scholar Thomas Homer-Dixon focused on 'acute conflict probability' – that is, the likelihood that environmental change and inadequate state responses would lead to large-scale violent conflict (Homer-Dixon and Blitt, 1998). These insights allowed Homer-Dixon and his research team to develop a generalizable model explaining the role that resource scarcity plays in directly inciting violence (Homer-Dixon, 1999). Despite Homer-Dixon's findings that environmental change in and of itself was unlikely to be a primary driver of conflict (particularly in the absence of other social drivers such as a history of warfare between states), and that in the area of renewable resources, sub-state violence that was persistent, diffuse and low level was far more likely as an outcome, an endless stream of 'resource wars' studies have been published, many of which remain light on empirical evidence but heavy on 'doom and gloom' predictions (Klare, 2001 being the seminal study in this regard).

The major check on this linear understanding of resource scarcity as a causal factor precipitating violence emerged from the realm of Political Ecology, which seeks to combine insights from political economy and the ecological sciences to better understand human-environment relations. Political ecologists challenged Homer-Dixon's Neo-Malthusian logic predicated on causal linkages between increasing populations, diminishing resources and resulting conflict (Le Billon, 2001; Peluso and Watts, 2001). Refusing to begin their analyses with the presumption of resource scarcity, these scholars argued that the study of environmental violence 'should begin with the precise and changing relations between political economy of access, control, and struggle over environmental resources' (Floyd, 2008: 5). Political ecologists sought to uncover the range of economic, social, cultural and political processes that structure the relationship between environment and violence, with particular emphasis on the inequities created by social and environmental change. Their goal was to produce empirically rich, detailed studies of the conditions that determine outcomes in a particular context, stressing 'the importance of historical, geographic, and spatial specificities of resource-related conflict, and their embeddedness within conflicts broader than the spaces of the resources themselves' (Peluso and Vangergeest, 2011: 354). Political ecologists further stressed that resource abundance could drive violence as much as scarcity (Watts, 2004; Le Billon, 2008), a reality driven home by larger statistical studies on the 'resource curse' or the 'paradox of plenty' (Sachs and Warner, 2001; Collier and Goderis, 2007). For our purposes, the most significant insights into the study of environmental security over the past decade concerns the dangers of securitization, which understands security as a form of 'social practice' that transforms the meanings and outcomes associated with it. Labelling the environment as a security issue limits the linguistic possibilities to those revolving around 'survival, urgency, and emergency. It allows for exceptional measures, the breaking of otherwise binding rules and governance by decrees rather than by democratic decisions' (Trombetta, 2008: 588). Once an issue is securitized, the logic of security necessarily follows: environmental issues normally handled in the democratic realm are transformed into emergency politics, which erodes transparency and accountability, instils fear, and curtails political freedoms (Newman, 2010). The real-world consequences of this transformation are significant: the discourse of securitization expands state monopolization of the issue and serves to legitimize the security agenda of the wealthy elite by targeting the poor as threats to both affluence and political stability (Barnett, 2000; Dalby, 2000). Security, Ken Booth reminds us, is a 'powerful political concept; it is the sort of word that energizes opinion and moves material power' (Booth, 2005: 23).

The general trends and spatial distribution of environmental change today looks much the same as it did when articulated so dramatically in the years immediately preceding Rio: climate change; deforestation; soil erosion, degradation and desertification; biodiversity loss; point source and diffuse air, land and water pollution; coastal and marine degradation; depletion of fish stocks (cf. Homer-Dixon, 1991; Matthew, Barnett and O'Brien, 2010). While the issues haven't changed, what has changed has been the increased depth and breadth of these problems, as well as the increasing alarmist rhetoric regarding their implications for global security (MEA, 2005). Simon Dalby (2009) ominously predicts that the scale of human influence on the biosphere has heralded a new era, the Anthropocene, in which the security implications of environmental change will be impossible to ignore.

A new world order: Human security and environmental change

The most significant change in terms of how issues of environment and security have been understood since the Rio conference has been the emergence of the paradigm of human security. Human security was first introduced by the United Nations Development Programme in its 1994 *Human Development Report*, which identified environmental, alongside economic, health, food, personal, community and political components, as a vital element of any individual's security, stressing the 'all-encompassing' and 'integrative' qualities of what it means to be secure (UNDP, 1994: 24). Human security thus shifted the referent object of security from the state to the individual, suggesting that true security can only be achieved if it moves beyond the long-standing focus on state-centric threats and national defence.

Human security represents a pluralizing of security to include considerations and concerns that were previously deemed to be beyond its purview (Dalby, 2002, 2009). It allows for analytical space to consider the myriad processes that can undermine security, including poverty, gender inequity, disease, malnutrition, environmental degradation, as well as insufficiencies in rights, justice and access. In this way human security becomes largely indistinguishable from human development, in recognizing that one's security is intrinsically connected to freedom and dignity (Matthew et al., 2010). This powerful recognition allows us to move beyond state-centric security orthodoxy to include considerations such as human rights, the impact of globalization, trade imbalances and the consumption patterns, which had previously been considered outside the scope of security studies. Human security thus opens up space for alternative strategies for achieving security, including redistributive mechanisms, reduced consumption or debt repayment.

In reality, though, the paradigm of human security has rarely attained its radical potential. Its most voracious critics are scholars of critical security studies who reject human security for its commitment to political realism, suggesting that its proponents shy away from more emancipatory possibilities for fear of losing touch with the policy world (Booth, 2007). Critics accuse human security of being statist and serving as a hegemonic discourse that furthers powerful interests by transforming political issues into security ones (Newman, 2010: 87). What is needed, these scholars suggest, is a more radical critique that understands knowledge as socially constructed, and is willing to challenge the prevailing order, values and institutions – such as the primacy of the nation state, and the importance of the military as the purveyor of security – that uphold and perpetuate the prevailing worldview of security, one that is 'top-down, statist, power-centric, masculinized, ethnocentric, and militarized' (Booth, 2005: 9).

The most important contribution to move beyond human security has been made by Jon Barnett, whose analytical approach shifted the focus from one premised on examining how environmental change threatened the privileged position of those living in security, to one which began with exploring the conditions that perpetuate a lack of security among vulnerable populations (Barnett, 2001, 2007, 2008). Barnett (2007: 5) thus succeeded in shifting the analytical focus from a study of environmental security to a study of environmental *in*security, that is, a focus on 'the vulnerability of individuals and groups to critical adverse effects caused directly or indirectly by environmental change'. He argues that environmental violence can be both direct (e.g. resource scarcity catalyzes conflict between groups, a la Homer Dixon) or structural (whereby vulnerable groups experience the negative implications of environmental change based on the 'inequitable distribution of economic opportunities, political freedoms, social opportunities, transparency guarantees, and protective security' (2007: 6). Within this formulation the problems of environmental degradation and insecurity become inseparable, both a function of meta-processes of development in the industrialized North at the expense of underdevelopment in the industrializing South. This emphasis on structural violence alongside direct violence allows for an approach to environmental insecurity that resonates with theories of environmental justice; to redress environmental insecurity means tackling issues of social injustice and inequality head-on. Such an approach implies 'that environmental security necessitates fundamental reform of the global political economy, and reform of the socially and ecologically degrading features of modernity' (Barnett, 2000: 8–9). True security can thus only be achieved by transforming the 'odious configurations of power and authority' that perpetuate these inequities (Williams, 2007: 1023).

Critical environmental security

Following Barnett, this volume seeks to de-essentialize and deconstruct prevailing claims about environmental security, while maintaining a balance between perspectives that are both critical and policy relevant (Krause and Williams, 1997). Our volume seeks to tackle Ken Booth's (2005: 9) challenge to 'rethink security from the bottom-up', by providing a holistic perspective on environmental insecurity: one that focuses simultaneously on cause (global, economic, political, modernity), context (history, culture) and effects (health, natural disasters, slow cumulative changes, accidents, conflict). Such an approach – which we term 'critical environmental security' – begins with analytical questions that are too often left out of studies premised on maintaining conditions of security.

Whose security is being secured? Who defines conditions of security? How do changing degrees of control and access over the environment contribute to insecurity? How can we transform the conversation over environmental security into one of environmental justice? We argue that such penetrating questions are best answered through empirically grounded, context-specific studies that underscore how issues of security reflect broader patterns of political struggle and social control. Take, for example, the declining coastal fisheries in Namibia in the 1990s. Namibia was newly independent in 1990 and had a demonstrated incapacity to defend and manage its coastal waters, particularly the deep sea which was rife with European commercial fishers who treated these resources as 'open access', so leading to a 'tragedy of the commons'. Some deep-sea stocks have never recovered. At the same time, the inland fishery was negatively affected by mid-1990s macro-ocean current events (e.g. El Nino Southern Oscillation or ENSO) resulting in temporary but significant declines in important commercial species such as pilchard and anchovy. Taken together, these events constituted a significant challenge to the Namibian society and economy (Moyo, O'Keefe and Sill, 1993). But were they 'security' issues?

The deep-sea fishery issue directly impacted marine biodiversity but did not directly affect the Namibian economy or society as neither was involved in the competition for these resources. However, what was at stake was the potential loss of future benefits (e.g. income, employment, economic diversification, wealth creation) that might accrue to the Namibian economy and society if and when national capacity to develop and manage the deep-sea fishery was improved. In addition, these deep-sea activities were a challenge to the new Namibian state's sovereignty, and were thus regarded as an important security issue by state actors.

Showing it had the capacity to police and defend its own borders became a priority for Namibia's government. Among other things, the government declared a 200 nautical mile exclusive economic zone and turned to several international organizations and donors to assist it in the establishment of this 'border'. Since then, the government has become an active member in numerous marine- and fisheries-related international and regional organizations and associations. It has developed a National Fisheries Master Plan that is structured around an 'ecosystem approach' in line with the terms and conditions of its various memberships (see http://www.fao.org/fishery/countrysector/FI-CP_NA/en, accessed on 17 June 2011). While there have been numerous ups and downs in developing this sector, the general result is a vibrant fishery that contributes significantly to national GDP, employment, food and livelihood security, and foreign exchange earnings. The government's focus on an integrated (land/sea) ecosystem approach is in recognition of the need to plan for periodic ecological disruptions to the fishery (e.g. the El Nino and La Nina southern oscillation events) and to land-based activities (e.g. due to drought and flood). Beyond the fisheries sector, Namibia also participates in regional climate-related and disaster management information sharing and capacity building activities. There is much speculation regarding climate change impacts on the ENSO, as well as land-based extreme weather events across Southern Africa (Mohamed-Katerere, 2010). How a state 'prepares' for unseen and little understood threats of an environmental nature requires a perspective considerably different from a direct challenge to a state's sovereignty through the plunder of its marine resources.

As a 'developing' country with a primarily arid environment, and a 2010 per capita GDP estimated at US$4149 (UNDP, 2010), Namibia's capacity to deal with recurrent, relatively predictable, or sudden, primarily unanticipated, or slow developing but large-impact climate changes is limited. The lessons learned from the early to mid-1990s resource 'war' (even if, in the Clausewitzian sense, it was 'by other means') and ENSO events suggest that state security as well as longer-term human security were enhanced by coordinated government response: Namibia's capacity to assert its sovereignty was improved, the fisheries sector has developed and shown both growth and stability, and the natural resource base is better managed. In the immediate term of the ENSO event, however, small fishers were driven out of the sector, many of whom migrated to urban areas in search of work. Boats and equipment were eventually sold to larger operators.

'Security' looks very different depending on the filter one uses to view and interpret these events. As described earlier, aside from 'policing' the 200 nautical mile EEZ, there seems to be very little role for the military – the traditional security actor. Indeed, 'sectoral restructuring' following a prolonged ENSO event is described by some as nothing more than the natural economic order of things: the strong survive. Privatization of the economy under neoliberal globalization is also regarded this way, despite the fact that 47% of the population suffer from 'multi-dimensional poverty' (UNDP, 2010: 162) and stand not to benefit from these processes (Levine, 2007). In the absence of a direct military threat from another state, Namibian 'state security' seems to revolve around enhancing the capacity of the economy to absorb a youthful labour force in meaningful employment. But how to do this? When faced with a discreet challenge, such as transgression of the EEZ, it is relatively easy for state actors to identify the 'threat' and to determine appropriate remedial action. But when the challenge is multifaceted and diffused – such as persistent, historically based underdevelopment – it is not clear how to move forward quickly with collective purpose particularly when the negative consequences of underdevelopment are unevenly distributed across the society. Namibia's Gini coefficient of income inequality is 74.3, making it the most unequal society on earth (UNDP, 2010: 153). Clearly, some actors benefit from economic stability and restructuring that may in fact reduce the livelihood choices and life chances of others. Put differently, one person's 'security' is another person's 'insecurity'.

The Namibian case underlines the importance of broadening our understanding of security beyond state-centrism in order to understand how environmental change impacts political, economic and social instability. Starting with questions surrounding the impetus of environmental change and the uneven implications of securitizing the environment reveals the unequal distribution of benefits that emerged in this case: this new framing produces both winners (the state's marine policing capacity, large fishing operations) and losers (poor fishermen driven out of the sector). Only through understanding the specifics of Namibian history and politics can we interpret the outcomes of its crisis of marine environmental insecurity.

This collection and its contributions

In our view, because of powerful actors' persistence for thinking about environmental security as the implications of changing resource endowments for state security, and as an issue primarily for powerful actors and their networks to deal with, alternative conceptions which focus on rights, justice and access remain marginalized within this state-centrist discourse. Our collection seeks to redress this limitation by privileging alternative conceptions and understandings of environmental security. Our aim is to encourage new ways of thinking about the theories and practices of environmental security, by focusing on three major themes.

Multi-scalar analyses and sensibilities

Many of the chapters in this book grapple with questions of the appropriate scale at which to begin piecing together the puzzle of environment and security. Contributors are unanimous in rejecting the primacy of the state as the preferred level of analysis for exploring these issues. Many stress the omissions and erasures that result from this tendency to privilege the national scale of analysis above all others. A trend in political ecology is to regard the state as an inadequate level of analysis for investigations of environmental (in)security. A state-centred focus marginalizes local complexities and livelihood (Peluso and Watts, 2001), which are key to understanding how lived realities are reconfigured by environmental insecurity (Camacho, 1998). Failure to appreciate local livelihood complexity has led to an over-prediction of possible violent conflicts (Barnett, 2000). At the same time, a statist ontology fails miserably in its visions for biosphere sustainability. This critique is most eloquently put forward by Deudney and Matthew (1999: 200): 'Privileging the nation directly conflicts with the "one world" and "global village" sensibility of environmental awareness ... In short, if environmental concerns are wrapped in national flags, the "whole earth" sensibility at the core of environmental awareness will be smothered.'

Contributors are equally suspicious of perspectives that seek to replace the state with another privileged lens of analysis. The current fashion is towards macro-studies of environmental change that investigate how large-scale events such as climate change will impact national governments' varied capacities to cope directly with these events (Matthews et al., 2010; Moran, 2011). The chapters in this book suggest that multiple scales must be taken into account simultaneously. Congruent with political ecology's emphasis on multi-scalar, or nested scales of analysis, these papers integrate international, national, community and individual perspectives in order to reveal the complex and layered interactions that determine environmental insecurity. Swatuk's (Chapter 5) analysis of water and security in Africa, for example, interrogates the assumption that interstate approaches to 'water security' will lead to continental peace and security. He argues that discourses of 'crisis' and 'conflict' privilege high-level interstate planning and action, to the exclusion of those most seriously affected by water insecurity – that is, the rural and peri-urban poor. Moreover, it leads state-makers towards high-modern solutions to water insecurity that appear to benefit sections of African states and societies that already enjoy a high degree of water security. Mulligan, in Chapter 8, interrogates the rhetoric of peak oil by examining the interplay between national and supranational scales in the same analytical frame, suggesting that these interactions across scales are key to understanding widespread reluctance to face impending energy shortages.

Environmental security as environmental justice

The second thread that connects these chapters is a desire to broaden the analytical field of environmental security to encompass questions of environmental justice. Peter Stoett's theoretically rich take on environmental justice serves as the linchpin of this collection (Chapter 2). Stoett's plea for a focus on environmental justice resonates among all of the contributors. Stoett takes issue with the narrow scope of concerns that emerge within the literature on environmental security. He proposes understanding environmental violence as transgressions of environmental justice, which offers both a better conceptual vantage point for understanding the links between the non-human environment and political violence, and a normative programme from which we can move forward with plans and policies to remedy situations where 'chronic inequality or sudden catastrophe have ensured ongoing harm to vulnerable populations'. This is in line with Barnett's (2000: 283) important observation that 'perhaps the more telling question to be examined then is why do people *not* resort to violence?'

Several of our case studies add empirical bricks and mortar to Stoett's theoretical frame by shedding light on the lived realities of vulnerable groups coping with environmental insecurity. Whitman (Chapter 7) narrates the brutal realities faced by women living in the eastern Kivu region of the Democratic Republic of Congo, arguing that the international demand for precious metals such as coltan and tantalum is largely responsible for unprecedented levels of sexual violence. Wiebe (Chapter 11) similarly focuses on the lived experiences of women coping with environmental insecurity among the Aamjiwnaag First Nations. She provides a theoretically rich and locally situated account that underscores how environmental violence literally inscribes itself upon peoples' bodies. Greaves (Chapter 4) focuses on community experiences of insecurity among the Inuit, arguing that dominant narratives of securitization exclude and ignore the environmental realities experienced by non-dominant populations. That these people's human and environmental insecurities are largely invisible in state-centric discussions of violence and environmental change suggests to us the importance of conducting more empirical work that challenges these silences and absences. It also suggests to us that we must challenge dominant discourses of 'security', 'vulnerability' and 'threat' that argue that peace between states is the only valid measure of a desirable world order (Williams, 2007). Following from Stoett, then, these contributions aim to transform the vocabulary of environmental security from one based on territories, threats and defence, to one based on rights, access and justice.

Questioning key assumptions

The third pillar of critical environmental security is a commitment to questioning some of the key assumptions that underpin much of the existing scholarly and policy research. The first pertains to geographic focus. Following in the tradition of Robert Kaplan's seminal essay 'The Coming Anarchy' (1994), widely recognized as the catalyst that popularized environmental issues among security and policy experts, much of the literature on environmental security locates the source of insecurity squarely in the Global South. Accordingly, most scholarly accounts come replete with dramatic projections of swelling numbers of environmental refugees ready to invade the North, or entrenched conflicts among resource poor pastoralists fighting over dwindling food supplies. The primary concern, in this view, is that instability in the South may spill over to threaten prosperity in the North (Dalby, 2002).

Contributors refuse to fall into this trap, emphasizing that environmental insecurity remains deeply embedded in supposedly secure states. The chapters by Arsenault (Chapter 10), and Le Billon and Carter (Chapter 9) both focus on Northern insecurities created by the Alberta Oil Sands. Touted in the United States as a secure alternative to dirty Middle East supplies, each chapter shows that Oil Sands development leads to variable forms of security and insecurity, partly dependent upon geographic proximity to extractive activities and direct dependence on the local natural environment. Contributions by Wiebe and Greaves focus on aboriginal Canadian communities, whose insecurities are often occluded by this bias against recognizing insecurity in supposedly secure states. This focus on 'insecurities of non-dominance', as Greaves puts it, is an attempt to redress this widely held assumption that insecurity can be neatly delineated along geographic lines.

Other contributions take aim at other deeply engrained assumptions that underlie much of the environmental security literature. Russill (Chapter 3) warns against accepting the rhetoric of securitization at face value, suggesting we need to critically interrogate the relationship between science and policy. Using the case study of climate change, his chapter investigates the representative process of securitization, demonstrating how scientific information is selectively incorporated by security agencies to further their own agendas. Arthur (Chapter 6) challenges the inevitability of the resource curse, suggesting that more accountable and transparent environmental governance can help Ghana avoid the trap that has befallen other oil-rich nations in Africa. Similarly, Mulligan challenges dominant representations of energy security, explaining not just how certain discursive formations emerge as dominant, but how other conceptualizations (such as that of peak oil) are suppressed.

Conclusion: Towards a critical environmental security

This collection adds support to the already rich literatures on political ecology and critical security studies whose primary concern is to find a new way of articulating the local and global environmental insecurities and injustices that affect us all, but unequally so. We hope that the reader will find here a few first steps towards articulating a critical analysis of environmental security that dislodges the state as the preferred level of analysis, seeking to understand threats to security in terms of rights, access and justice, and questioning key assumptions that underlie much of the existing literature. Through this lens the focus shifts from environmental security to environmental *in*security, as we attempt to move attention towards understanding how individuals, groups and communities become disadvantaged in terms of their environmental entitlements and how these impact their human security. This will not be easily done, as the hypothesized violence that most animates state actors is the stuff that makes blockbuster Hollywood films. The 'violence' we are talking about, however, often takes a structural form, and is located at the margins of interstate actions and discourses. It is the not-so-tasty, mundane and everyday fare. Locating our analysis within this rubric of insecurity implies a deep level of self-confrontation that connects these essays: a willingness to critically examine our own role (as citizens, as scholars, as activists) in creating conditions of insecurity, and to participate meaningfully in helping to answer Simon Dalby's (2002) foundational question: what kind of social order will we secure for the future?

References

Barnett, J., 2000. 'Destabilizing the Environment-Conflict Thesis'. *Review of International Studies* 26: 271–88.
Barnett, J., 2001. *The Meaning of Environmental Security*. London: Zed Books.
Barnett, J., 2007. 'Environmental Security and Peace'. *Journal of Human Security* 3: 4–16.
Barnett, J., 2008. 'Peace and Development: Towards a New Synthesis'. *Journal of Peace Research* 45: 75–89.
Booth, K., 2005. 'Critical Explorations'. In K. Booth, ed., *Critical Security Studies and World Politics*. Boulder, CO and London, UK: Lynne Rienner Publishers, 1–20.
Booth, K., 2007. *Theory of World Security*. Cambridge, UK: Cambridge University Press.
Camacho, D. E., ed., 1998. *Environmental Injustices, Political Struggles: Race, Class and the Environment*. Durham and London: Duke University Press.

Collier, P. and B. Goderis, 2007. 'Commodity Prices, Growth, and the Natural Resources Curse: Reconciling a Conundrum'. *CSAE Working Paper Series 2007-15*. Oxford: University of Oxford.
Dalby, S., 2000. 'Jousting with Malthus' Ghost: Environment and Conflict after the Cold War'. *Geopolitics* 5: 165-75.
Dalby, S., 2002. *Environmental Security*. Minneapolis: University of Minnesota Press.
Dalby, S., 2009. *Security and Environmental Change*. Cambridge: Polity Press.
Deudney, D. H. and R. A. Matthew, eds, 1999. *Contested Grounds: Security and Conflict in the New Environmental Politics*. Albany: SUNY Press.
Floyd, R., 2008. 'The Environmental Security Debate and its Significance for Climate Change'. *The International Spectator* 43: 51-65.
Homer-Dixon, T., 1991. 'On the Threshold: Environmental Changes as Causes of Acute Conflict, *International Security* 16(2): 76-116.
Homer-Dixon, T., 1999. *Environment, Scarcity and Violence*. Princeton: Princeton University Press.
Homer-Dixon, T. and J. Blitt, eds, 1998. *Ecoviolence*. New York: Rowman & Littlefield.
Kaplan, R. D., 1994. 'The Coming Anarchy'. *Atlantic Monthly* 273(2): 44-76.
Klare, M., 2001. *Resource Wars: The New Landscape of Global Conflict*. New York: Henry Holt and Company.
Krause, K. and M. C. Williams, 1997. 'Preface: Towards Critical Security Studies'. In K. Krause and M. C. Williams, eds, *Critical Security Studies: Concepts and Cases*. Minneapolis: University of Minnesota Press, vii-xxi.
Le Billon, P., 2001. 'The Political Ecology of War: Natural Resources and Armed Conflicts'. *Political Geography* 20(5): 561-84.
Le Billon, P., 2008. 'Diamond Wars? Conflict Diamonds and the Geographies of Resource Wars'. *Annals of the Association of American Geographers* 98(2): 345-72.
Levine, S., 2007. *Trends in Human Development and Human Poverty in Namibia. Background paper to the Namibia Human Development Report*. Windhoek: UNDP (October).
Matthew, R. A., J. Barnett, B. McDonald, K. L. O'Brien, eds, 2010. *Global Environmental Change and Human Security*. Cambridge, MA: MIT Press.
Millennium Ecosystem Assessment (MEA), 2005. *Ecosystems and Human Well-Being: Synthesis*. Washington, DC: Island Press.
Mohamed-Katerere, J., 2010. 'Climate Change, Natural Resource Governance and Human Security in Africa: Charting New Paths'. In B. Kessleman, T. Hughes, C. Kabemba, F. Matose and D. Rocha, eds, *Natural Resource Governance and Human Security in Africa: Emerging Issues and Trends*. Pretoria: Pax-Africa, 85-126.
Moran, D., ed., 2011. *Climate Change and National Security: A Country-Level Analysis*. Washington, DC: Georgetown University Press.
Moyo, S., P. O'Keefe and M. Sill, 1993. *The Southern African Environment: Profiles of the SADCC Countries*. London: Earthscan.
Newman, E., 2010. 'Critical Human Security Studies'. *Review of International Studies* 36: 77-94.
Peluso, N. and M. Watts, eds, 2001. *Violent Environments*. Ithaca: Cornell University Press.
Peluso, N. and P. Vandergeest, 2011. 'Taking the Jungle out of the Forest: Counter-Insurgency and the Making of Natural Reserves'. In R. Peet, P. Robbins and M. J. Watts, eds, *Global Political Ecology*. New York: Routledge, 254-84.

Sachs, J. and A. Warner, 2001. 'The Curse of Natural Resources'. *European Economic Review* 45(4–6): 827–38.
Trombetta, M. J., 2008. 'Environmental Security and Climate Change: Analysing the Discourse'. *Cambridge Review of International Affairs* 21: 585–602.
UNDP (United Nations Development Programme), 1994. *Human Development Report: New Dimensions of Human Security*. New York and Oxford: Oxford University Press.
UNDP (United Nations Development Programme), 2010. *Human Development Report: The Real Wealth of Nations: Pathways to Human Development*. New York and Basingstoke: Palgrave Macmillan.
Watts, M., 2004. 'Resource Curse? Governmentality, Oil and Power in the Niger Delta, Nigeria'. *Geopolitics* 9(1): 50–80.
Williams, P. D., 2007. 'Thinking about Security in Africa'. *International Affairs* 6: 1021–38.

2
What Are We Really Looking For? From Eco-Violence to Environmental Injustice

Peter Stoett

Introduction

The literature on eco-violence and environmental conflict, and its future as an interdisciplinary subfield, has a foundational problem if it is really based on the study of violence. This is because there is no accepted definition of 'violence' itself, and because the use of the term for any purpose other than strictly observing harm is misleading, especially if it is employed as a dependent variable (and it almost invariably is). However, there are conceptions of violence which are very useful indeed to ponder as they relate to the work of those studying eco-violence. In particular, the divide between agential and structural violence is pertinent, and I suggest there are various forms of ecocide which illustrate the dubiousness of their analytic separation (much in line with most resolutions, however unsatisfactory, of the agent-structure debate within International Relations (IR)). I then proceed to suggest that the theme of justice is as, if not more, important as the theme of violence in this work. Scarcity may cause conflict which is manifested in violence. Of course, violence may result in environmental degradation, which in further turn leads to conflict, and I have referred elsewhere to the image of a circle of ecocide derived from this empirically observable chain of events (Stoett, 2000).

But I will argue here that environmental justice is, in fact, a better conceptual vantage point to look for the trouble we seek when examining the links between environmental issues and anthropocentric violence. While interpersonal and other forms of agential violence take place in all contexts, our concern is much more oriented towards structural violence which is shaped by the processes (including agential violence) which contribute to environmental degradation. It is, admittedly, too easy to say that violence, or even the more limited term 'political violence', is best viewed as injustice (or, rather, that injustice, or more specifically environmental injustice, is violence, or eco-violence). But I will end there regardless, with a plea for further reflection on how we can breathe normative life into our collective project. This is not an innovative intervention so much as a call back to basics.

Of course, common sense would dictate that war and extreme exploitation cannot be non-violent, but there is much less consensus about the acceptability of such strategic or instrumental violence (means versus ends arguments) and how all this relates to nature and ecology. Even this brief discussion makes it clear that consensus would be impossible to achieve.[1] We face the additional question, however, of how all this relates to the environment, and to a political geography of violence. I should be clear at the outset that even the less direct terminology often employed, 'environmentally induced conflict' is regarded by many as 'fundamentally flawed, as it relies on preconceived causalities, intermingles eco-centric with anthropocentric philosophies, and neglects the motivations and subjective perceptions of local actors' (Hagmann, 2005: 2). Yet it does direct our attention towards possible links between 'violence' and 'environmental degradation', which is obviously an important association if we value either human life or nature (or both), so we had better have some sort of common understanding about what the former term means. I will begin, however, with what I would argue it does not mean.

Nature is violent: Eco-violence as order and scarcity as causal

I will do my best to dispense with this first as it holds little promise for advancing human or environmental security, but, after a short leap from Hardin (1968) and company, does push us closer to what I consider a vulgar social Darwinism fixated on fantasies about population control. Invasive species, predatory killers, the stalking lioness, the battling rams, bloodthirsty bats, flesh-tearing sharks: no shortage of film footage here, much of it genuine but much more orchestrated to accommodate the camera. The water hole goes dry and all predatory bets are off. And of course there is Hitler's famous statement about the cruelty of nature, which has resonated since Treblinka and Auschwitz changed (almost) everything; Nietzsche's will to power, shallowly interpreted; the need to cull herds on occasion, and slash and burn for the sake of future generations of genetic winners. Eco-violence is not a problem, inherently, and it is often a good thing, and not only because of its evolutionary inevitability: after all, if the spectre of eco-violence can add prescriptive urgency and pragmatic value to the promotion of environmental protection, it can help raise the awareness needed to save our own species from destroying the nest.

I would not venture into the hostile arena of debate over original sin, sociobiology or psychoanalysis without several years more reading as protective clothing. However, I will argue that this perspective is, thankfully, the antithesis of the normative project which animates most research in the area of environmental crises and social conflict today. Though it may well be that '[w]e and the beasts are kin' (Seton, 1898: 12; see also Noske, 1997), the ethical questions raised by invasive species offer an interesting example of how futile a perspective which equates us with them actually is: while they are certainly problematic for the indigenous species they overcrowd, overshadow, devour or out-mate, this does not mean bioinvaders have anything but the best of intentions – survival. It is difficult to pin moral agency on them, even for the most bio-centric of thinkers. However, they are often the result of either accidental or purposeful introductions by human beings (usually through trade and tourism, but also often through military activity; see Stoett, 2007). We routinely speak of responsibility, negligence, even malfeasance, in this respect. At the same time of course we have a vested interest in protecting ourselves from microbial invasions and this extends to the protection of local ecosystems from exogenous bio-assault. (Though many technical responses to bioinvasion are quite ecocidal in nature, they are deemed by most observers to serve a greater good.) We may revert to petri-dish ethics in relation to human population movements, but the array of moral ascriptions is hardly uniform. Moral agency remains both foundational and optically fundamental.

In short, human history (and thus its natural history as well) moves along a continuously evolving path constituted by competing conceptions of justice, not just pecking orders and harem maintenance. Certainly, violence has been a central feature in the journey. Yet this does not preclude thinking outside the limited confines of the neo-Malthusian box of presumptions based on eco-scarcity, especially if it avoids what I refer to as the optical demographic dilemma: blaming population growth for global environmental problems is too easy, ignoring it is too ridiculous. Blaming it is in itself an injury to the human rights and dignity of those people living in overcrowded areas, and its ancillary solutions, including birth control and other depopulation measures, are hardly without their own controversial conceptual frames and historical records of unjust application. But, even if imbalances of wealth and power are taken into account, there is little doubt that population is a factor that cannot be overlooked by conflict analysts.[2]

More to the point perhaps, scarcity itself is not a trustworthy independent variable. As Conca and Wallace suggest, 'much of the eco-conflict literature has invoked "scarcity" without paying attention to how social relations create the conditions for resource capture or other forms of social scarcity.' Conversely, 'the precise mechanisms by which resource wealth may induce or sustain violence remain disputed' (both quotes by Conca and Wallace, 2009: 488). Other studies have suggested there is limited explanatory power to the 'eco-scarcity theory', but poverty and 'dysfunctional institutions' remain central independent variables (Theisen, 2008). Another widespread assumption, that conflict over natural resources is key to explaining the 'new wars' (i.e. civil wars involving a broad range of stakeholders we want to distinguish from the decolonization phase), has also hit obstacles when subject to empirical analysis. Welsch (2008: 503), for example, found that resource conflict did matter, but that the 'negative effect of agricultural resources on conflict probability is almost twice as large as the positive effect of mineral resources' (in other words, scarcity matters, but more in terms of agricultural productivity as a mitigating factor than mineral wars as a causal factor). To be fair to Homer-Dixon's work, he is well aware of the variations on the theme, and I am certainly not equating the scarcity agenda with social Darwinism.[3] Nor do I wish to enter an empirical debate at this stage but merely to accentuate the fact that, while humans are likely to fight over diminished life-sustaining resources, basing an entire subfield of scholarly enquiry on this easy presumption does not provide us with any prescriptive value other than the obvious need to avoid situations where life-sustaining resources are threatened with extinction (an imperative already dictated either by the quest for survival or humanitarian concern). We still need an overarching view of what constitutes violence and justice to give this analytic context and normative animation.

Agential and structural eco-violence

The widely referenced World Health Organization's definition of violence is emblematic of an agential position: 'The intentional use of physical force or power, threatened or actual, against oneself, another person, or against a group or community, that either results in or has a high likelihood of resulting in injury, death, psychological harm, maldevelopment or deprivation' (*World Report on Violence and Health: Summary*, 2002: 4).

The keyword here, of course, is 'intentional'. Structural understandings of mass atrocities often split on this point, since not all participants are intending the effected outcome of the event. Interpersonal violence 'refers to violence between individuals, and is subdivided into family and intimate partner violence and community violence. The former category includes child maltreatment; intimate partner violence; and elder abuse, while the latter is broken down into acquaintance and stranger violence and includes youth violence; assault by strangers; violence related to property crimes; and violence in workplaces and other institutions' (5–6). Collective violence 'refers to violence committed by larger groups of individuals and can be subdivided into social, political and economic violence' (5–6).

There are at least three subtypes of agential eco-violence, or purposeful infliction of harm on ecosystems: ecocide, ecological sabotage and the deliberate or neglectful harm of animals. I will not expand on the last, since this falls within the category of psychopathic behaviour and/or is a manifestation of the food industry which, while quite violent to some, is considered quite routinized and even beneficial to others. The animal rights literature is vast, challenging and beyond the scope of this paper (see Regan, 1983). Elsewhere I have explored both maximalist and minimalist definitions of ecocide (see Stoett, 2000). The former includes everything from driving SUVs, flying to academic conferences and eating dubiously farmed salmon. The latter refers exclusively to the deliberate destruction of nature as part of a military strategy aimed not at destroying nature, but at subjugating an enemy.[4] This is classic agential violence (regardless of the 'just war' question) in which ecosystems suffer, but the end result is of course the prolonged suffering of human populations, and thus an act of indirect collective violence is also committed.

In between we have military preparation, which was an especially deleterious activity during the heights of the Cold War and remains a significant factor today, especially if we include incidentals such as greenhouse gas emissions resulting from military production, weapons shipments, problems related to stored toxic wastes and others. 'Ecological sabotage' refers largely to terrorist activity (conducted by individuals, states or other actors) designed to harm or frighten human populations, but the term is also often used to refer to the actions of radical ecologists resorting to the sabotage of property to protect the natural environment itself.

The study of ecocide in particular needs a resurgence, despite its spiking after the US' Vietnamese campaign as a justice issue and photos of burning oil wells in Kuwait. While most of the eco-violence literature has focused on the Homer-Dixon analytic route (also referred to as the Toronto School in some publications, which may be a first in IR for Canada, though Robert Cox's work has generated such city-based recognition), or 'whether and why environmental scarcity, abundance, or dependence might cause militarized conflict, less research has focused on the environmental impacts of violent conflict, war or military activities' (Khagram and Saleem, 2006: 395). Post-conflict analysis has certainly provided empirical evidence of the environmental costs of war. The UNEP's Post-Conflict and Disaster Management Branch has identified numerous sources of concern in the 17 states it has been charged with investigating, from depleted uranium weaponry in Iraq and Bosnia and Herzegovina to hazardous wastes in Somalia to illegal forestry to Afghanistan (see Conca and Wallace, 2009). Meanwhile, we are moving much closer to an established body of literature on the impact of the ecological costs of displacement resulting from warfare, including competition over local resources between refugees and host communities (Martin, 2005). This includes of course the long-term psychological damage caused by displacement from traditional lands, which 'harms the ecological self and therefore creates an internal sense of alienation' (Ramanathapillai, 2008: 114), further blending the line between agential and structural violence.

It is a fine line, indeed, between the two, especially for social scientists looking at events/contexts from afar (less fine, no doubt, to those in the immediate grip of agential violence, but they would themselves no doubt often refer to the injustice of the situation to contextualize it). One of the foremost theorists on structural violence, J. Galtung paints a 'violence triangle' which consists of direct violence (an event), cultural violence (a permanent phenomenon, as it only changes as cultures change) and structural violence (a process, which fluctuates with power shifts) (1990: 294). He argues that 'violence can start at any corner in the direct-structural-cultural violence triangle and is easily transmitted to the other corners' (302). Violence is defined as 'avoidable insults to basic human needs, and more generally to life, lowering the real level of needs satisfaction below what is potentially possible' (Galtung 1990: 292). The keyword here may be well be 'avoidable'. Again, this raises justice-related questions, since we would not have a concept of justice if we assumed that injustice was unavoidable. Furthering the theme, Uvin argues 'the concept of structural violence draws our attention to unequal life chances, usually caused by great inequality, injustice, discrimination and exclusion and needlessly limiting people's physical, social and psychological well-being' (Uvin, 1998: 105).[5] And Coomaraswamy, quoting Govind Kelkar, in reference to gender-based violence, says: 'A narrow definition of violence may define it as an act of criminal use of physical force. But this is an incomplete concept. Violence also includes exploitation, discrimination, unequal economic and social structures, the creation of an atmosphere of religiocultural and political violence. While violence against women is part of general violence found in the social structures such as class, caste, religion and ethnicity, and in the way the state controls people, it also encompasses aspects of structural violence and forms of control and coercion exercised through hierarchical and patriarchal gender relationships in the family and society' (1995: 21; quote is from Kelkar, 1992).

Audi argues that what Garver (1975) defines as 'quiet institutional violence' (such as systemic social inequalities) should not be defined as violence because 'it confuses the issue to use the emotively loaded word "violence" when the grievance can be better described and treated under another name', such as inequality, because 'misnaming the disease can lead to the use of the wrong medicine – or none at all' (1974: 37–8). I would humbly suggest that our concern with the nexus linking environmental and social conflict should similarly move us away from confusing the occurrence of agential violence and the impacts of structural violence with a mythical separate category labelled 'co-violence'. If Keane's critique of Galtung's definition of structural violence as coming to 'resemble an injustice detector' instead of being a concrete definition (2004: 32) is meaningful, it begs a meaningful question: so what? And why would we not include violence against nature itself within our analytical realm? The meaning of violence itself is framed by dominant elites who control media outlets, educational systems and life opportunities of vulnerable populations. Ridgeway and Jacques (2002) refer to the 1994 Zapatista uprising in Chiapas, Mexico, in this light: the uprising was violent, but the poverty and marginalization which preceded it was not, since it was structural and thus not 'direct' violence. Of course, widespread sympathy for the Zapitistas was perhaps evidence of the widespread recognition of the pernicious nature of structural violence in the first place, as well as its ecological impacts. Yet the support was only a major factor after the violent response to NAFTA's demands became a mass media event. Surely the outrage over the response of Burma's military government to Cyclone Nigris, and the revealed helplessness of the Haitian people following the recent earthquake there, can serve as other prominent examples.

Environmental injustice and systematic eco-violence

Only by defining eco-violence as environmental injustice do we capture both the agential and structural violence, with or without direct intent, described earlier, while emphasizing the importance of links between humans and ecosystems, differentiated spatial and virtual communities, and universal needs and individual responsibilities. Of course, environmental justice has been defined in competing fashions as well (see Schlosberg, 2007) but the crux of the concern here is that certain populations (or individuals) are more likely to be harmed by or suffer the risks associated with environmental problems than others, and this social question needs rectification if we are to deal effectively with those problems. In a concise survey of GIS-related efforts to provide empirical data on this barometer of fundamental inequality, Maantay defines environmental injustice as the 'disproportionate exposure of communities of color and the poor to pollution, and its concomitant effects on health and environment, as well as the unequal environmental protection and environmental quality provided through laws, regulations, government programs, enforcements and policies' (2002: 161). Let us add violence to this equation: agential, when deliberate harm is caused to ecosystems, as well as structural, as when oppressed people suffer disproportionately when environmental conditions worsen by indirect change. Le Billon (2001), for example, writes of the vulnerability resulting from resource dependence (rather than conventional notions of scarcity or abundance) and the opportunities it presents to those prone towards violent assertion of their superiority (including opportunities of armed insurgency).

Maantay's definition is typical of the American environmental injustice movement, much of which has been focused on race as determinative factor (see also Rajan, 2001 for a treatment of the concept in a global context with reference to the Bhopal, India calamity). While it would be problematic to speak categorically of an environmental justice *movement*, the last several decades have seen the rise of increased concern over the fairness implications of pollution in particular, and in both the northern and southern hemispheres, and in both the East and West, before and especially after the advent of what Ulrich Beck has famously referred to as the 'risk society' where risk producers suffer less than risk victims, or those more vulnerable to its deleterious effects (1992). The pursuit of environmental justice is associated with achieving intergenerational justice (Almond, 1995) and interspecies justice (Hayward, 1994; Low and Gleeson, 1998), but it is mostly associated with 'debates about distributional inequalities and the actions needed to address them' (Illsley, 2002: 70). Definitions vary: it is considered 'the fair treatment and meaningful involvement of all people regardless of race, colour, national origin or income, with respect to the development, implementation and enforcement of environmental laws, regulations and policies' (Bullard, 1999: 7); more succinctly, the 'just distribution of environmental goods and bads among human populations' (Dobson, 1998: 20; see also Dobson, 2003).[6]

Much of the literature links racism with differentiated environmental policy, while some borrow from feminist literature (Di Chiro, 1992) and some are more driven by concerns with income and class. When taken as the critical examination of norms, it is fair to say that applying the concept to an international perspective that is enhanced by various critical theories of global politics is an obvious step, one already taken by many analysts concerned about the long-term impact of colonialism and imperialism, the cultural impact of market economies, the effects of various forms of discrimination on life opportunities, the environmental impact of globalization, the necessity of social networking innovations (on rhizomatic organizing see Schlosberg, 1999) and a plethora of other questions. I add political ecology to this formula, which seeks to understand, in Peluso and Watts' words, 'ways that specific resource environments (tropical forests or oil reserves) and environmental processes (deforestation, conservation, or resource amelioration) are constituted by, and in part constitute, the political economy of access to and control over resources' (2001: 5; parenthesis in original). Obviously, the environmental justice approach is based largely on the conceptual acceptance of structural violence as both cause and outcome of inequality. This mirrors the 'environmental conflict thesis' put forth best by political ecologists, perhaps best summarized by Robbins, and takes us back to Homer-Dixon's discussion of resource capture:

> Increasing scarcities produced through resource enclosure or appropriation by state authorities, private firms, of social elites accelerate conflict between groups (gender, class, or ethnicity). Similarly, environmental problems become 'socialized' when local groups secure control of collective resources at the expense of others by leveraging management interventions by development authorities, state agents, or private firms. So too, existing and long-term conflicts within and between communities are 'ecologized' by changes in conservation of resource development policy.
>
> Robbins (2004: 173)

So we are to some extent back to human rights (social responsibility, equity) and this concerns not only present rights (including entitlements and obligations), but must reflect past justice issues and possible future scenarios, which raises untidy questions about the applicability of reparations and intergenerational justice recently explored by international environmental ethicists such as Steve Vanderheiden (2008). Indeed, spurred by the climate change debate – where an international dialogue is unavoidable – many authors are treating ecopolitics as an aspect of environmental justice, at the local to global levels (Boyle and Anderson, 1998; Athanasiou and Baer, 2002; Roberts and Parks, 2007).

Though some deep ecologists and animal welfarists remain critical of the anthropocentricism of international human rights law (see Redgwell, 1998), it is fairly widely accepted that the right to a safe environment is a fundamental human right. As Dinah Shelton suggests, a human rights approach to environmental protection seeks 'to ensure that the natural world does not deteriorate to the point where international guaranteed rights such as the rights to life, health, property, a family, a private life, culture, and safe drinking water are seriously impaired. Environmental protection is thus instrumental, not an end in itself' (2003: 1). However, one can position this in opposite terms, suggesting that the 'legal protection of human rights is an effective means to achieving the ends of conservation and environmental protection' (Anderson, 1998: 3). Water is of course a prime example. Access to clean water is often recognized as a human right of the first order; its denial, whether through occupation, usurpation or privatization, is at the root of an increasingly visible if politically limited water justice movement. Thus arguments persist, for example, for an international agreement that explicitly guarantees water as a universal human right in order to reduce looming water-related conflicts (see Davidson-Harden, Naidoo and Harden, 2007).

If environmental justice has become a major normative force today, we are equally concerned with environmental rights (including animal welfare) as factors proscribing certain types of human behaviour, and prescribing obligations towards those most affected. 'These claims may be based either upon the specific attribution of responsibility to the countries of the North for the carbon emissions which are responsible for global warming, or upon a human rights-based claim that the wealthy must assist those who are at risk of large-scale rights deprivation and are effectively unable to help themselves' (Steiner, Aston and Goodman, 2007: 1454), such as tropical islanders displaced by rising sea levels. The failure to pursue environmental justice at an international level can only lead us further on the path towards a world defined by *bioapartheid*: a systemic physical separation of people who have suffered the deleterious impacts of the health threats related to climate change, infectious diseases and even the malnourishment resultant from absolute poverty, from those with the means to escape these threats to human security, who are free to roam wherever their transnational capital can take them. This may or may not involve the application of military power to maintain such separation; it may or may not overlap with religious war; it may or may not assume a visibly racial character.

I would suggest that a variety of factors make the consideration of *global environmental justice* the new ethical frontier, the nexus between ecological thought and International Relations theory we need to further develop and promote in order to avoid the complete dissolution of global society today. Significantly, global environmental justice is not merely related to the mitigation of the anthropomorphic causes of climate change, biodiversity loss, toxic pollution or the oceans crisis; it also demands that adaptation measures undertaken by states and other actors do not further marginalize already vulnerable groups, and that their voice is heard in the precautionary balance sheet. This does not, of course, negate the fact that some extreme weather events, infectious diseases, genetic mutations and other manifestations of environmental problems will ultimately affect both rich and poor; but they most certainly will not be similarly or equally affected so long as the former have adequate resources and the latter have little but communal ties to assist them.[7] Surely the lesson of Hurricane Katrina, which after all affected one of the most prosperous and powerful states in the international system today, is that poverty kills. In a text that should, I believe, prove to be a must-read for anyone concerned with climate change policy, J. Timmons Roberts and Bradley Parks (2007) offer widespread evidence that this is the case on the global level as well.

Indeed, environmental justice as a theme and a movement is in danger of extinction as 'climate justice' (Klinsky and Dowlatabadi, 2009) pushes it out of public view. This is unfortunate in my view, not only because of the tenuous analytic nature of links between climate change and violence (Salehyan, 2008), its inevitable securitization (Barnett, 2003; Podesta and Ogden, 2007), the perpetually inconclusive nature of efforts at global climate change policy and governance, and the debate over the scientific validity of the more distressing geophysical predictions, but because there are so many other issues (albeit interlinked) that demand attention. This in no way diminishes what should be vigilant concerns, and research into, the links between climate change and environmental justice, from the phenomenon of environmental refugees and migrants[8] to the cultural impact of rapid changes in local ecosystems. Reuveny argues that environmentally induced migration can lead to conflict when it is coupled with competition over scarce resources, ethnic tensions between groups, distrust between migrants and host communities and the presence of socio-economic 'fault lines' or 'auxiliary conditions' such as political instability (2007: 659). These are certainly, as Barnett and Adger argue, human security concerns of the first order (2007). But they are also social and environmental justice issues, since they involve vulnerability, unequal power relationships and potential avenues towards emancipation from these conditions. As Brown, Hammill and McLeman argue in the African context, the degree to which climate change will actually result in violent conflicts depends upon 'a given area's susceptibility to conflict and the capacity of the population to adapt to changing conditions' (2007: 1149).[9] Similarly, Salehyan argues that it is not environmental factors alone that can predict conflict, but instead it is 'the *interaction* between environmental and political systems [that] is critical for understanding organized armed violence' (2008: 318) Environmental justice also allows us to focus on situations and events that are not within the usual humanitarian intervention context. Most instances of what is traditionally considered eco-violence would escape the Responsibility to Protect (R2P) doctrine, which demands genocide, war crimes, ethnic cleansing and crimes against humanity, though there is some room to manoeuvre within all of these categories.

A final reason to focus on environmental (in)justice is that it provides a normative platform from which we can move on to concrete unapologetic policy prescriptions to remedy situations where chronic inequality or sudden catastrophe has ensured ongoing harm to vulnerable populations; recent events in Haiti certainly underscore this point, whether viewed from country-specific or global lenses. While the more traditional eco-violence literature typically leads to calls for greater state capacity to 'manage' situations, environmental justice concerns typically advocate more fundamental shifts in power relations and access to natural resources. Though such calls can be unrealistic and even counter-productive if they challenge the entire status quo, if articulated in a measured manner they can be quite reasonable demands based on the enlightened self-interest of all stakeholders. Of course, some of the self-anointed clergy of the more radical branches of the movement would consider this a sacrilegious concession to the rich and greedy.

But as political ecology continues its evolutionary curve towards mainstream social significance, and yet capitalism continues to prove its resilience despite economic crises and technological change, it seems much more like the art of the possible than the clarion call for a global revolution the poor will continue to die waiting for.

Conclusion

This chapter has made several points relevant to the study of eco-violence and environmental conflict. Firstly, it is very difficult to arrive at anything even approaching a widely shared conception of what, precisely, 'violence' means as an operable term in social science. The distinct explications put forth in the essay are but a few of the competing understandings. If we cannot arrive at a common definition, then it is better to embrace a wider concept, such as environmental justice, to set our sights on. Secondly, the proposition that nature itself is violent and, therefore, violence attributed to environmental problems is natural also, does little to enhance our understanding of eco-violence and in fact serves to legitimize forms of structural violence and delegitimizes contemporary human rights norms. Thirdly, agential violence committed with specific intent to harm the environment (or wilful negligence) can be observed throughout history, and constitutes a violation of environmental justice. Fourthly, structural violence that persists over time and that either results in the degradation of environmental conditions or leads to situations where agential/instrumental violence is employed is also a violation of environmental justice. It follows that we should be looking for environmental injustice if we wish to examine the links between ecological conditions, power and anthropocentric violence, not just as possible predictors of the latter, but as evidence of them.

If eco-violence is seen as transgressions of environmental justice, we are able to adopt a more concrete programme of analysis and emancipation. We are able to limit the scope of enquiry and yet raise its implications. We are able to wed humanitarianism and environmentalism. Otherwise, given its causal limitations, I am not sure the eco-violence/eco-conflict literature achieves much beyond observational interest. The fixation on observed violence, or predictions thereof, so sexy in the twilight of the Toronto studies, certainly turned the Clinton-Gore crank. But we need to fixate on something with broader applicability, less definitional and causal uncertainty, and greater humanitarian resonance, and that is environmental injustice.

Notes

1. For a very good anthology on the meaning of violence (sans Hannah Arendt (1969), who should also be consulted), see Bufacchi (2009).
2. Ridgeway and Jacques go so far as to argue that the standard to approach 'environmentally-induced regional conflict ... posits population growth as the primary cause of environmental scarcity and/or degradation, which then results in violence' (2002: 599). I am not sure this is an accurate characterization, however.
3. The most damning indictment of Homer-Dixon's work (1994, 1999) is certainly the excellent Peluso and Watts text (2001), and in particular the chapter by Betsy Hartmann (2001). Although the book did not make a big splash in the waters of IR studies (unsurprisingly, given its emphasis on political ecology, agrarian studies and anthropology), it remains largely unanswered.
4. Note the significant ecological footprint of going to war/occupation: according to *The Economist*, 'American forces consume more than 1m [one million] gallons of fuel a day in Afghanistan, and a similar quantity in Iraq', and the British army '[c]alculates that it takes seven gallons of fuel to deliver one gallon to Afghanistan'. See 'Greenery on the March', *The Economist Technology Quarterly*, 12 December 2009, p.3.
5. Uvin offers a sophisticated concision, but neglects ecology:: 'For poor people, meaningful development is not simply about increases in income but also about improved access to the means of production; reduction in insecurity and vulnerability, and the creation of a sustainable and hopeful future; empowerment through participation, justice, freedom, and access to information and education; overcoming physical weakness through access to health and nutrition; and social relations characterized by human dignity, cooperation, and a sense of equity ... [the] systematic absence [of these processes] for certain groups, especially under conditions of macroeconomic growth, can be called structural violence' (Uvin, 1998: 107).
6. Of course, social ecologists would reject any human hierarchy as part of the problem; justice could only be truly found under anarchic conditions (see Bookchin, 1982). Most proponents of environmental justice, however, are not anarchists but would use the state as an agent in the realization of environmental justice claims and any resultantly necessary redistribution of wealth.
7. We should not underestimate the importance of those ties, however. As Michael Thompson puts it, 'Environmental security ... is all about solidarities. If the appropriate solidarities are not there, and they are not interacting with one another in appropriate ways, then the pressure-cooker model will be valid' (1999: 137).
8. Ironically, perhaps, efforts at conserving nature are also possible sources of environmental injustice, and there is a little information on the level of displacement caused by conservation projects, including indigenous and non-indigenous person (see Brockington, Igoe and Schmidt-Soltau, 2006). For an historical treatment see Warner (2006).
9. According to political geographers Nordas and Gleditsch: 'the prospect of human-induced climate change encourages drastic neomalthusian scenarios. A number of claims about the conflict-inducing effects of climate change have surfaced in the public debate in recent years. Climate change has so many

potential consequences for the physical environment that we could expect a large number of possible paths to conflict. However, the causal chains suggested in the literature have so far rarely been substantiated with reliable evidence. Given the combined uncertainties of climate and conflict research, the gaps in our knowledge about the consequences of climate change for conflict and security appear daunting' (2007: 627). See Obioha (2008) for a Nigerian case study. Meanwhile Raleigh and Urdal conclude that while 'population growth and density are associated with increased risks, the effects of land degradation and water scarcity are weak, negligible or insignificant. The results indicate that the effects of political and economic factors far outweigh those between local level demographic/environmental factors and conflict' (2007: 674).

References

Almond, B., 1995. 'Rights and Justice in the Environment Debate'. In D. Cooper and J. Palmer, eds, *Just Environments*. London: Routledge.
Anderson, M., 1998. 'Human Rights Approaches to Environmental Protection: An Overview'. In A. Boyle and M. Anderson, eds, *Human Rights Approaches to Environmental Protection* Oxford: Clarendon Press, 1–23.
Arendt, H., 1969. *On Violence*. New York: Harcourt, Brace, and World.
Athanasiou, T. and P. Baer, 2002. *Dead Heat: Global Justice and Global Warming*. New York: Seven Stories Press.
Audi, R., 1974. 'Violence, Legal Sanctions and Law Enforcement'. In S. M. Stanage, ed., *Reason and Violence: Philosophical Investigations*. Oxford: Basil Blackwell, 29–49.
Barnett, J., 2003. 'Security and Climate Change', *Global Environmental Change* 13: 7–17.
Barnett, J. and W. N. Adger, 2007. 'Climate Change, Human Security and Violent Conflict'. *Political Geography* 26: 639–55.
Beck, U., 1992. *The Risk Society: Towards a New Modernity*. Trans. Mark Ritter. London: Sage.
Bookchin, M., 1982. *The Ecology of Freedom: The Emergence and Dissolution of Hierarchy*. Palo Alto, CA: Cheshire Books.
Boyle, A. and M. Anderson, eds, 1998. *Human Rights Approaches to Environmental Protection*. Oxford: Clarendon Press.
Brockington, D., J. Igoe and K. Schmidt-Soltau, 2006. 'Conservation, Human Rights, and Poverty Reduction'. *Conservation Biology* 20(1): 250–2.
Brown, O., A. Hammill R. McLeman, 2007. 'Climate Change as the "New" Security Threat: Implications for Africa'. *International Affairs* 83(6): 1141–54.
Bufacchi, V., ed., 2009. *Violence: A Philosophical Anthology*. New York: Palgrave Macmillan.
Bullard, R. D., 1999. 'Dismantling Environmental Racism in the USA'. *Local Environment* 4(1): 5–19.
Conca, K., and J. Wallace, 2009. 'Environment and Peacebuilding in War-torn Societies: Lessons From the UNEP's Experience with Postconflict Assessment'. *Global Governance* 15(4): 485–504.
Coomaraswamy, I., 1995. 'Some Reflections on Violence Against Women'. *Canadian Women Studies / Les Cahiers de la Femme* 15(2 and 3): 19–23.

Davidson-Harden, A., A. Naidoo and A. Harden, 2007. 'The Geopolitics of the Water Justice Movement'. *Peace, Conflict, and Development* 11: 1–34.
Di Chiro, G., 1992. 'Defining Environmental Justice: Women's Voices and Grassroots Politics'. *Socialist Review* 22(4): 93–130.
Dobson, A., 1998. *Justice and the Environment: Conceptions of Environmental Sustainability and Theories of Distributive Justice.* Oxford University Press.
Dobson, A., 2003. *Citizenship and the Environment.* Oxford: Oxford University Press.
Galtung, J., 1990. 'Cultural Violence'. *Journal of Peace Research* 27(3): 291–305.
Garver, N., 1975. 'What Violence Is'. In R. Wasserstrom, ed., *Today's Moral Problems* New York: Macmillan, 410–23. Reprinted from *The Nation* (24 June 1968), 817–22.
Hagmann, T., 2005. 'Confronting the Concept of Environmentally Induced Conflict'. *Peace, Conflict and Development* 6: 1–22.
Hardin, G., 1968. 'The Tragedy of the Commons'. *Science* 162: 1243–8.
Hartmann, B., 2001. 'Will the Circle Be Unbroken? A Critique of the Project on Environment, Population, and Security'. In N. L. Peluso and M. Watts, eds, *Violent Environments.* Ithaca: Cornell University Press, 39–62.
Hayward, T., 1994. *Ecological Thought: An Introduction.* Cambridge: Polity Press.
Homer-Dixon, T., 1994. 'Environmental Scarcities and Violent Conflict: Evidence from Cases'. *International Security* 19(1): 5–40.
Homer-Dixon, T., 1999. *Environment, Scarcity and Violence.* Princeton: Princeton University Press.
Illsley, B., 2002. 'Good Neighbour Agreements: the First Step To Environmental Justice?' *Local Environment* 7(1): 69–79.
Keane, J., 2004. *Violence and Democracy.* Cambridge/New York: Cambridge University Press.
Kelkar, G., 1992. 'Stopping the Violence Against Women: Fifteen Years of Activism'. In M. Schuler, ed., *Freedom from Violence.* New York: UNIFEM.
Khagram, S. and S. Saleem, 2006. 'Environment and Security'. *Annual Review of Environment and Resources* 31: 395–411.
Klinsky, S. and H. Dowlatabadi, 2009. 'Conceptualizations of Justice in Climate Policy'. *Climate Policy* 9: 288–108.
Le Billon, P., 2001. 'The Political Ecology of War: Natural Resources and Armed Conflicts'. *Political Geography* 20: 561–84.
Low, N. and B. Gleeson, 1998. 'Situating Justice in the Environment: The Case of BHP and OK Tedi Copper Mine'. *Antipode* 30(3): 201–26.
Maantay, J., 2002. 'Mapping Environmental Injustices: Pitfalls and Potential of Geographic Information Systems in Assessing Environmental Health and Equity'. *Environmental Health Perspectives* 110(2): 161–71.
Martin, A., 2005. 'Environmental Conflict Between Refugee and Host Communities'. *Journal of Peace Research* 42(3): 329–46.
Nordas, R. and N. P. Gleditsch, 2007. 'Climate Change and Conflict'. *Political Geography* 26: 627–38.
Noske, B., 1997. *Beyond Boundaries: Humans and Animals.* Montreal: Black Rose.
Obioha, E. E., 2008. 'Climate Change, Population Drift and Violent Conflict Over Land Resources in Northeastern Nigeria'. *Journal of Human Ecology* 23(4): 311–24.
Peluso, N. L., and M. Watts, eds, 2001. *Violent Environments.* Ithaca: Cornell University Press.

Podesta, J. and P. Ogden, 2007. 'The Security Implications of Climate Change'. *The Washington Quarterly* 31(1): 115–38.
Rajan, S. R., 2001. 'Toward a Metaphysic of Environmental Violence: The Case of the Bhopal Gas Disaster'. In N. L. Peluso and M. Watts, eds, *Violent Environments*. Ithaca: Cornell University Press, 280–398.
Raleigh, C. and H. Urdal, 2007. 'Climate Change, Environmental Degradation and Armed Conflict'. *Political Geography* 26: 674–94.
Ramanathapillai, R., 2008. 'Modern Warfare and the Spiritual Disconnection from Land'. *Peace Review* 20(1): 113–20.
Redgwell, C., 1998. 'Life, the Universe and Everything: A Critique of Anthropocentric Rights'. In A. Boyle and M. Anderson, eds, *Human Rights Approaches to Environmental Protection*. Oxford: Clarendon Press, 71–87.
Regan, T., 1983. *The Case for Animal Rights*. Berkeley: University of California Press.
Reuveny, R., 2007. 'Climate Change-Induced Migration and Violent Conflict'. *Political Geography* 26: 656–73.
Ridgeway, S., and P. Jacques, 2002. 'Population-Conflict Models: Blaming the Poor for Poverty'. *The Social Science Journal* 39: 599–612.
Robbins, P., 2004. *Political Ecology: A Critical Introduction*. Oxford: Blackwell Publishing.
Roberts, J. T. and B. Parks, 2007. *A Climate of Injustice: Global Inequality, North-South Politics, and Climate Policy*. Cambridge, MA: MIT Press.
Salehyan, I., 2008. 'From Climate Change to Conflict? No Consensus Yet'. *Journal of Peace Research* 45: 315–26.
Schlosberg, D., 1999. 'Networks and Mobile Arrangements: Organisational Innovation in the US Environmental Justice Movement. *Environmental Politics* 6(1): 133–48.
Schlosberg, D., 2007. *Defining Environmental Justice: Theories, Movements, and Nature*. New York: Oxford University Press.
Seton, E. T., 1898. *Wild Animals I Have Known*. New York: Scribners.
Shelton, D., 2003. 'The Environmental Implications of International Human Rights Tribunals'. In R. Picolotto and J. Taillant, eds, *Linking Human Rights and the Environment*. Tucson: University of Arizona Press, 1–30.
Steiner, H., P. Aston and R. Goodman, 2007. *International Human Rights in Context: Law, Politics, Morals*, 3rd Edition. Oxford: Oxford University Press.
Stoett, P., 2000. *Human and Global Security: An Exploration of Terms*. Toronto: University of Toronto Press.
Stoett, P., 2007. 'Counter-Bioinvasion: Conceptual and Governance Challenges'. *Environmental Politics* 16(3): 433–52.
Theisen, O. M., 2008. 'Blood and Soil? Resource Scarcity and Internal Armed Conflict Revisited'. *Journal of Peace Research* 45: 801–18.
Thompson, M., 1999. 'Security and Solidarity: An Anti-Reductionist Analysis of Environmental Policy'. In F. Fischer and M. Hajer, eds, *Living With Nature: Environmental Politics as Cultural Discourse*. Oxford: Oxford University Press, 135–50.
Uvin, P., 1998. *Aiding Violence: The Development Enterprise in Rwanda*. Connecticut: Kumarian Press.
Vanderheiden, S., 2008. *Atmospheric Justice: A Political Theory of Climate Change*. Oxford: Oxford University Press.

Warner, R., 2006. 'The Place of History in International Relations and Ecology: Discourses of Environmentalism in the Colonial Era'. In E. Laferriere and P. Stoett, eds, *International Ecopolitical Theory: Critical Approaches*. Vancouver: UBC Press, 34–51.

Welsch, H., 2008. 'Resource Abundance and Internal Armed Conflict: Types of Natural Resources and the Incidence of "New Wars"'. *Ecological Economics* 67: 503–13.

World Health Organization, 2002. *World Report on Violence and Health: Summary*. Geneva: WHO.

3
Climatic Security and the Tipping Point Conception of the Earth System

Chris Russill

> Now it is time for us to rise to our newest and biggest challenge: to fight the first great war of interdependence, the struggle for climate security.[1]

> And I think that, from this day forward, the words 'climate change' and 'international security' will be forever linked.[2]

Abrupt and dangerous climate change is now a significant concern for many people, and the recent and very rapid reconfiguration of some mainstream scientific, environmental, regulatory and security discourses by claims of increasing climatic instability deserves close attention. Perhaps not surprisingly, the notion of an insecure or unstable climate system is itself a shifting and ambiguous construct, one assembled from diverse cultural and scientific elements, and invested with multiple meanings depending on the context and purposes for which it is invoked. These elements are sometimes of ancient origins, and marked by different histories and debates, as suggested by Mike Hulme, Simon Dalby, Jon Barnett, Max Boykoff, Paul Edwards and others.[3] Nothing is gained in over-simplifying this point. Yet, the current discourse on climatic instability is quite new in many respects, at least in the form that underpins the surge of interest in 'climate security' shown by Western intelligence, security and military planning agencies. It is the relationship between recent efforts to reconfigure popular notions of climate change – as abrupt, as tipping point laden, as dangerous, as a security issue – and the national security interests of the US and UK governments that are explored here.[4]

One obvious and popular manifestation of this 'climate security' phenomenon is the new fascination with 'climate wars'. Among the most notable examples is the 2003 report, 'An Abrupt Climate Change Scenario and its Implications for United States National Security', produced by Global Business Network (GBN) for the US Department of Defense, which generated considerable interest when abridged in *Fortune Magazine* in 2004.[5] By selectively interviewing abrupt climate change scientists, and by reinterpreting their work via 'scenario planning' to generate security implications, GBN challenged conventional climate policy approaches. Similar warnings and more imaginative scenarios soon proliferated.[6] Today, Friends of the Earth claims, 'Warming Means War,' and Gwynne Dyer hypothesizes nuclear war as a consequence of climate change.[7] Nor are climate war scenarios confined to our future. Darfur, it is claimed, represents the world's first climate war. If so, climate wars date back to around 2003 at the latest.

How should one respond to such alarming scenarios? A number of critics have raised objections and counselled scepticism. In the sober words of Barnett, climate wars discourse 'is excessively general, and poorly if at all informed by evidence'.[8] Hulme makes a similar observation regarding the most widely disseminated claims, which sensationalize the association between climate change and violent conflict by using simple and 'deterministic' frameworks.[9] Barnett and Hulme are right to question the authority accorded to climate war projections, and to worry that security agencies are seeking to appropriate public concern over climate change to advance the inequitable and dangerous reconfiguration of geopolitical space.

While we might quickly decide that the current fascination with climate wars is unfortunate, some argue that this work represents only a partial snapshot of the emerging climate security discourse.[10] In fact, in recent years, it has become clear that the main proponents of climate security prefer an ambiguous pluralism infused by complexity and chaos science. Threat multipliers and interconnected metrics for security form the background of many contemporary studies, and causal determinants of war and violence do not dominate these analyses. If we concentrate on the more sensational claims of violent conflict, we obscure other ways that military, intelligence and security agencies are prioritizing ideas of climatic instability to reconfigure institutional, infrastructural and cultural sites of environmental concern.

In order to understand how this works, we must avoid facile conceptions of the relationship between security and scientific work on environmental change. In particular, we must abandon the idea that climatic instability is an ideological fabrication of paranoid national security agencies or a fiction of worrywart environmentalists, one bereft of scientific merit or impossible to legitimize through scientific means.[11] The idea of climatic instability – and the associated terminology like 'tipping points', 'thresholds', 'irreversibility', 'abrupt change', 'rapid change', 'flickering', etc. – is good science published by established researchers at strong universities in recognized journals.

It is not, however, environmental science as it is usually conceived. It is not significantly funded via close contact with the characteristic environmental issues of the last 40 years. It is not usually discussed in terms of 'limits to growth' or the international law regulating industrial pollution. And it has not shaped – or been shaped in turn – by the usual policy and media processes, which are sites where environmental concerns are especially pronounced.[12] United Nations Intergovernmental Panel on Climate Change (IPCC) assessment reports, for example, have not prioritized such science or the notion of climate 'surprises' it seems to entail.[13] Nor did these reports include chapters on climate security. In this respect, we might say (quite tentatively) that abrupt climate change science is an as yet 'un-socialized' scientific perspective; environmentalist concerns, policy demands or democratic traditions of social change have not strongly shaped its public expression.[14] Indeed, such work is the offspring of what Ronald Doel suggests is the hidden second parent of environmental science: the geophysical and earth science communities linked to the military and its foreign policy needs during the Cold War.[15]

Securitizing climate

The question of social influence on science and its adoption in policy circles is a complex one. I argue here that abrupt climate change concerns are a primary vehicle for re-conceptualizing the notion of environmental 'precaution', and that questions of precaution have become subsumed by security perspectives in the discussion on climate security. Precaution, in this case, is no longer animated by an effort to limit industrial despoliation of living environments through international law and democratic forms of negotiation, which were the characteristic concerns of the 'first parent' of environmentalism, or led by those supposedly professing 'watermelon politics'.[16] Instead, arguments for precaution are now oriented to the boundary conditions necessary for prevailing political-economic orders to function. This represents a significant shift in the way policy-relevant science is imagined and abrupt climate change warnings, which until recent years have been elided from mainstream policy discussions as too improbable or as too ineffective in raising public concern with climate change, are a significant aspect of this displacement of conventional environmentalist thinking. Though dating from the 1980s, these warnings have remained discursively available for new actors to use to enter the processes through which social implications are generated from climate science. The reinterpretation of these warnings in light of security concerns, I argue next, relies on a unique 'discourse-image' of the earth.[17]

If this is the case, proposals to reconfigure observing/modelling systems and environmental policy around this discourse-image of the earth demands our close attention and critical appraisal. A distinctive feature of the earth in this framework is a threshold-based notion of change, which finds policy expression in the desire to identify safe distances from dangerous tipping points in the earth system. A good example of how this works is the conflict in Darfur, a frequent touchstone in the climate security debate.

Darfur is sometimes used as an example of climate wars to come. However, proponents of climate security do not rely on a simple relationship between climate change and violent conflict to motivate concern. Instead, complexity is emphasized, and climate change is envisioned as a horizon upon which the social and political factors influencing conflict are rendered still more complex and ambiguous. For example, in the words of CNA Corp (2007), 'Darfur provides a case study of how existing marginal situations can be exacerbated beyond the tipping point by climate-related factors.'[18] Similarly, in the words of Neil Morisetti, a Rear Admiral and UK climate security envoy for the Ministry of Defence,

> Climate change on its own is unlikely to start a conflict, but when you add it to all the other stresses you see around the world; food shortages, water shortages, poor health, loss of livelihood, weak governance; there's a potential for it to be a tipping point to cause conflict.[19]

The important point is that a tipping point conception is used to reinterpret the Darfur example. It is an intellectual exercise, and not simply a public relations ploy to build support for international climate regulation. Instead, the Darfur example signals a deeper argument: social-political decisions must become responsive to an emerging 'climate knowledge infrastructure', which is far-flung, global in orientation and perhaps not as tightly bound to the policy goals of the United Nations as was once envisioned.[20] It is this expansive infrastructure – which represents the oldest, the most intense and perhaps the most assimilative example of an 'informational-globalist imperative' – to which we should direct our attention.[21]

The question is whether climate information produced by this knowledge infrastructure can become 'actionable,' or usable by security actors.[22] In a world of climate change-related tipping points, new forms of observation, knowledge and planning are needed, since the current modelling, policy and legislation have been designed in ignorance of tipping points. This is often presented as an epistemic shift – 'we need more and different knowledge' – yet, I argue, it entails an ontological shift, or the adoption of a different discourse-image of the earth. In this respect, the effort to rethink environmental danger via tipping points has implications not only for climate change, but also the broader relationship of environmental observation, intelligence gathering, policy and management – or what Edwards refers to as an infrastructure. Security analysts clearly realize that climate knowledge, as currently produced for UN policy institutions, is not 'actionable' in a security sense. Climate security discourse, then, is a 'demand signal' to producers of climate information.[23]

In their Foucauldian analysis of earth system science, Lövbrand, Stripple and Wiman emphasize that 'A new political space for government intervention is also in the making.'[24] What does it mean to treat planetary systems as objects of governance and political strategy, and how do proposals for tipping point warning systems advance such thinking? In addressing such questions, I argue that the danger of the security interest in climate change is its capacity to produce truths consonant with specific visions of geopolitical order, not the penchant or ability to circulate untruth, manufacture public fear or distort science. I am hypothesizing that the contemporary interest in climatic instability is shaped by security agencies drawing selectively on scientific discourses of climate change in order to amplify the elements of this science that comport well with their geopolitical visions of the world.[25] Just as new images of catastrophically abrupt climate change achieved popular salience around 2005, so too we witnessed a strong interest in reframing climate change as a security matter in the UK and US. The relationship is not coincidence, or environmental lobbyists simply recasting their framing strategies to build a coalition in the usual manner.

The depiction of climate change as dangerous has led to a re-conceptualization of environmental precaution from security perspectives. In many cases, the threats illustrated by geophysical science are interpreted as a failure of democratic institutions generally, and this is easily converted into an argument that new thinking and new institutions are needed to plan and prepare for climate change. The arguments underpinning this interpretation are many and raised later in this chapter.[26] The effect is that we find new prominence accorded to the concepts, methods and actors concerned with security. Concepts, like CNA Corporation's (2007) idea of a 'threat multiplier', become touchstones for interpreting the impacts of climate change. Methods, like GBN's scenario planning, are drawn upon in news discourse to raise alarm, and in planning exercises to envision future possibilities. Actors, like the UN Security Council, or the US and UK departments of defence, become the vehicles through which the social implications of the science are worked out. These are intellectual efforts to produce security implications from climate change knowledge.

Before proceeding, some important qualifications are in order. First, the full range of relationships between national security institutions and mainstream environmental institutions – which are varied and complex – cannot be seriously examined. Instead, I focus on one of the more pronounced and interesting trends, which is the displacement of the environmentalist framing of climate change by security discourse in significant political and policy forums. Second, I focus primarily on the US and UK contexts, and I do not seek to appraise the interest in climate security against other recent turns in climate change discourse. Third, my intent in sketching out the elevated prominence of security concerns is not meant to suggest that geophysical or resilience theory researchers are warmed-over cold warriors, or personally driven by ideological visions of the world. The research communities hoping for a trans-disciplinary earth systems perspective are internally complex endeavours marked by the respective methodologies, disciplinary fields and national contexts in which they emerge. The recent effort to integrate geophysical and ecological research under the sign of earth systems science and via the 'planetary boundaries' proposal does not – yet – indicate anything more than a provisional hope for unity among the geophysical, life and social sciences.[27] Moreover, by definition, any emergent phenomenon cannot be explained fully by reference to its constituent parts, and no single discipline, methodology or vision for the future of such science can be taken as definitive. Yet, having said all that, I do not wholly remove the discussion of geophysical science from its historical context, or shelter it from the searching criticism of Ronald Doel, James Fleming and others.[28]

In the following section, I discuss how critical discourse analyses of climate change communication help explain the emergence of public and political concern with climate security. Building on the tradition of analysis[29] established by John Dryzek, Ron Greene, Maarten Hajer, Karen Litfin, Sheila Jasanoff, Anabel Carvalho, as well as Boykoff, Hulme and their respective collaborators, we can account for and explain the prominence of specific perspectives in the 'epistemological hierarchy' of climate change discourse.[30] Then in the next section, I describe the popular emergence of climate security and the discourse-image that is privileged, namely, the tipping point vision of the earth system. In the later section, I offer some reflections on the science-policy interface to raise questions regarding the way societal implications are generated from climate change and earth system science. I conclude by situating this discussion among attempts to engage questions of climate security more broadly.

'Epistemological hierarchy' and climate change communication

There are many ways of depicting the earth system and climatic change. The dominant way of discussing different depictions is through the concept of framing, which argues that in the communication of a complex phenomenon certain aspects are emphasized in order to guide perception, to suggest responsibility, and to direct preferences regarding the underlying problem and best solution.[31] Frames, in a sense, are pre-packaged interpretations that fit events to familiar examples or experiences. In climate change communication, specific discourse-images of the earth facilitate the use of particular frames.

The discourse-image of a stable and resilient earth system characterized by negative feedbacks and self-correcting mechanisms, for example, are often drawn upon to dampen concern over industrial pollution – anthropogenic CO_2 emissions, CFC emissions or dumping in the ocean is of minimal concern in discourses governed by this view of the earth. The use of this enduring image of the earth system in contemporary politics is pronounced. It is notable, for example, that perhaps the most prominent climate sceptic, Richard Lindzen, repeatedly emphasizes the role of negative feedbacks as self-correcting mechanisms in his treatments of anthropogenic climate change as a trivial concern.[32] Al Gore, in *An Inconvenient Truth* (Guggenheim, 2006), devoted much of his lecture to overturning this discourse-image of the earth.

More recently, we have witnessed the rise of a competing conception of the earth system, one closely allied with concerns over catastrophic climate change. Within this view, our current period of relative stability is the exception, not the usual condition. Our belief in stable environmental systems characterized by incremental, gradual and manageable change is derived from our experiences with a terribly minute slice of earth systems change, and this experience is by no means the norm. In fact, if examined in geological time scales and through paleoclimatic evidence, the most significant forms of environmental change are better characterized as abrupt, rapid, flickering, cascading, threshold-based, tipping, irreparable and irreversible on human time scales. There are 'monsters' and 'ornery beasts' in the climate system.[33] In these discussions, the role of positive feedbacks is emphasized to suggest that climate change is potentially much worse than previously anticipated.

In the last five to seven years, this conception of the earth system has been intermixed with the idea of tipping points and a catastrophic framing of climate change, and this 'compound' has gained extraordinary salience in a range of cultural sites, most notably the mainstream news media in the US and UK (where the interest in climatic security has also emerged). Although I have suggest this a unique discourse-image of the earth system, there is debate regarding the novelty of this notion of climate change: some argue that the tipping point concept is merely 'old wine in new bottles', an idea long familiar to those working in ecological and complexity science, whereas others insist such ideas imply a new paradigm for geophysical understanding.[34]

One thing is clear: the contemporary salience of such views of the climate system in mainstream media *is* new. As a consequence, the discourse-image of an unstable, insecure climate system has delegitimized or even pushed aside competing understandings of environmental and climatic change, and the discursive availability of this discourse-image has authorized actors and institutions not commonly involved in defining the terms of debate for climate change to make claims regarding the management and governance of global spaces.

The notion of an 'epistemological hierarchy' is helpful in conceptualizing how the competitive jostling among framings of climate change works. I borrow the concept from Saffron O'Neill and her collaborators who state that 'There is an emerging recognition that different institutions promote certain types of climate change knowledge production, whilst other types are marginalized; a situation we term an "epistemological hierarchy".'[35] On this view and in the earlier work of Mike Hulme, climate change discourse is a complex and heterogeneous field of struggle among different disciplinary perspectives and framings, and we can study how different ensembles of knowledge practice and institutional imperative coalesce into a framing strategy designed to gain public, political and policy influence.

Discourse analysis is useful for establishing the state of play among frames, discourse-images, knowledge practices and institutions, and for tracking the reconfiguration of the hierarchy over time and in a range of cultural sites. In a series of important studies, Max Boykoff has illustrated the way climate change sceptics have reframed climate science as a 'scientific debate' in prestige US news media.[36] Carvalho has also tracked the way the UK government structures the terms of climate discourse in mainstream press systems over time.[37] In my previous research, I signalled the effort of researchers, the CDC, Health Canada and the WHO to redefine climate change as a 'public health' issue, and I suggested new saliency for discussions of climate change and human health as the vehicle for advancing such frames in mainstream news media.[38] In these cases, prestige news media were the vehicle through which institutional claims-makers sought to reconfigure the epistemological hierarchy for climate change discourse.

The new proliferation of the 'abrupt and catastrophic climate change' frame is evident in several sites of interest. In their study of the 2009 Copenhagen Congress– a precursor to the COPS meeting in November 2009 – O'Neill et al. (2010) illustrated the dominance of geoscientific frames of climate disaster. Although a range of different frames were made available during the conference, O'Neill et al. noticed that the media strategies of conference organizers emphasized 'geoscience research through a catastrophic frame', and they suggested this preference was reflected in media coverage of the event.[39] Other research has found the same preference in the UK and US print media coverage of climate change more generally.[40] In appraising the trend towards catastrophic scenarios in climate change discourse, they offer this conclusion:

> Catastrophic reporting reinforces the hierarchical pre-eminence of the geosciences and, conversely, the knowledge claims of the geosciences provide legitimacy and credibility to catastrophic framing. This serves to reinforce the message of climate change as an unfolding, almost pre-determined, disaster.[41]

It should be evident from this discussion that media are a site where framing competitions play out, as well as a means through which the 'epistemological hierarchy' is refigured across a whole range of sites, including IPCC reports, COPS meetings and policy deliberations, UN Security Council debates, among others.[42] The main difficulty is not illuminating media influence – or efforts to gain influence – but in evaluating the merits and consequences of any given perspective in the contemporary configuration of the epistemological hierarchy. It often looks nefarious or uncouth to seek media dissemination for a particular perspective. Yet, few if any conclusions should be drawn simply from the desire or effort to gain media attention for one's position or preferred frame, nor is success in achieving wide dissemination or interest a useful indicator or criterion for assessing the quality of a scientific perspective. How then can we evaluate the quality or standing of a perspective in the hierarchy of climate change discourse? One criterion is the degree to which the configuration of the epistemological hierarchy comports with the assessment reports of the UN IPCC. Boykoff and Boykoff, for instance, demonstrate that the standing of sceptics in media discourse did not reflect their standing in the IPCC reports, in professional society statements, or in National Academy of Science publications.[43] In this respect, the success of skeptics in achieving media influence distorted public perceptions of climate change by framing the science as a subject of intense and polarized debate. Barnett suggests a similar criterion in suggesting that conjectures regarding climate change and violent conflict should be deemphasized.[44] Finally, Hulme noted that tipping point conceptions of climate change, and of looming danger or catastrophe, were not warranted by IPCC assessments, and were instead the result of a discourse of catastrophe used for policy campaigning and for securing big science budgets.[45]

A different criterion for evaluation is suggested in Hulme's later work and in the conclusion of O'Neill et al. (2010), where they state that 'an epistemological hierarchy exists in the framing of climate change whereby the geosciences disproportionately influence the representation of climate change as primarily an environmental issue'.[46] On this perspective, the geoscientific perspective is criticized for dominating climate change discourse, and for an inability to encourage a broader range of frames to intermix with when generating appraisals of danger; since climate change is as much sociocultural and geopolitical as it is geophysical, this disproportion is damaging if not distorting.

I agree with this position. However, I suggest the security interest is also advanced by defining climate change primarily in geophysical terms, and that we might anticipate the displacement of the environmental framing by security insofar as the slice of geophysics emphasizing abrupt earth systems change becomes more prominent or even dominant in defining the dangers of climate change.

The popular emergence of climate security

> The key point about the operation of securitization is precisely that it refers to pressing and immediate situations that normal political life cannot address.[47]

The relationship between an emergent climate security discourse, the broader environmental security perspectives initiated in the 1980s and 1990s, and the longer history of climate and weather modification is not yet evident.[48] There is one clear difference between the environmental modification schemes of the 1950s envisioned by General Electric, the Weather Bureau and the US military, and contemporary security discourse: attention to non-linear and chaotic forms of change. These concerns are evident, for example, in Homer-Dixon's frequently referenced article, 'On the Threshold: Environmental Changes as Causes of Acute Conflict'.[49] Inspired by Wallace Broecker's warning of angry beasts in the climate system, Homer-Dixon suggested nothing short of a 'new paradigm' for interpreting data and policy options with respect to environmental change.

Homer-Dixon's 'threshold' article reached a wide audience when it was drawn upon by Robert Kaplan in his famous 1994 piece for *The New Atlantic*, 'The Coming Anarchy', which was an extended argument for placing environment at the centre of US foreign policy. In Kaplan's view, Homer-Dixon was the new 'X' for the post-Cold War era.[50] Kaplan filtered Homer-Dixon's work through a pessimistic perspective inspired by Thomas Hobbes to generate doubts regarding the future of liberal democratic systems. In reimagining US foreign policy to encompass Homer-Dixon's views of environment, developing countries and violent conflict, Kaplan accepted the narrowing of security to violent conflict that Homer-Dixon had recommended as a simplified starting point. Indeed, Kaplan's heading, 'The Environment as Hostile Power', was none too subtle. Despite such gestures, Kaplan's prioritizing of environmental scarcity as the cause of violent conflict was exceedingly simplistic, and climate change remained an afterthought in an article designed to advance a new image of environmentally driven, tribal war. Thus, it is easy to forget that Homer-Dixon's (1991) prognostications were driven by his belief that emerging earth system science perspectives would transform the perception of environmental problems.

By most accounts, it is only in the last five to seven years that a distinctive climate security perspective has been generated from earth system science perspectives, which seeks to span ecological and geophysical disciplines in an all-encompassing fashion. It is fair to say that Broecker's work has once again been a primary heuristic through which security implications have been generated. There is the aforementioned 'Pentagon' report authored by GBN, and other reports have drawn on this work, yet one event in particular stands out: The 'Avoiding Dangerous Climate Change' conference convened in Exeter, UK, February 2005, at the Hadley Centre of the UK

MET (the national weather service of the United Kingdom and operated as a trading fund of the Ministry of Defence). The conference sought to legitimate the earth systems science that would underpin the UK effort to move climate policy discussions into the G8, UN Security Council, and military and security planning institutions in the UK, US and Canada. Most notably, the conference served as the strategic means through which abrupt climate change gained salience in public discourse, and it helped reconfigure the epistemological hierarchy in climate change claims-making by elevating pieces of science that did not previously feature prominently in climate policy deliberations. In this respect, we can focus on some specific examples of strategic use of media, public interest and political leadership, before examining how climate science is resituated in climate security discourse.

In terms of *media*, Fred Pearce (2007), the widely acclaimed environmental science reporter, served as an embedded journalist for the conference, and spoke in urgent and glowing terms of the 'maverick' scientists who were suddenly receiving attention and gaining influence. In the book based on the perspectives he acquired during the conference, *With Speed and Violence: Why Scientists Fear Tipping Points in Climate Change*, Pearce drew a distinction between Type I (gradualist) and Type II (abrupt) climate change, and canvassed a variety of environmental situations to discuss the implications of substituting Type II climate change for the assumptions of Type I climate change. It is an idea Pearce rightly connects to Broecker, 'one of the high priests of abrupt planetary processes', and Pearce emphasizes the sudden prominence of this worldview.[51] In the case of scientist after scientist, Pearce emphasizes their maverick, outsider or previously out-of-step research, and this depiction includes Broecker, Michael Schlesinger, 'who has been making Broecker's case', and others.[52] Pearce's stylized portrait of Schlesinger is a microcosm of the book's larger message. According to Pearce, Schlesinger, still stuck in 1950s fashion, has subsisted on the margins of mainstream climate policy and criticized the IPCC for failing to take seriously abrupt climate change threats for over a decade.

> But in Exeter, Schlesinger was back in vogue ... Although he had been saying much the same thing for a decade, he was now considered mainstream enough to be invited across the Atlantic to expound his ideas at a conference organized by the British government.[53]

Pearce is a very good environmental reporter. He honestly locates the impetus to his work in the 2005 Exeter Conference, and he does not shy away from emphasizing the new discourse-image of the planet that climate change tipping point warnings seem to entail. His sense of fear is palpable. Yet, he uncritically interjects such warnings into public discourse on the basis that the interest of the UK government represents the mainstreaming of this knowledge. Perhaps most interestingly, at the time of the conference, there was no primary science published on climate change tipping points; thus, the conference and its political and media uptake helped generate public concern with tipping point warnings of climate change danger in advance of the primary science – which followed in subsequent years.

In terms of *public interest*, Hulme argued initially that the conference 'served the government's purposes of softening up the G8 Gleneagles summit,' by 'stage-managing' discussion of the implications of abrupt climate change.[54] In a more reflective moment, Hulme tempered his prose, yet without stepping back from his assessment:

> The Exeter Conference signaled a step-change in the ways in which the risks associated with climate change were conceived, presented and debated in the public sphere. Previously, climate change had usually been discussed in terms of incremental changes to the average conditions of climate; incremental changes to which it might – at least in some regions and with some foresight – be possible to adapt ... But the Exeter Conference opened up to a wider public a third category of climate change risks: abrupt or rapid changes in the climate.[55]

How significant was this step-change? Like Pearce, Hulme emphasizes that abrupt change warnings are part and parcel of a different paradigm, and one not represented in IPCC assessment reports. Tracing such warnings to Broecker's work, Hulme notes that 'new thinking about climate change in the late 1980s was to lead scientists to find new ways of conceiving, representing and modelling climate change'.[56] Indeed, as noted previously, this was the work inspiring Homer-Dixon's reflections in 1991. Importantly, Hulme adds, 'Ideas such as threshold, abrupt and non-linear changes, and 'tipping points' became part of the new paradigm of Earth system science,' and he states that 'It remains to be seen how durable and powerful these new conceptions of climate change, pioneered by Broecker and like-minded colleagues, will prove to be.'[57]

In terms of *political leadership*, there is enough evidence to suggest Hulme's suspicions of government interest were well placed, and that the Exeter Conference was called by the Blair government to lay the groundwork for an effort to prioritize climate change at the July 2005 G8 Summit, and to support the UK's contention that the UN Security Council should debate both the implications and possible responses to climate change.[58] In 2005, British PM Tony Blair wrote an open letter to the heads of the G8, 'We have a window of only 10–15 years to take the steps we need to avoid crossing a catastrophic tipping point', a point of emphasis underlined by his then Environment Secretary, Margaret Beckett: 'The thing that is perhaps not so familiar to members of the public ... is the notion that we could come to a tipping point where change could be irreversible.'[59] The terrorist attack in London during these G8 meetings would dominate global discourse, and Blair never convinced US President George Bush to embrace climate change, but the intent of the Blair government to reframe climate change as a security issue was evident with their forceful insistence that the UN Security Council debate the matter for the first time in April 2007.[60]

In the days leading up to the Security Council meeting, CNA Corp published 'National Security and Climate Change', which was produced by exposing retired admirals and generals to climate change science in order to interpret its security implications. The role of the US military in advising the analysis was reported widely. In the words of Gwynne Dyer, 'What they are selling is a mission. The next mission of the U.S. Armed Forces is going to be the long struggle to maintain stability as climate change continually undermines it.'[61]

Margaret Beckett, serving as UK Foreign Secretary in 2007, spoke the day before the Security Council meeting by invoking Winston Churchill's famous title, 'The Gathering Storm'. The first challenge, according to Beckett, was to avoid the 'trap' of an environmentalist understanding of the issue, an interesting suggestion from a former Environment Secretary.[62] John Aston, Special Representative for Climate Change for the UK, suggested in unsubtle terms that Darfur was as an example of the future to come: 'the security implications of climate change are bigger than we thought even two or three years ago. Their effects can already be seen in Darfur.'[63] In the years since, retired generals and admirals from US and UK have hit the lecture circuit with these claims, especially the idea of climate change as a threat multiplier. Thus, it is probably fair to conclude that the Exeter Conference was an initial step in the development of climate security policy discourse.

The preceding discussion was intended to underline two points. First, abrupt climate change scenarios have transformed the perception of climate change in key sites, and been used as the basis of claims that we are approaching a dangerous situation. The warnings were quite consciously presented as a divergence from IPCC assessments, and this remains the case; indeed, since these warnings precede the formation of the IPCC in 1988, it is obvious this discourse-image has been excluded for one reason or another. It is also true that tipping points are absent from the first four IPCC assessment reports. Yet, since 2005, the concept of climate change tipping points emerged, and has been used primarily to argue that the prevailing discourse-images of climate change are encouraging a false sense of security.[64] Second, the partial reconfiguration of the epistemological hierarchy through this discourse-image of an earth system laden with tipping points owes something significant to the political and media strategies of the Blair government, which used this science to underpin (if not authorize) their efforts to move the discussion of climate change to sites not dominated by environmental concerns, namely the G8 summits and UN Security Council.

Situating the science

> All of this suggests that, by the 1960s, two distinct 'environmental sciences' had emerged: one biology-centered, focused on problems in ecology and population studies, and funded in part by agencies and managers concerned about human threats to the environment; the other geophysics-centered, focused on the physical environment, and responsive to the operational needs of the military services that supported it.[65]

One of the more remarkable findings in recent histories of the geophysical sciences is the extent to which our knowledge of the earth system reflected not only the Cold War context but also the specific operational and foreign policy demands of military actors. In fact, the very term 'environmental sciences' appears to predate the emergence of 1960s civilian-scientist research and 1970s regulatory institutions to originate instead from specific projects in the US military.[66] In Ronald Doel's account, the result is two rather distinct strands of environmental science, and a pervasive military influence on geophysical/earth science research that remained less public – 'often "born classified"' – and effectively separated from the biological and activist traditions of research.[67]

Abrupt climate change work is much more clearly rooted in the less public side of environmental sciences. The 'maverick' or 'lone wolf' accounts of prominent researchers in the fields most relevant to abrupt change research are almost always emphasized – whether it is colourful accounts of idiosyncratic and unconstrained personalities, or gleeful descriptions of circumventions of bureaucratic and science policy processes – and this is accurate to a degree.[68] As stated, it is clear that abrupt climate change has not shaped the mainstream environmental depiction of climate change until very recently. Yet, such tales can obscure several features of the history, funding and appropriation of this science that raise interesting questions.

An example of this problem is found in Mark Bowen's useful account of abrupt climate change research. Bowen attributes the nascent military interest in climate security that was evident in 2005 to Broecker's bluster, force of personality and timely press releases. In particular, Bowen takes issue with Broecker's article, 'Thermohaline Circulation, the Achilles' Heel of our Climate System', which was published in *Science* on the eve of the Kyoto Protocol negotiations and circulated widely via a 'vivid press release'. In directing our attention to these details, Bowen argues that Broecker introduced 'outlandish speculations' to seize media attention for his preferred theory at an opportune moment. In Bowen's assessment: 'Even the military bought into it.'[69]

Bowen's suspicions illustrate the importance of media. Yet, this explanation is too partial and obscures the deeper military interest in the knowledge infrastructure necessary for climate change science. Abrupt climate change research is hardly unconnected from the military interest in geophysics. Of course, the question of military patronage is a difficult one, and piling up circumstantial detail is insufficient for drawing broader conclusions. Is the mere use of Army Corps drilling technology, military planes and transport, or space in military encampments and research facilities evidence of substantial influence? Is a history of funding, consultation or advising to military actors enough to establish such conclusions? In the passages that follow, my intention is to illuminate how military interest in the knowledge infrastructure necessary for climate change – which is currently influenced by the practices and norms of international law and democratic practice – might be redirected if climate security concerns are taken more seriously.

It is this broader perspective that leads Doel to some interesting observations. In his assessment of influence of military and foreign policy imperatives on geophysical sciences during the Cold War, Doel makes special mention of Lamont Geological Observatory at Columbia University as '[a] particularly revealing case'.[70] Lamont, the career home of Broecker and the most well-recognized if not dominant place for abrupt climate change research, was almost entirely dependent on military contracts for the first 25 years of its existence. Is this evidence of unseemly influence or an irrelevant historical detail? Doel's knowledge of this particular institution is extensive – he helped lead an oral history project dedicated to it – and he uses the case to illuminate some general conclusions. These conclusions focus mainly on how the pathways established by military interest elevated particular forms of geophysical research and made it available to foreign policy strategists. Scientists doing work consonant with the security concerns driving military funding found their *fields* elevated, and research opportunities expanded, while the range of political perspectives permitted to infuse such work was tightly circumscribed. Thus, 'those earth scientists who could not conform (or were perceived not to conform) to the secrecy policies of the national security state often did not receive research opportunities or ship time'.[71] Access to the earth science infrastructure was shaped by security demands.

We cannot easily adapt these insights to the contemporary situation for many reasons. In particular, the trend towards commercialization, private-public partnerships, and 'dual-use' military-civilian applications has transformed the infrastructure for such science, and sensitized us to look for the interpenetration of military/corporate/civilian interests. Strong, pervasive military influence of the sort demonstrated during the Cold War seems antiquated. Indeed, in the case of Broecker, it was private entrepreneurial support that elevated his work and the field generally in public discourse. Gary Comer, the founder of Lands' End, sought to quickly raise the research capacity and public profile of abrupt change research, with the caveat that such work needed to shape mainstream discourse and integrate with US government funding opportunities. Comer did this by directly funding scientists and projects hand-selected by Broecker. On one account, Comer 'changed the field'; on another account, he may have doubled the amount of research money targeted for abrupt climate change in the US.[72] As a result, this research entered into policy discourse differently than other forms of environmentalist concern.

The example illustrates how a shifting political economy of climate research has reoriented public and policy priorities. The pressure for scientific activity to be policy-relevant or usable/operational for deep-pocketed interests is severe. The most obvious example is the trying history of NASA's long desired, satellite based, climate-observing system – nominated the Earth Observing System (EOS)[73] in the wake of emerging earth systems science perspectives. Scientists sought to fit the proposal to shifting political and policy imperatives – in Eric Conway's work, we find the EOS variously hitched to weather satellite infrastructures, the shuttle program, robotics, and the policy agenda of the IPCC.[74] Similarly, the Earth Systems Modeling Framework (ESMF) has been designed to facilitate interoperability among the various systems involved in the climate knowledge infrastructure. Whether one interprets such intentions as part of an admirable open-source ethos, or as an effort to make the framework an 'obligatory point of passage' for climate knowledge producers, the ESMF is designed to be responsive to contemporary policy demands and to produce information of socio-economic value from earth system observations.[75] Demand signals from users concerned with 'policy-relevance' are sure to shape the future of this infrastructure.

Juxtaposing military and commercial influence on climate science to celebrate the liberalization of such information is a mistake. As Lisa Parks' important work makes clear, the declassification and commercial sale of intelligence activities like remote sensing hardly represents an end to securitization. Indeed, public display of previously classified activities would seem to align public interests with the discourse-images and knowledge practices of security institutions, which in the case of remote sensing often entails literally adopting the point of view of military analysts. Moreover, the commercial availability of satellite imaging means the US military can buy exclusive rights to what is now considered proprietary information, while reserving the ability to unilaterally restrict all imagery produced for a specific region via 'shutter control' authority.[76]

These examples touch briefly on select elements of the climate knowledge infrastructure. What bearing do they have on the emergence of the tipping point conception of the earth system or its relationship to climate security discourse? Both Parks and Edwards emphasize how images of the earth are not free-floating, discourse-neutral depictions of reality; both insist that an epistemological system or knowledge infrastructure produces and is reinforced by particular ways of apprehending the planet. In this chapter, I have suggested the concomitant rise of a new discourse-image of the earth system and a more authoritative role of security, intelligence and military institutions with respect to climate change. I have emphasized how warnings of a new threat – or a threat only now appreciated – has aroused an interest in securitization with respect to climate change. This threat is based on reorganizing our sense of precaution around tipping points and uncertain thresholds for environmental danger.

In this respect, the tipping point concept is quite significant – it has become a focal point for generating security implications from climate change science. How did Broecker's abrupt climate change paradigm translate into a generalized concern with earth system tipping points? Climate change tipping point warnings emerged publically in 2005, and the prominence of this concept in public discourse developed from the public statements of prominent scientists warning of danger.[77] Of course, Broecker's warnings of angry beasts and Achilles heels in the climate system were intended to gain attention and raise concerns as well, and his insistence that climate change would be experienced through surprising events that emerged abruptly rather than gradually was not unnoted. Yet, Broecker does not speak in terms of crossed tipping points. The translation of tipping points for Broecker's Achilles heel and the proliferation of prospective tipping points in the earth system originates in the earth system science vision of German physicist John Schellnhuber.

Schellnhuber is a prominent policy voice, a climate science advisor to German Chancellor Angela Merkel, and perhaps most importantly given the concerns of this paper, a scientific convener for the 2005 Exeter Conference and editor of its publication, *Avoiding Dangerous Climate Change*. In his own words, he 'prepared a conference for Tony Blair for the 2005 G8 summit in Gleneagles'.[78] Schellnhuber's conception of tipping point advances the epistemic shift that Broecker hopes to motivate, yet his own work in ecological systems and chaos theory underpin a more expansive application of non-linear and abrupt change scenarios.

The origins of the tipping point concept in climate change are not fully clear. In one account, Schellnhuber borrows the term from business terminology to interpret the threat of non-linear change for the media: 'In a conversation with a BBC journalist, I said "these are, more or less, tipping points" [in climate change].'[79] This is clearly a metaphorical use. In another account, the notion is introduced to the scholarly community in a 2001 paper co-authored with Hermann Held,[80] and developed through an expert elicitation exercise at a 2005 conference convened by the British Embassy in Germany. This resulted in several scientific publications using the concept between 2008 and 2010. The most important of these papers, 'Tipping Elements in the Earth's Climate System', quite forthrightly seeks to fit abrupt change work to contemporary political and policy demands by reframing abrupt change warnings around the concepts of tipping elements and tipping points. The goal is to unlock a policy pathway for climate change and to advocate for an early warning system. Indeed, the paper presents itself as a work of synthesis, and reorganizes a range of earth system work in terms of a tipping point framework sensitive to political timelines and policy demands. Its conclusion sounds a familiar message: 'Society may be lulled into a false sense of security by smooth projects of global change.'[81]

What is most remarkable about the tipping point concept is not its synthetic scientific ambitions or desire to infuse non-linear and abrupt change scenarios into policy-relevance, public discourse and political strategy. What is remarkable is that the novelty of tipping points for reorganizing the discourse-image of climate change is never remarked upon. The idea of dangerous and proximate climate change tipping points is not only novel, by which I mean the terminology was not previously applied to climate change or related geophysical research, but their detection, avoidance and amelioration requires new observing, modelling and managerial systems.[82] In this respect, tipping point warnings marry a new discourse-image of the earth to an infrastructural argument, one that abandons the fragmented systems and laws guiding global sustainability to pursue earth system management in a new way. In Schellnhuber's account, this new discourse-image represents human awareness of an unfolding 'second Copernican revolution,' one brought about by new observational technologies.[83]

The promise of a new Copernican revolution derives from Schellnhuber's earlier proposals for 'controlling the earth system' through earth system analysis.[84] The idea is that earth system observation and governance will emerge conjointly through a newly conceptualized 'global subject', a digitally constituted Leviathan. Constituted via a real-time updating network of planetary sensors, computer simulations, and space-based earth observing systems, this 'global subject will reign for centuries to come'.[85] The primary merit of this enthusiastic proposal is a stark recognition of the insufficiency of international approaches to global sustainability, a problematic condition Schellnhuber coupled to demands for a remarkable expansion of cybernetic control frameworks – indeed, from its origins in understanding atmospheric dynamics to better direct anti-aircraft weaponry, the entire planet is now brought within a cybernetic control framework.

If one is tempted to write off such proposals as the characteristic hubris of physicists wandering into fields of study they grasp only superficially, or as typical of 1990s dot-com bubble fantasies, then there is a long-list of examples to which Schellnhuber's might be added. Yet, the remarkable salience of tipping point warnings over the last five to seven years should prompt us to more carefully consider the future direction of earth observing systems and earth systems modelling in the climate knowledge infrastructure. The level of investment and integration across disciplinary, methodological and national science institutions touching upon earth systems change over the last ten years is significant.[86] This infrastructure hardly controls the earth system on behalf of a global leviathan; yet, it is a remarkable confluence of knowledge systems of global scope.

This raises two points of concern. First, the scientific discussion on climate change tipping points is designed primarily with policy-relevance in mind, and would demand a pervasive observational and intelligence processing network to succeed in even the crudest sense. There is every indication these warnings are taken seriously, and the scientific papers using the notion have been widely noted, even if a detailed treatment of the implications of reorienting policy around tipping points has not yet emerged. I have suggested in this paper that security analysts have embraced this discourse-image of the earth to reinterpret climate change as a security problem. In this respect, 'tipping points' have become a prominent concern for the US and UK military, intelligence and security planners; thus, the implications of this discourse-image of the earth – an increasingly prominent one that demands reorienting key components of the climate knowledge infrastructure – could have significant pathways determined by contemporary trends in security discourse. It is obvious, for example, that tipping point warning systems designed to identify both thresholds of danger and opportunities for geophysical intervention into planetary processes open up a new space for political strategies involving foreign policy considerations.

Second, the imagined policy-relevance is not environmental regulation or global sustainability as typically envisioned; in fact, we should interpret the last five years of climate security discourse as sidelining rather than supplementing processes of international law and democratic deliberation, which are based in a different discourse-image of the earth. Precaution, in the securitized conception, is reoriented around the identification of thresholds that demarcate safe operating conditions from danger zones, and which propose to manage the boundaries of socio-economic systems in concert with the ecological and geophysical conditions required for their satisfactory or optimal functioning. In Schellnhuber's initial proposal, the planet was envisioned as a cybernetic control problem; in the more sophisticated 'planetary boundaries' proposals forwarded today, it is a space for securing the prevailing political order organized on industrial and capitalist models.

In this respect, the rhetorical shift from 'climate surprises' to a 'false sense of security' is worth noting, as the effort to carve out a policy space for a new discourse-image of the earth system via tipping point warnings has generated security implications from climate science in interesting ways. The difference in speaking of surprise rather than security seems initially slight, yet the condition producing 'surprise', the unknown and the unexpected, is now interpreted as cause for alarm and a source of insecurity. Technologically, on this view of the earth system, the requirements are staggering in terms of the monitoring required for such a warning system, and I will leave it to other analysts to determine whether the panoptic potential of such infrastructure is frightening or science fiction. Conceptually, however, insecurity becomes the norm. In the 'planetary boundaries' proposal, earth system processes are divided into two states – safe operating space and danger zones – that are defined in terms of thresholds or boundaries. [87] The idea is to manage the resiliency of the earth system by avoiding proximity to thresholds where shifts to alternative states become possible. The assumption is that managing resiliency is easier than managing an abrupt shift in circumstances, the unknown nature of the transition, and the unknown nature of the alternative state into which we might settle.

Insecurity, in this sense, would be permanent, at least for the foreseeable future. This is not only due to the provisional nature of climate change impacts knowledge, or a judgement regarding the inherently unstable nature of industrial models of production. It results from the fact that policy-relevant thresholds are not inherent to the earth system; rather, thresholds, or the boundaries drawn around proposed tipping points, imply judgements of permissible risk and the ability of society to modify planetary systems in response to warnings, and it implies determining thresholds in concert with the institutions most likely to guide such responses.

Who, then, is the global subject, and which institutions are capable of observing, monitoring and intervening in the earth system? While it is too much to reinterpret this condition through the heuristic of Kaplan's historical reference to 'X', or Kennan's inspiration for the Cold War containment strategy, it takes little imagination to envision a future where geopolitical strategy guides earth system interventions to secure resources in line with foreign policy imperatives.

Conclusion

> A planetary early-warning system for tipping elements should be designed and put into place. Finally, assuming early warning can be achieved, the international community should critically evaluate what climate engineering options (if any) it could reasonably deploy, at short notice, to protect certain elements from tipping.[88]

In 2003, Jon Barnett speculated on the future contours of climate change discourse in perspicuous fashion, and raised questions regarding the implications of framing climate change as a security issue. While recognizing the way security discourse encapsulated 'danger' better than sustainability or environmental perspectives, Barnett argued that 'national security discourse and practice tends to appropriate all alternative security discourses no matter how antithetical ... in ways that neutralise their efficacy whilst maintaining the power of the security establishment'. In Barnett's opinion, the most promising path was 'a grounding in the findings of the

Intergovernmental Panel on Climate Change', through which climate security discourse 'could better resist appropriation from conventional national security'. Thus, 'If used by IPCC scientists a change-security discourse will have a legitimacy that renders it less amenable to appropriation and rewriting by conventional national security institutions'.[89]

It remains to be seen whether the tipping point conception of climate change will be wholly embraced by the next IPCC assessment report, and if so, whether this would have the desired effect hoped for by Barnett, as opposed to carrying the interests and goals of Anglo-American security into mainstream climate change discourses. Several security analysts have sought to avoid emphasizing tipping point dangers to develop implications from the IPCC AR4 in a credible fashion.[90] Others have proliferated abrupt change scenarios as if they derive directly from IPCC assessments while generating security implications through the discourse-image of the earth system discussed in this chapter.[91]

Thus, the intellectual pathways for generating security implications from climate change are not yet well defined. The refreshingly blunt talk of a new 'Leviathan' or 'Global Subject' is unlikely to win out in unrevised form, but it does raise questions regarding which agencies will make determinations regarding the thresholds between safety and danger zones, and whether the exercise of such power can be shaped by the less iconoclastic pillaging from Western traditions of political and democratic theory. George Dyson's idea of Thomas Hobbes as forerunner and inspiration for the digital sentience was a neat one; as a political model for earth system governance, however, we should wonder. In particular, if we are to avoid making a wide range of geological, biological and cultural practices susceptible to securitization while entrenching the socio-economic systems pushing ecosystems to dangerous boundaries, then we must interpret the implications of earth systems science through a wider range of perspectives. Otherwise, the instability of the earth system created by industrial infrastructures will be used as evidence of the insufficiency of democratic and participatory traditions of decision-making. As Dalby notes, 'The key point about the operation of securitization is precisely that it refers to pressing and immediate situations that normal political life cannot address.'[92] If precautionary measures are deemed situations of this sort, then the recent concerns with the 'state of exception' type reasoning – where democratic processes are suspended to cope with emergencies – will gain a rather depressing new example.

In conclusion, I recognize that this article has done little more than lay out some suggestive directions for studying climate security discourse. A more rigorous and wide-ranging study is needed to confirm the impressionistic view offered here regarding the prioritizing of abrupt and catastrophic earth system science in those institutions and documents most likely to shape the future of such climate security discourse. This study would need to be better attuned to the struggle between national security and human security perspectives over the last 20 years or so, and recognize the differences in national context between UK, US and other places earth system science has a foothold, like Germany, and those countries invested in resilience management. Finally, it is not my intent to promote an overly homogenous view of the community of earth system, resilience science researchers, national security institutions or environmentalists; I am definitely not suggesting that abrupt change scholars are warmed-over cold warriors. Schellnhuber is not Dr Strangelove. Instead, I'm intrigued by the way the securitization projects of the last decade have shaped the contexts in which the most pressing matters of the day are imagined, debated, funded and entered into public discourse, and I cannot imagine that this deep cultural shift is without consequence for climate change discourse. It is because I believe that complexity and resilience theories are invaluable that I suggest we attend to the questions treated here, and that we strive to articulate a much more robust 'human security' perspective when advancing the discourse-image of earth system discussed before.

Acknowledgements

I would like to thank Jeremy Packer and Matthew Schnurr for their interest in this work and for their incisive yet encouraging questions. Conversations or email exchanged with Simon Dalby, Sabrina Schultz, Shane Gunster, Brett Nicholls, Chris Waddell and Steve Schwarze were also helpful. Obviously, no one mentioned here is responsible for the contents of this chapter.

Notes

1. Margaret Beckett, 2007, 'Climate Change: "The Gathering Storm"', Annual Winston Churchill Memorial Lecture, New York, 16 April, available at http://collections.europarchive.org/tna/20080205132101/http://www.fco.gov.uk/servlet/Front?pagename=OpenMarket/Xcelerate/ShowPage&c=Page&cid=1007029391629&a=KArticle&aid=1176453874175 (accessed January 2, 2011).
2. Rep. Anna Eshoo (D-CA), National Intelligence Assessment on Climate Change, Joint Hearing Before The Select Committee on Energy Independence and Global Warming and Subcommittee on Intelligence, Community Management, Permanent Select Committee on Intelligence, House of Representative, One Hundred Tenth Congress, Second Session, June 25, 2008, Serial No. 110-41.

3. My own partial effort to trace the long history of abrupt climate change emphasizes the point that deeply embedded temporal assumptions orient evaluations of the danger of climate change, and I suggest that many familiar points of dispute might be indexed to different visions of time and change. See Chris Russill, 2010. 'Temporal Metaphor in Abrupt Climate Change Communication: An Initial Effort at Clarification', in W. Leal Filho, ed., *The Economic, Social, and Political Elements of Climate Change*. New York: Springer, pp. 113–32.
4. News and public discourse sources are too numerous to list. I have consulted the following reports in developing this manuscript: The National Intelligence Council's available material on the US national security implications of climate change and its subsequent reports on China, Russia, Africa, Mexico, the Caribbean, Southeast Asia and Pacific Islands (its initial report was a classified assessment produced in 2008); US Department of Defense, 2010, *Quadrennial Defense Review Report*; UK Ministry of Defence, 2008, *Climate Change Strategy*; Chad Michael Briggs, 2009, *Environmental Security, Abrupt Climate Change and Strategic Intelligence*, US Department of Energy; CNA Corp, 2007, *National Security and the Threat of Climate Change*, CNA Corp; Peter Schwartz and Doug Randall, 2003, *An Abrupt Climate Change Scenario and its Implications for United States National Security*, Global Business Network; Nils Gilman, Peter Schwartz and Doug Randall, 2007, 'Impacts of Climate Change', Global Business Network; Joshua Busby, 2007, *Climate Change and National Security: An Agenda for Action*, New York: Council of Foreign Relations; Kurt Campbell, Jay Gulledge, J. R. McNeill, John Podesta, Peter Ogden, Leon Fuerth, R. James Woolsey, Alexander T. J. Lennon, Julianne Smith, Richard Weitz, and Derek Mix, 2007, *The Age of Consequences: The Foreign Policy and National Security Implications of Global Climate Change*, Washington, DC: Center for Strategic and International Studies; Kurt Campbell, 2008, *Climate Cataclysm: The Foreign Policy and National Security Implications of Climate Change*, Brookings Institution Press; Pew Center, 2008, *National Security Implications of Global Climate Change*, Pew Center on Global Climate Change; Will Rogers and Jay Gulledge, 2010, *Lost in Translation: Closing the Gap between Climate Science and National Security Policy*, Center for a New American Security; Alan Dupont, 2008, *Climate Change and Security: Managing the Risk*, Garnaut Climate Change Review.

I have also consulted Geoffrey Dabelko, 2008, 'An Uncommon Peace: Environment, Development, and the Global Security Agenda', *Environment: Science and Policy for Sustainable Development*; Joshua Busby, 2008, 'Who Cares about the Weather? Climate Change and U.S. National Security,' *Security Studies*, 17: 468–504; Gwynne Dyer, 2008, *Climate Wars*, Toronto: Random House; Simon Dalby, 2009, *Security and Environmental Change*, London: Polity; James Lee, 2009, *Climate Change and Armed Conflict: Hot and Cold Wars*, London: Routledge; Cleo Paskal, 2010, *Global Warring*, Toronto: Key Porter Books; Jeffrey Mazo, 2010, *Climate Conflict*, London: Routledge and IISS.
5. David Stipp, 'The Pentagon's Weather Nightmare', *Fortune Magazine*, 9 February, 2004; Schwartz and Randall (2003).
6. On the origins and style of the scenario planning methodology of GBN with respect to its corporate and military clients, see Fred Turner, 2006, *From Counterculture to Cyberculture*, Chicago, IL: University of Chicago, pp. 181–92.

7. In the later case, it seems we have come full circle from the 'nuclear winter' concerns of the mid-1980s (when it was thought that nuclear war would induce civilization-threatening climate change, not vice versa). For 'Warming Means War,' see http://www.globalclimatesecurity.org/about and Dyer (2008).
8. Jon Barnett, 2009, 'The Prize of Peace (is Eternal Vigilance): A Cautionary Essay on Climate Geopolitics', *Climatic Change* 96(1–2): 1–6.
9. Mike Hulme, 2007, 'Climate Security: The New Determinism', 20 December, available at http://www.opendemocracy.net/article/climate_change/the_new_determinism (accessed January 2, 2011).
10. Cf. Dabelko (2008). Similarly, Mazo argues that the raft of reports on climate security in the early twenty-first century 'often focus on worst-case rather than the most likely scenarios', and he seeks to integrate security perspectives into public discussion by generating implications for security from an interpretation of the 2007 IPCC AR4 (Mazo, 2010, p. 10).
11. I am not suggesting that Barnett or Hulme draw this conclusion.
12. On this point, see Mike Hulme, 2003, 'Abrupt Climate Change: Can Society Cope?' *Philosophical Transactions of the Royal Society* 361: 2001–21.
13. There is work on 'large-scale discontinuities' referenced in the IPCC assessment reports, and it is a component of the infamous 'burning embers' visual used to depict risk. In 2005, Hansen's dissatisfaction with this perspective on risk prompted his first warning of climate change tipping points.
14. For a compelling example of the intricate relationship between atmospheric science and US environmental politics, see Eric Conway's authoritative history of atmospheric science and climate change study at NASA. Erik M. Conway, 2008, *Atmospheric Science at NASA*, Maryland: Johns Hopkins University Press.
15. Ronald E. Doel, 2003, 'Constituting the Postwar Earth Sciences: The Military's Influence on the Environmental Sciences in the USA after 1945', *Social Studies of Science* 33(5) (October): 635–66.
16. 'Watermelon politics' is a pejorative term that suggests proponents of environmental regulation are pursuing socialistic politics indirectly.
17. I use the term 'discourse-image' to acknowledge the important role of visual material. The term is inspired by Paul Edward's compelling work on 'data-images' of the earth. Paul Edwards, 2010, *A Vast Machine*, Cambridge, MA: MIT Press.
18. CNA Corp (2007: 16); also cited in Mazo (2010: p. 81).
19. UK Foreign and Commonwealth Office, 2010, 'Climate Change and Security: Tipping Point for Conflict', available at http://www.fco.gov.uk/en/news/latest-news/?view=News&id=21781162 (Accessed January 2, 2011).
20. Cf. Edwards (2010). I use Paul Edwards' idea of a 'climate knowledge infrastructure', and I follow his general thinking on infrastructural development and appropriation in this chapter.
21. See Edwards (2010: 24).
22. See Rogers and Gulledge (2010).
23. See Rogers and Gulledge (2010).
24. E. Lövbrand, J. Stripple and B. Wiman, 2009, 'Earth System Governmentality: Reflections on Science in the Anthropocene', *Global Environmental Change* 19(1), February: 7–13. James Rodger Fleming, 2010, *Fixing the Sky: The Checkered History of Weather and Climate Control*, New York, NY: Columbia University Press, offers an even bleaker assessment of the historical relationship between security agencies and geoscientists.

25. I have described this process elsewhere in terms of generative metaphor, and I argue that that such work can produce cognitive innovation; indeed, the application of tipping points to climate systems is one such example. Yet, the importance of metaphor and media for such innovation is usually disguised or elided. Cf. Chris Russill and Zoe Nyssa, 2009, 'The Tipping Point Trend in Climate Change Communication', *Global Environmental Change* 19(3): 336–44; Russill (2010).
26. There is the epistemic argument which claims poor or partial knowledge of the earth system is the problem. There are also political arguments that question the capacity of democratic practices. In some accounts, the public is unwilling or unable to handle abrupt change warnings without paralysing in fear or defaulting to fatalism. In other accounts, the UN system is too polarized politically, and international law is unenforceable. The Copenhagen meeting was widely interpreted as a failure of the UN system and of democratic diplomacy, and the Copenhagen Accord is often depicted as a departure from the inclusive process initiated by the 1992 Framework Convention on Climate Change.
27. Johan Rockström, Will Steffen, Kevin Noone, Åsa Persson, F. Stuart Chapin, III, Eric F. Lambin, Timothy M. Lenton, Marten Scheffer, Carl Folke, Hans Joachim Schellnhuber, Björn Nykvist, Cynthia A. de Wit, Terry Hughes, Sander van der Leeuw, Henning Rodhe, Sverker Sörlin, Peter K. Snyder, Robert Costanza, Uno Svedin, Malin Falkenmark, Louise Karlberg, Robert W. Corell, Victoria J. Fabry, James Hansen, Brian Walker, Diana Liverman, Katherine Richardson, Paul Crutzen, Jonathan A. Foley, 2009, 'A Safe Operating Space for Humanity,' *Nature* 461, 24 September: 472–75.
28. See Doel (2003) and Fleming (2010).
29. By discourse, I follow in the research tradition of Litfin, Hajer, Greene and my colleague, Graham Smart. My definition follows Smart and his use of Hajer's definition of discourse, 'an ensemble of ideas, concepts and categorizations through which meaning is given to social and physical phenomena, and which is produced, reproduced, and transformed in a particular set of practices' (available at http://www.maartenhajer.nl/index.php?Itemid=19&id=17&option=com_content&task=view).
30. Saffron J. O'Neill, Mike Hulme, John Turnpenny and James Screen, 2010, 'Disciplines, Geography and Gender in the Framing of Climate Change', *Bulletin of the American Meteorological Society* 91: 997–1002, available at http://journals.ametsoc.org/toc/bams/0/0. (Accessed 2 January 2011).
31. My definition draws from the work of Mike Hulme, 2009, *Why We Disagree About Climate Change*, Cambridge: Cambridge University Press. It is worth noting that the work of Matthew Nisbet has become a frequent point of departure for framing analysis.
32. See Conway (2008) for Lindzen and a good account of the debate over positive and negative feedbacks in climate science.
33. For the term 'monsters', see Fred Pearce, 2007, *With Speed and Violence: Why Scientists Fear Tipping Points in Climate Change*, Boston, MA: Beacon Press; 'beasts' is a well-known phrase of Wally Broecker (1999).
34. The situation is made complex by the tendency to retrospectively re-describe previous research in terms of 'tipping points' (cf. Russill and Nyssa, 2009; Russill, 2010; and Hulme, 2009).
35. O'Neill et al. (2010), p. 3.

60 *Climatic Security*

36. Max Boykoff and J. M. Boykoff, 2004, 'Balance as Bias: Global Warming and the US Prestige Press', *Global Environmental Change* 14: 125–36. By 'prestige press,' Boykoff and Boykoff mean newspapers such as *The Wall Street Journal*, *The New York Times*, *The Washington Post*, and *Los Angeles Times*.
37. Anabel Carvalho, 2005, 'Representing the Politics of the Greenhouse Effect: Discursive Strategies in the British Media,' *Critical Discourse Studies* 2(1): 1–19.
38. Chris Russill, 2008, 'Tipping Point Forewarnings of Climate Change: Some Implications of an Emerging Trend', *Environmental Communication* 2(2): 133–53.
39. O'Neill et al. (2010), p. 5.
40. Cf. Russill and Nyssa (2009).
41. O'Neill et al. (2010), p. 5.
42. A few clarifications are in order. In this paper, I do not deal with the methodological questions involved in determining the current configuration of an 'epistemological hierarchy' in any given cultural space, and deal only implicitly with the difficult theoretical questions of the interrelationships of scientific, public, policy and political sites where the configuration of the hierarchy might differ. Moreover, there remain difficult questions regarding whether or not the simple proliferation of more frames is a good thing, and whether and how subjugated knowledge can be made more salient in political struggles over environmental space.
43. See Boykoff and Boykoff (2004).
44. Jon Barnett, 2003, 'Security and Climate Change', *Global Environmental Change* 13: 7–17.
45. Mike Hulme, 2006, 'Chaotic World of Climate Truth', 4 November, available at http://news.bbc.co.uk/2/hi/6115644.stm. (Accessed 2 January 2011).
46. O'Neill et al. (2010) and Hulme (2009) are seeking to broaden the range of perspectives permitted to make credible statements regarding climate change.
47. Simon Dalby, 2009, 'Anthropocene Security', available at http://http-server.carleton.ca/~sdalby/papers/DalbyAnthropoceneISA2009.pdf. (Accessed 11 January 2011).
48. See Dabelko (2008) and Dalby (2009) on environment and security; see Edwards (2010) and Fleming (2010) for relevant remarks on meteorology and weather modification.
49. Thomas Homer-Dixon, 1991, 'On the Threshold: Environmental Changes as Causes of Acute Conflict,' *International Security* 16: 76–116.
50. Robert Kaplan, 1994, 'The Coming Anarchy', *Atlantic Monthly*, pp. 44–76. George Kennan was the 'X' of the famous *Foreign Policy* article, which is often taken as inspiration for the policy of containment applied to US-Soviet relationships during the Cold War.
51. See Pearce (2007: xxv).
52. See Pearce (2007: 145).
53. See Pearce (2007: 145–46).
54. Hulme, 2006, 'Chaotic World of Climate Truth', 4 November.
55. See Hulme (2009: 178–9).
56. See Hulme (2009: 60).
57. See Hulme (2009: 60).

58. See Carvalho (2005) for an account of how the UK government structures media discourse on climate change.
59. Cited in Chris Russill, 2008, 'Tipping Point Forewarnings of Climate Change: Some Implications of an Emerging Trend', *Environmental Communication* 2(2): 133–53.
60. See Tony Blair, 2010, *A Journey: My Political Life*, Toronto: Knopf.
61. Dyer (2008: 10).
62. See Beckett (2007). Beckett was Secretary of State for Environment, Food, and Rural Affairs from 2001 to 2006, and Foreign Secretary from 2006 to 2007, during which she shepherded the UK effort to situate climate change as a security issue. When Gordon Brown replaced Blair as PM, Beckett was removed as Foreign Secretary and replaced by David Miliband, who had taken Beckett's position as Environment Secretary.
63. Cited in Mazo (2010: 73).
64. Hansen offers one way to reconcile the divergent views in his discussion of climate sensitivity. Hansen expresses great confidence in his estimate of climate sensitivity, but points out that it holds only for the present state of the earth system; if relevant tipping points are crossed, and if we flip into alternative climate states, then all bets are off, and the sensitivity will vary widely, even to the point of threatening runaway climate change or Snowball Earth scenarios. In this respect, I expect that the Earth Systems Science perspective does not represent a new paradigm for Hansen, at least if the paradigm shift requires the kind of sudden conversion experience prioritized in Kuhn's work. Instead, the main difference between Hansen's work now and his work in the 1980s is the finding that positive feedbacks are much quicker and more dominant than previously thought: 'The most startling advances in recent understanding of climate change involve the realization that the dominant slow feedbacks are not only amplifying; they are not nearly as slow as we once believed.' See James Hansen, 2009, *Storms of My Grandchildren*, New York: Bloomsbury Press, pp. 44–5.
65. See Doel (2003: 653).
66. See Doel (2003: 636, 657, note 2).
67. See Doel (2003: 653). It would seem that military interest in climate change emerges with proposals for weather modification (cf. Fleming, 2010; Edwards, 2010), whereas public interest was articulated from within a 'pollution' framework.
68. Cf. Fred Pearce (2007) and Mark Bowen (2005). Thin Ice: Unlocking the Secrets of Climate Change in the World's Highest Mountains. New York: Henry Holt and Company.
69. See Bowen (2005: 298).
70. See Doel (2003: 641). It has been renamed and is currently called Lamont-Doherty Earth Observatory.
71. See Doel (2003: 654).
72. Richard A. Kerr, 2006, 'An Entrepreneur does Climate Science,' *Science* 311, 24 February: 1088–90; citations from 1088. Comer's involvement should not be interpreted as the interjection of hawkish views into abrupt change research. I mention it to indicate how much impact an external influence could have on getting specific studies produced and interjected into mainstream channels – an influence symbolically noted by the inclusion of

Comer on peer-reviewed science publications, which the primary authors insist was not merely honorific.
73. See Conway (2008: 1999).
74. Cf. Conway (2008).
75. On the notion of an 'obligatory point of passage', see Michel Callon, 1986, 'Elements of a Sociology of Translation: Domestication of the Scallops and the Fishermen of St Brieuc Bay', in John Law, ed., *Power, Action and Belief: A New Sociology of Knowledge?* London: Routledge, pp. 196–233; on the move to orient the ESMF to production of socio-economic information for weather- and climate-affected industry, see Anthony Hollingsworth, Sakari Uppala, Ernst Klinker, David Burridge, Frederic Vitart, Jeanette Onvlee, J. W. De Vries, Ad De Roo, and Christian Pfrang, 2005, 'The Transformation of Earth-System Observations into Information of Socio-Economic Value in GEOSS', *Quarterly Journal of the Royal Meteorological Society* 131: 3493–512.
76. Lisa Parks, 2006, 'Planet Patrol: Satellite Imaging, Acts of Knowledge, and Global Security', in Andrew Martin and Patrice Petro, eds, *Rethinking Global Security*, New Jersey: Rutgers University Press, pp. 132–50.
77. Cf. Russill and Nyssa (2009).
78. Kasper Mossman, 2008, 'Profile of Hans Joachim Schellnhuber', *Proceedings of the National Academy of Sciences of the United States of America*, available at http://www.pnas.org/content/105/6/1783.full. (Accessed 2 January 2011).
79. Cited in Mossman (2008).
80. *Science Watch*, 2009, 'Hot New Papers 2009', available at http://sciencewatch.com/dr/nhp/2009/pdf/09julnhpLentET.pdf. (Accessed 2 January 2011).
81. Timothy M. Lenton, Hermann Held, Elmar Kriegler, Jim W. Hall, Wolfgang Lucht, Stefan Rahmstorf, and Hans Joachim Schellnhuber, 2008, 'Tipping Elements in the Earth's Climate System,' *Proceedings of the National Academy of Sciences* 105(6): 1786–93; citation on p. 1792.
82. Cf. Russill and Nyssa (2009).
83. See Schellnhuber (1999: C19).
84. Schellnhuber (1999: C22).
85. Schellnhuber (1999: C22).
86. Cf. Edwards (2010).
87. Rockström et al. (2009).
88. Tim Lenton and Hans Joachim Schellnhuber, 2007, 'Tipping the Scales', *Nature Reports Climate Change*, available at http://www.nature.com/climate/2007/0712/full/climate.2007.65.html. (Accessed 2 January 2011).
89. Barnett (2003: pp. 14–15).
90. See Busby, 2008; UK Ministry of Defence (2008); Mazo (2010).
91. See GBN (2007).
92. See Simon Dalby, 'Anthropocene Security'.

References

Guggenheim, D. (2006) An Inconvenient Truth: A Global Warning. DVD. Beverly Hills: Participant Productions.
Broecker, W. S. (1999) "What If the Conveyor Were to Shut Down? Reflections on a Possible Outcome of the Great Global Experiment," GSA Today 9(1): 1–7.

4
Insecurities of Non-Dominance: Re-Theorizing Human Security and Environmental Change in Developed States

Wilfrid Greaves

Introduction

Contemporary human security theory often characterizes people as secure or insecure based largely upon the 'security' of their respective states. Although some research explicitly notes that human insecurity can arise in developed and developing states, seldom does it pay the former more than cursory attention; repeatedly, the unspoken assumption is that citizens of developed states don't actually experience, or experience very little, human insecurity (see, for example, Thomas and Wilkin, 1999; ICISS, 2001; Hampson et al., 2002; CHS, 2003; Roberts, 2008).[1] Such an approach, however, assumes generally uniform security conditions within a given state, and depends upon gendered characterizations of 'secure' states in the Global North exporting or promoting human security to 'insecure' states in the Global South. Consequently, it obscures conditions of insecurity experienced by minority or marginalized groups within otherwise 'secure' states and societies. As a result, human insecurity within developed states remains under-theorized and under-examined.

Given the particular, and worsening, hazards associated with environmental changes, this chapter proposes a framework for explaining environmentally driven human insecurity in developed states based on societal relations of dominance/non-dominance (Greaves, 2009).[2] Centrally, it identifies non-dominance as a constitutive factor for insecurity due to the inability of marginalized groups to 'securitize' locally experienced environmental hazards to their human security. Such an approach avoids the state-centrism inherent in much of the human security literature, and provides a mechanism for identifying, examining and mitigating human insecurity within developed states.

This chapter proceeds in three parts. First, it critically engages contemporary human security theory, and asserts the need for a broad and non-statist conception of human security. It identifies the concept of insecurity(ies) of non-dominance and situates it within a broad human security framework. Second, it examines the particular constitution of non-dominance within Canada as an example of a developed state. Third, it examines how environmental changes underlie and multiply the human insecurity of non-dominant groups in Canada. In particular, it surveys economic, physical and societal insecurities constituted by environmental changes and non-dominance in the Canadian Arctic.

Human security and insecurities of non-dominance

Human security emerged from the geopolitical and conceptual opening offered by the end of the Cold War. It sought to change the ontology of security from one concerned primarily with the survival and interests of states to one focused upon the survival and well-being of people. Since their inception, however, human security theory and practice have been bifurcated between two distinct approaches: a 'narrow' school concerned primarily with violent threats to people's well-being, and a 'broad' school which asserts that, because human lives and livelihoods are integrally affected by non-violent as well as violent means, 'the problem of human security ... cannot by its very constitution be approached in a narrow manner' (Roberts, 2008: 16). Instead, the broad school contends that human security must extend to other hazards that can threaten the economic, social, cultural and physical aspects of human life (UNDP, 1994; CHS, 2003). Although this debate has not been entirely resolved, the broad school appears to have gained more traction in scholarly and practical circles, and there seems to be a general recognition that human security cannot be limited *a priori* to violent security hazards without excessively limiting the remit and utility of the concept.[3]

Central to most human security theory is the assumption that the state remains a, if not *the*, central provider of security for its citizens (Price-Smith, 1999; Shani, Sato and Pasha, 2007). Although the literature notes the potential and likelihood for predatory, despotic or unstable states to pose a threat to their citizens' security, most policy-oriented human security studies still promote the establishment of effective sovereign states able to fulfil the 'responsibility to protect' their citizens (DFAIT, 2002; CHS, 2003; UN, 2005). According to Krause and Williams, for instance, 'security is synonymous with citizenship'

(1997: 43), such that creating effective states capable of delivering the goods of citizenship is the *sine qua non* of providing human security. In examining states that lack the capacity to provide security for their citizens, however, scholars have overwhelmingly focused upon so-called fragile, failing and failed states concentrated in particular regions of the Global South. This has resulted in two problematic and related trends within the human security field.

First, human security research has often retained a state-centrism that is antithetical to the basic purpose of human security, namely employing *people* as the referent object of security analysis (e.g. Thomas and Wilkin, 1999; Hampson et al., 2002). Whether in the developing world, such as the ongoing turmoil in the Great Lakes region of Africa, or the developed or semi-developed world, such as the overflow of drug violence from Mexico into the southern United States, human security hazards clearly transcend state borders. Analytical and policy state-centrism, such as the reduction of regional violence to a 'civil war' within the Democratic Republic of Congo, or the designation of cross-border drug problems as a 'Mexican' drug war, denies the multifaceted causes, transmission and impacts of security hazards across state boundaries. Moreover, it obscures the variegated effects of those hazards within societies; to take two similar examples, discussions of violence associated with 'Mexico's drug war' or 'Brazilian gangs' omit the reality that violent crime throughout most of both countries has been declining for decades (UNODC, 2010). Overlooking trans- and sub-state insecurities merely compounds the flaws of 'the dominant state-centric security orthodoxy [that has] provided at best a very partial representation of reality and at worst completely misunderstood, misrepresented, or ignored other important security concerns' (Thomas and Wilkin, 1999: 9). This state-centrism is further compounded within the narrow approach, since restricting human security's focus to violence necessarily privileges state structures that defend, fail to defend or actively endanger the lives of civilians. In many ways, the narrow school thus attempts to discipline the radical potential of the human security framework by 'securing security' from alternative, that is, non-state, ontologies (Hoogensen and Rottem, 2004: 160).

Second, while a robust research focus on the developing world is appropriate given that it contains the most severe and pervasive cases of human insecurity, the ongoing paucity of human security analysis in/of the developed world suggests a widespread view of human security as being a problem *only* in/for the developing world. Contemporary human security studies often employ and reinforce a dichotomy according to which people's security is largely determined by the 'security' of their respective state (Peou, 2002; Thomas and Tow, 2002; Riddell-Dixon, 2005).[4] The dichotomy arises from a view of human security not 'as a concept that is relevant the world over ... but as a service offered by the global north to the global south, defined by the global north (scholarship and policymaking) and distributed by the global north' (Hoogensen and Stuvoy, 2006: 216). This approach thus employs gendered characterizations of 'secure' states in the Global North exporting or promoting human security to 'insecure' states in the Global South, and is subject to standard critical and feminist critiques of mainstream security theory (Hoogensen and Stuvoy, 2006; Hoogensen and Rottem, 2004; Sjoberg, 2009). In particular, dichotomous North-South/secure-insecure conceptions of human security mirror what Iris Marion Young (2003: 2, 4) termed the 'bargain of masculinist protection':

> In this patriarchal logic, the role of the masculine protector puts those protected, paradigmatically women and children, in a subordinate position of dependence and obedience ... Central to the logic of masculinist protection is the subordinate relation of those in the protected position.

Not only does such logic perpetuate power/knowledge relations that privilege Northern polities and their citizens – with developed societies treated as aspirational for all others – it obscures conditions of insecurity that exist *within* developed states.

By characterizing developed states as 'secure', and by collocating human security with the existence of effective states, conventional human security theory cannot explain conditions of insecurity for minority or marginalized groups within wealthy states with high security-provision capabilities, particularly if they are caused *by* the state. It more or less presumes human security for citizens of the developed world, uncritically accepting that states which can secure their citizens will. That such conditions exist is axiomatic of social and economic policies aimed at mitigating unequal distributions of resources and providing essential services to vulnerable and marginal groups. It is also empirically demonstrated by quotidian instances of intra-developed state poverty, violence, ethno-social tension, injustice, etc., such as, to take but one example, a 2004 national homicide rate of 5.5/100,000 across the United States, but a rate of 48.5/100,000 in the city of Baltimore, one of the poorest and most heavily African American metropolitan areas in the United States (FBI, 2008). State-centric approaches to human (in)security, combined with a presumption of homogenous security conditions within states, especially developed states, lead to the conceptual restriction of human insecurity to those states that cannot provide for their citizens, rather than those which, for whatever reason, do not. By contrast, a broad approach to human security provides an epistemology for examining (in)security beyond the confines of violent and statist analysis. Conceptually, it suggests that traditional notions of security lack relevance in a world of transnational phenomena capable of affecting a wide variety of human referent objects. The security of people, intimately linked with the security of their respective states during the Cold War, can no longer be examined by employing the state as the referent object of analysis. Instead, '"human security" seeks to place the individual – or people collectively – as the *referent* of security, rather than, although not necessarily in opposition to, institutions such as territory and state sovereignty' (Newman, 2001: 239). Thus, human security can only be understood by specifying a level of analysis – individual, collective or societal – and uncovering hazards to some element of the specified group's existence. As people are, in most societies, only rarely threatened through the overt exercise of military force, it is necessary to examine hazards arising from a multitude of sources, analytically divided into different 'sectors' of security analysis (Buzan, 1991; Buzan, Waever and de Wilde, 1998; Nef, 1999). Hazards affecting any of these areas – such as the physical, economic, environmental and cultural sectors – are potential sources of insecurity and valid subjects of security analysis.

In this chapter, human security is defined by two critical elements: the multi-sectorality of security hazards, as identified before, and the intersubjectivity of security for human communities. Intersubjectivity – shared understandings among a group of people – determines communal identity, since it is individuals' mutual understandings of membership, 'being' part of a group and 'belonging' to it, that distinguish a community from other observable human collectivities (Anderson, 2006). Community derives from shared understandings of common interests and common identity among a group of people; without a shared identity, a sense of 'we-ness', there is no community. In this sense, we discuss 'community not as a matter of feelings, emotions and affection, but as a cognitive process through which common identities are created' (Adler, 2005: 195). Human communities are therefore 'imagined communities' (Anderson, 2006), socially constructed and intersubjectively understood by their members. Communal identity, moreover, is an essential component of broad human security; although a critic of a human security approach, Barry Buzan has observed that, as social creatures, 'individuals are not free standing, but only take their meaning from the societies in which they operate' (Buzan, 2004: 370). Communitarian human security, as a level at which to conduct security analysis, overlaps with the idea of 'societal security' pioneered by Buzan and Waever, which centres on 'identity, the self-conception of communities, and those individuals who identify themselves as members of a particular community' (Wæver, 1995: 67; Wæver, et al., 1993; Buzan, Waever and de Wilde, 1998). Using this framework, the referent object is the community – including the identity(ies) that link its members – rather than the individuals who comprise its membership. Identity is central: some hazards might threaten a human collectivity irrespective of the social relations that exist between its members, but others can only be understood in terms of their impact upon the shared identities that constitute a particular community. Since communal identities are socially constructed, so too must be the hazards by which societal human securities are considered threatened. Only members *of* a group can designate threats *to* that group, but the designation of 'threat' must be intersubjectively understood by the group's members. 'Threats to identity are thus always a question of the *construction* of something as threatening some "we" – and often thereby actually contributing to the construction or reproduction of "us"' (Buzan, Waever and de Wilde, 1998: 120). Accordingly, different communities experience particular hazards in different ways, 'depending upon how their identity is constructed' (Buzan, Waever and de Wilde, 1998: 124).

Whether or not changes to a particular communal identity are translated into *security* hazards, however, is a function of the power relations between that community and other securitizing actors. Securitization – the process of designating an issue a security threat 'requiring emergency measures and justifying actions outside the normal bounds of political procedure' (Buzan, Waever and de Wilde, 1998: 24) – is one from which no actor is entirely excluded, but to which a small number have privileged access. Sociopolitical and state elites, through their greater control of political and economic resources, mass media and the instruments of government authority, occupy a dominant position within securitization processes that privileges their – that is, statist and elite – conceptions of security over those of non-dominant actors. As such, identities that are shared by these elites or that are strongly linked with national identity are privileged as more security-worthy than competing or marginal sub- and trans-state identities. Beyond hazards to a particular identity, then, identities matter for security. As Hoogensen and Stuvoy (2006: 219) note, 'relations of dominance and non-dominance determine who defines norms and practices and who must follow them; who is important and who is not; who sets the parameters of the debate and who does not; who is valuable and who is not;' who is to be secured and who is not. This cleavage between the security and securitization-capacities of dominant and non-dominant groups exists at both the international and sub-national levels, and reaffirms the limitations of statist forms of security analysis. Non-dominance is constituted in multiple ways along multiple societal cleavages dependent upon the societal context, and not all non-dominance translates into insecurity. Examining human security at the state level risks conflating the (in)security of the dominant social group within a state with (in)security for all groups within the state, precluding serious possibility of secure and insecure groups cohabiting the same space. Employed this way, human security merely reinforces the tired and false dichotomy between secure developed states and insecure developing ones (Cheung-Gertler, 2007). As Edward Newman notes, such an approach obscures the reality that 'citizens of states that are "secure" according to the traditional conception of security can be perilously insecure to a degree that demands a reappraisal of the concept' (Newman, 2001: 240). Conversely, it overlooks an elite transnational socio-economic class originating from the developing world whose security is unaffected by the insecurity of the majority of their fellow citizens. Crucially for this paper, reifying human security within developed states 'denies relations of dominance and non-dominance within the global north itself. People that are located in the north but that do not reap the benefits of the dominant group – such as, for example, indigenous peoples or marginalized communities – vanish within such a security approach' (Hoogensen and Stuvoy, 2006: 216). The security and identities of dominant social groups are privileged within any security analysis that does not delve into sub-national insecurities that exist even within developed states; minority and marginalized concerns remain omitted.

Such an epistemic basis for security analysis dramatically alters the way in which security is understood, studied, distributed and pursued. If security hazards occur within and across state borders, the state's utility as a level of analysis diminishes. Since human security is experienced differently by peoples and groups within polities, the structures and variables that determine who is secure and who is not must be uncovered, and the processes that lead to or perpetuate insecurity examined. If state action can be both cause and corrective of human insecurity, analysts must consider insecurity 'not as some inevitable occurrence but as a direct result of existing structures of power that

70 *Insecurities of Non-Dominance*

determine who enjoys the entitlement to security and who does not' (Thomas and Wilkin, 1999: 3). For research to truly reflect conditions of human (in)security within a given polity, it must examine the security of those groups most removed from political and economic power, and most marginalized from securitization discourse and the exceptional mobilization of state resources to address their security concerns.

Non-dominance in Canada

As a wealthy developed state that has also been a pioneer in the conceptual and policy development of human security, albeit through a consciously narrow approach, Canada is a particularly suitable candidate for (in)security analysis (DFAIT, 2002; Cheung-Gertler, 2007; Huliaris and Tzifakis, 2007). It also typifies two examples of societal non-dominance that, in the face of an environmental hazard, can result in insecurity. Two dominant/non-dominant cleavages appear particularly relevant for human (in)security analysis in Canada: a geographic division between rural and urban Canadians and a racial one between aboriginal and non-aboriginal Canadians. Canada is highly urbanized, and the economic and political power is concentrated in a few urban regions across the country.[5] In political representation, per capita income, socio-economic indicators of well-being and influence upon major public-policy debates, rural residents are quantitatively or substantively inferior to city dwellers (Mitura and Bollman, 2003; Singh, 2004). Although the relationship between rural and urban in determining public policy is complex, Simon Dalby notes that 'the urban view of things frequently reduces rural concerns either to a backward society in need of modernisation or to a source of resources for the industrial modern sector controlled in the metropoles' (2003: 196). Rural Canadians are a non-dominant group relative to their urban counterparts; their numerical minority and political and economic marginalization render them less able to affect policy decisions regarding their particular needs and concerns, including security. In political decision-making, this can be understood as the power of metropolitan and mid-sized urban areas vis-à-vis smaller urban areas and rural communities.

A second social cleavage exists between the dominant non-aboriginal and non-dominant aboriginal populations. Though broad, this implicates a racialized power distinction between the non-aboriginal majority and the aboriginal minority that exists on multiple political and social levels. At the level of the Canadian state, aboriginal non-dominance is evident: the capacity of Native groups to pursue their rights and assert their interests against Ottawa and the provinces is circumscribed by their inferior legal and constitutional status. The Indian Act of 1876 and subsequent legislation established a fiduciary relationship between the federal government and First Nations, Inuit and Métis peoples that has marginalized and infantilized aboriginals, making so-called 'Indians a special class of persons, legal dependents on the crown, [and] children in the eyes of the law' (Harring, 1998: 263). This legal regime informed racist, exclusionary and assimilationist practices directed by the state against aboriginal peoples for at least the subsequent century of the Canadian nation-building project (Harring, 1998: 263). The Constitution Act of 1982 stipulates that aboriginal groups possess a set of unspecified rights vis-à-vis the state, of which 'self-government' has been the primary focus of Government and Native bands' rights efforts (Green, 2001: 722). In practice, though, as an expression of aboriginal peoples' self-determination, self-government has struggled to overcome 'the very configurations of colonial power that Indigenous peoples' demands for recognition have historically sought to transcend' (Coulthard, 2007: 439). The non-dominance of Canadian aboriginals has been enshrined in successive constitutional and legal instruments, and has been implicated in the substantially lower socio-economic conditions experienced by Native populations both on- and off-reserve, as identified by, among others, the 1996 Royal Commission on aboriginal Peoples (Government of Canada, 1996).

The implications of racialized relations of non-dominance in a developed-state context are particularly significant because they have often escaped security analysis. As Debra Thompson (2008) has observed, Canadian political science has generally under-examined the significance of race. She notes that 'dominant approaches to the study of English Canadian political science are unlikely to acknowledge race as a political production or phenomenon', despite the fact that 'institutions that avoid race according to the principles of colour blindness serve to solidify existing social hierarchies' (Thompson, 2008: 537–38). This is apparent with respect to Canadian security studies, in which the overwhelming disciplinary preoccupation is with security policy and practices abroad, rather than any particular conception of insecurity at home. Indeed, precisely because it generally does not employ a human security lens, security studies of much of the developed world seem to omit any serious discussion of race. Like insecurity itself, race is seen to be more relevant 'out there' than it is 'here at home'.

A notable exception in Canadian security studies is recent work by Kyle Grayson, who not only incorporates race into his study of the production of Canadian domestic security and drug policy, but also observes the highly racialized nature of (in)security in Canada. Grayson challenges dominant perceptions of Canadian identity as 'civilized, unified, progressive, and tolerant' (Grayson, 2008: 100) and, though with specific respect to state practice towards illegal drugs, notes: 'the substances, those who use them, and the spaces in which it is claimed they are exclusively produced/used have been subject to a series of securitizations that have marginalized specific individuals and entire communities' (Grayson, 2008: 247). Given the litany of Native abuses over Canada's colonial and postcolonial history, an aboriginal/non-aboriginal cleavage appears particularly relevant to studies of Canadian human insecurity since, as Heather Smith has observed, 'human security remains an aspiration for too many First Nations people in Canada' (Smith, 2006: 80–1). Race is thus seen to be an important variable in the distribution of (in)security, perhaps especially in a developed context such as Canada, where strong state security-provision capabilities mitigate insecurity for large portions of the population. In such a state, insecurities of non-dominance may be especially apparent in relation to the security of dominant social groups.

Environmentally driven human insecurity

Although there exist clear societal cleavages in Canada and other developed states that suggest certain groups are disproportionately unable to securitize hazards to their local human security, it remains that, in many observable ways, people in developed states are more secure than those living elsewhere. Effective state structures can indeed mitigate insecurity for citizens; particularly in democracies, state responsiveness to citizens' concerns provides perhaps the greatest defence against insecurity. However, increasingly, security conditions within all states, including developed ones, are being undermined by environmental changes, a category which captures both 'natural' (including the effects of anthropogenic climate change) and man-made (including pollution, ecological degradation and resource depletion) hazards. There is a substantial and growing literature about environmentally driven human insecurity in the developing world, but increasingly scholars and policymakers are also recognizing the insecurity facing the states, and citizens, of the developed world (UNDP, 1994; CHS, 2003; Dodds and Pippard, 2005; Wisner et al., 2007). A high-level report in the United States, for instance, noted that the magnitude of environmental change is now such that it has 'the potential to disrupt our way of life and to force changes in the way we keep ourselves safe and secure' (CNA Corporation, 2007: 6). The increasing seriousness of global environmental changes is generating a renewed awareness of the maxim of environmental security scholarship that 'the environment, modified by human interference, sets the conditions for socio-political-economic life. When these conditions are poor, life is poor' (Buzan, Waever and de Wilde, 1998: 84). Thus, it is *environmental* hazards that are increasingly likely to confront non-dominant groups within developed states, since these groups' relative inability to securitize emerging threats makes them less able to deal with environmental changes that affect them but not, or not yet, dominant groups.

Given the suggested relationship between non-dominance and insecurity in developed states, the logic of non-dominance suggests that insecurity will be greatest where forms of non-dominance overlap and coincide with an environmental hazard. In Canada, this suggests that the most acute human insecurity will exist in the Arctic, which primarily comprises rural and aboriginal communities and is experiencing some of the most significant environmental change in the world (ACIA, 2004; IPCC, 2007). In the Arctic, non-dominance is partly structured by the territorial status of the Yukon, Northwest Territories and Nunavut. Unlike provinces, whose powers derive from the Constitution, territorial governments have no inherent jurisdiction; their mandates and powers are delegated by the federal government. A federally appointed commissioner heads each territorial government, and though the territories have the highest per capita representation in Parliament, in absolute terms they are by far the least significant jurisdictions in the House and least regionally represented in the Senate. The territories also have the highest proportion of aboriginal populations among any Canadian jurisdictions, with Nunavut and the Northwest Territories both possessing aboriginal majorities. While progress has been made in the realization of Northern aboriginal self-government, including the resolution of the Nunavut Land Claims Agreement and establishment of the Nunavut Territory, these jurisdictions with aboriginal majorities continue to be denied full incorporation into the Confederation. Thus, though self-government remains the watchword of federal-territorial relations, 'direct rule from Ottawa denies them the regional political representation and authority enjoyed by the majority in the south' (Burnet, 1987: 185). The consequences of this configuration of federal/ territorial, aboriginal/non-aboriginal power relations extend beyond issues like the settlement of land claims and the devolution of authority over natural resources. As a result, 'the North can be studied as a society – actually a set of several societies – but it can only be understood as a colony ... A society is colonial to the extent that major decisions affecting it are made outside it ... [and] the North is totally dependent constitutionally on Ottawa' (Dacks, 1981: 208). The political dependence of the region in Canadian politics, and the racial and geographic non-dominance of its inhabitants, makes it unable to effectively respond to the hazards of environmental change.

Of the different dimensions of human (in)security, the economic, physical and societal sectors appear especially relevant in the Arctic. The author has argued elsewhere that all aspects of security are underpinned by conditions of environmental security (Greaves, 2009), but environmental changes seem most directly to affect Arctic human security in these three sectors: economic security because environmental changes are undermining traditional economic activities and the subsistence capacities of communities and individuals; physical security because Northerners experience greater risk of harm, impairment and threats to their survival as a result of environmental change; and societal security because Inuit and other Northern aboriginal cultures and identities rooted in a connection with the natural environment are eroded by changes to that environment. These insecurities are empirically linked and conceptually interdependent, and the purpose in distinguishing them is not to fully separate each from the others. Rather, it is to identify 'a multiplicity of [in]securities flowing concurrently [so] we can then start to recognize ways in which these [in]securities are linked to one another, rather than isolating them from one another and prioritizing them individually' (Hoogensen and Rottem, 2004: 168–9).

Economic insecurity in the Canadian Arctic

In its 2009 *Human Development Report*, the United Nations Development Programme identified 'five key transmission mechanisms' that link environmental change to reversals in human development: food security, water stress and water security, rising sea levels and exposure to climate-driven disasters, ecosystem disruption, and human health (UNDP, 2009: 9). Although the report's focus is conditions within the developing world, these mechanisms also contribute to human insecurity in the Canadian North. For instance, there are strong links between these mechanisms and economic human security in the Arctic. At its most basic, 'economic security requires an assured basic income – usually from productive or remunerative work' (UNDP, 1994: 25). This income is essential for the purchase of food, the mitigation of vulnerability to weather and climate events, and the maintenance of health. In other words, economic security is integral to resisting the negative effects of the environmental transmission mechanisms identified by UNDP. One of the challenges in the Arctic, however, is that socio-economic modernization has substantially displaced traditional economic systems. Though modernization drives positive and negative economic trends, for many aboriginal Northerners modernization has supplanted traditional economic activities with a mixed wage-subsistence economy in which they remain disadvantaged. In 2001, for instance, the unemployment rate for Inuit was 22% compared to 6% for non-aboriginal Northerners; the average income among non-aboriginal adults in Nunavut was $52,864 but only $19,686 among Inuit, a stark example of economic inequality (Statistics Canada, 2006: 15–16). The purchasing power of Northern incomes is further reduced because store-bought foods are two to three times more expensive than in the South but provide less nutrition than traditional country foods (Statistics Canada, 2006: 9). Economic modernization has thus not only failed to greatly benefit many Inuit, but in absolute terms it has also weakened their economic self-sufficiency. According to Simon Dalby (2003: 190), 'the increasing dependence of native peoples in the far north on commercial markets in the global economy may ironically reduce their resilience and ability to adapt because their modes of life and resource extraction have become so dependent on fuel, clothing and other necessities provided by the market system.'

Although not caused solely by environmental change, Northerners' economic insecurity is multiplied by it. Country foods remain an important part of most Inuit's regular diet, with more than half of all meat and fish consumed coming from traditional harvesting (Statistics Canada, 2006: 13). However, as Arctic ecosystems change as a result of climate change, thinning sea ice, changing vegetation, altered migration patterns for caribou herds and increased variability and unpredictability in weather and climate all reduce the accessibility and availability of traditional foods (ACIA, 2004). In some places, 'reduced quality of food sources, such as diseased fish and dried up berries, are already being observed' (ACIA, 2004: 16). Given the higher cost and reduced benefit of packaged foods in Northern communities, a decrease in the availability of country foods as a result of environmental change is economically impossible for many Northerners to replace, further implicating their food and economic security. Simultaneously, climate change is facilitating industrial development to extract natural resources from the Arctic, particularly minerals and fossil fuels. However, in many cases 'these large-scale activities are totally separated from the regional socio-economic environment. They are carried out on an autonomous basis and have practically no economic impact on the permanent communities in the vicinity' (AHDR, 2004: 71). In such cases, the environmental facilitation of extractive economic activity in the North is likely to perpetuate the disparity between aboriginal and non-aboriginal groups.

Physical insecurity in the Canadian Arctic

Physical security refers to personal survival and the conditions for ongoing human existence. It too is clearly implicated by reduced access to food and water, exposure to extreme weather events, and chronic and acute health issues. In the North, physical insecurity is particularly manifest in endemic levels of public and private health issues. Arctic communities suffer lower life expectancies and access to medical care but substantially higher levels of depression, domestic violence, physical abuse, infant mortality and suicide than anywhere else in Canada, with the exception of certain other aboriginal groups (Statistics Canada, 2006: 15–16). For instance, in 2001 average life expectancy for all Canadian men was 77 years, while for Inuit men it was 62.6 years; the gap between all Canadian and Inuit women's life expectancies was more than 10 years (Statistics Canada, 2005). Hazards to physical security are not freestanding, however, but linked to phenomena in the economic and societal sectors that pose hazards in their own right: economic subsistence and affordability and accessibility of food, for instance.

The relationships can also be more complex. The fact that Arctic communities have unemployment levels 30% above the Canadian average, with mean incomes 30% below, is linked with the dislocation of traditional economic activity; local and regional climate change also affect opportunities for traditional hunting and harvesting, especially when combined with societal loss of traditional skills and knowledge (Statistics Canada, 2006: 15–16). These factors contribute to an Inuit suicide rate of approximately 135/100,000, more than 10 times the rate for non-Inuit (Kirmayer, et al., 2007). Thus, while a physical security hazard, 'this pattern [of suicide] has been associated with a view of young males not seeing a future for themselves as hunters and contributors to their community and at the same time not fitting into the cash employment structures that are becoming the dominant lifestyle' (ACIA, 2004: 157). Clearly, human (in)security analysis must consider the mutual constitution of hazards in different sectors in order to fully grasp their impacts upon human collectivities.

As with economic insecurity, physical insecurity in the Arctic is generally not caused by environmental changes, but is strongly affected by them. Though there are significant and growing physical security hazards due to increased lake temperatures, permafrost thawing, stress on plant and animal populations, melting of glaciers and sea ice, and damage to essential infrastructure, for the moment their impacts are primarily transmitted through their effects upon other sectors. Environmental hazards that more directly impact Northerners' physical security include the well-documented effects of trans-boundary pollution and persistent organic pollutants (POPs) (Downie and Fenge, 2003). Though virtually none of these pollutants originate in the Arctic, high levels of POPs 'have been linked to cancer, birth defects, and other neurological, reproductive, and immune-system damage in people and animals' (Johansen, 2003: 82) throughout the circumpolar North. These toxins bioaccumulate within individual animals and biomagnify up the Arctic food chain by 'as much as 10-fold from one "link" to the next' (VanderZwaag, Huebert and Ferrara, 2002: 136), resulting in human consumption of concentrated chemical and organic pollutants such as PCBs, DDT, mercury and other heavy metals. The level of certain toxins found in the blood and fatty tissue of some Canadian Inuit is five to ten times higher than the national average, including 'the highest levels of PCBs ever found, except for victims of industrial accidents' (Johansen, 2003: 84). These pollutants may originate from southern industries, but the physical environment is implicated because 'the Arctic's cold climate slows the natural decomposition of these toxins, so they persist in the Arctic environment longer than at lower latitudes' (Johansen, 2003: 82). The environment cannot be separated from the constitution of physical human security hazards in the Arctic, either.

Societal insecurity in the Canadian Arctic

Societal insecurity in the Canadian Arctic is strongly linked to how aboriginal identities and cultural practices are affected by changes to the natural environment. Many aboriginal peoples share a close relationship between their communal identities and natural environments: 'cultural survival, identity and the very existence of indigenous societies depend to a considerable degree on the maintenance of environmental quality. The degradation of the environment is therefore inseparable from a loss of culture and hence identity' (Cocklin, 2002: 159). The intersubjective understanding of Northern aboriginal cultures is one in which the social and physical realms are intimately connected.

aboriginal peoples have traditionally regarded themselves as central to the order and balance of the natural world, and their cultural and spiritual well-being depends upon maintaining their relationship with the land. Thus, 'damage to the land, appropriation of land, and spatial restrictions may all constitute assaults on the individual and collective sense of self of those who adhere to this ecocentric world view' (Kirmayer et al., 2007: 60). Physical changes to the land that alter the ways aboriginal peoples subsist, and which undermine the accumulated generational knowledge of weather and climate patterns, animal movements, and methods of hunting and gathering, can have wide-reaching implications for aboriginal cultures and identities.

Societal (in)security clearly also overlaps with hazards in other sectors. Reduced quality and availability of country foods as a result of the changing environment affect Northerners' food security and physical health, but also contribute to the erosion of cultural practices. 'To hunt, catch, and share these foods is the essence of Inuit culture. Thus, a decline in [country foods] ... threatens not only the dietary requirements of the Inuit, but also their very way of life' (ACIA, 2004: 94). Similarly, high rates of young male suicide have widespread implications for communities' societal security. The relationship between societal and physical insecurities is two directional: hazards to communal identity can contribute to physical insecurity for the individual, just as an individual's physical insecurity can affect the ties that bind a community together. Whole communities can be affected by the insecurity of individuals, particularly when that insecurity stems from shared community experiences. Thus, throughout the North, older men and 'women of all ages inevitably share in and suffer from the demoralization of the [young] men in the community' (Kirmayer et al., 2007: 64). Here the significance of the racial cleavage in the Canadian Arctic is emphasized again, because non-aboriginal Northerners who do not share traditional systems of belief and whose societal security is not rooted in a collective identity tied to the land will not experience the same societal insecurity as a result of environmental change.

Conclusion

This chapter has provided a critical analysis of contemporary human security theory, and has proposed a non-dominance framework for explaining and studying human insecurity within developed states. Particularly with respect to natural and man-made environmental changes, insecurities of non-dominance will increasingly expose non-dominant societal groups to environmental insecurity. This framework has been demonstrated through an analysis of non-dominance and insecurity in the Canadian Arctic where, despite significant and growing impacts of environmental change, and increasing calls from Inuit and aboriginal leaders for action to protect their peoples' human security (CBC News, 2009), the ongoing non-securitization of climate change reflects the non-dominance of Northerners and Northern aboriginals most immediately affected by it. This framework suggests that human (in)security is, and will increase as, a relevant mode of analysis within and across all states in both the developed and developing worlds.

Notes

1. The insecurity of non-citizen residents of developed states has been noted, however; see Lowry (2002); also Swatuk and Whitman in this volume. Wiebe (this volume) provides a compelling case of insecurity in the Global North.
2. I have previously proposed a four-part typology of different sources of insecurity. For this chapter, however, I will employ the term 'hazards' to refer to all observable immediate, likely and potential sources of insecurity.
3. A notable exception is official Canadian policy towards human security, which has continued to employ a narrow approach centred on 'violent threats to people's rights, safety, or lives' (see DFAIT, 2006).
4. This is particularly the case when human security is associated or conflated with humanitarian intervention or a political 'human security agenda' (see Behringer, 2005). For a non-dichotomous approach, see O'Brien and Leichenko (2007).
5. According to 2006 census data, over 80% of Canadians live in urban areas defined as having more than 1000 residents; 59% live in urban areas defined as having more than 100,000 residents (Statistics Canada, 2006).

References

ACIA, 2004. *Impacts of a Warming Climate: Arctic Climate Impact Assessment*. Cambridge: Cambridge University Press.
Adler, E., 2005. 'Imagined (Security) Communities: Cognitive Regions in International Relations'. In E. Adler, ed., *Communitarian International Relations: The Epistemic Foundations of International Relations*. New York: Routledge, 178–199.
AHDR, 2004. *Arctic Human Development Report*. Akureyri: Steffanson Arctic Institute.
Anderson, B., 2006. *Imagined Communities: Reflections on the Origin and Spread of Nationalism*. London: Verso.
Behringer, R. M., 2005. 'Middle Power Leadership on the Human Security Agenda'. *Cooperation and Conflict* 40(3), 305–42.
Burnet, P., 1987. 'Environmental Politics and Inuit Self-Government'. In F. Griffiths, ed., *Politics of the Northwest Passage*. Montreal: McGill-Queen's University Press, 181–99.

Buzan, B., 1991. *People, States and Fear: An Agenda for International Security Studies in the Post-Cold War Era*. Boulder: Lynne Rienner Publishers.
Buzan, B., 2004. 'A Reductionist, Idealistic Notion that Adds Little Analytical Value'. *Security Dialogue*, 35(3), 369–70.
Buzan, B., O. Waever and J. de Wilde, 1998. *Security: A New Framework for Analysis*. Boulder: Lynne Rienner.
CBC News, 2009. 'Inuit Leaders Demand Action at Climate-Change Conference' (18 November). Available at http://www.cbc.ca/canada/north/story/2009/11/16/inuit-climate-change.html, Accessed on January 1 2011.
Cheung-Gertler, J., 2007. 'A Model Power for a Troubled World?' *International Journal* 62(3), 589–607.
CNA Corporation, 2007. *National Security and the Threat of Climate Change*. Alexandria, VA: The CNA Corporation.
Cocklin, C., 2002. 'Water and "Cultural Security"'. In E. A. Page and M. Redclift, eds, *Human Security and the Environment: International Comparisons*. Northampton: Edward Elgar, 154–76.
Commission on Human Security (CHS), 2003. *Human Security Now*. New York: United Nations Press.
Coulthard, G. S., 2007. 'Subjects of Empire: Indigenous Peoples and the "Politics of Recognition" in Canada'. *Contemporary Political Theory*, 6(4), 437–60.
Dacks, G., 1981. *A Choice of Futures*. Toronto: Methuen.
Dalby, S., 2003. 'Geopolitical Identities: Arctic Ecology and Global Consumption'. *Geopolitics* 8(1) (Spring), 181–202.
Department of Foreign Affairs and International Trade (DFAIT), 2002. *Freedom from Fear: Canada's Foreign Policy for Human Security*. Ottawa: DFAIT.
Department of Foreign Affairs and International Trade (DFAIT), 2006. *Human Security – Cities: Freedom From Fear in Urban Spaces* (Leaflet). Ottawa: DFAIT.
Dodds, F. and T. Pippard, eds, 2005. *Human and Environmental Security: An Agenda for Change*. Sterling: Earthscan Publications.
Downie, D. and T. Fenge, eds, 2003. *Northern Lights Against POPs: Combatting Toxic Threats in the Arctic*. Montreal: Queen's-McGill University Press.
Federal Bureau of Investigation (FBI), 2008. 'Expanded Homicide Data'. *Crime in the United States, 2008*. Available at http://www2.fbi.gov/ucr/cius2008/offenses/expanded_information/homicide.html, Accessed on January 1 2011.
Government of Canada, 1996. *Report of the Royal Commission on Aboriginal Peoples*. Ottawa: Government of Canada.
Grayson, K., 2008. *Chasing the Dragon: Security, Identity, and Illicit Drugs in Canada*. Toronto: University of Toronto Press.
Greaves, W., 2009. 'The Essential Condition: A Stable Environment, Global Security, and Sustainable Peace'. In A. Livingstone, ed., *Environmental Conditions for Building Peace: The Pearson Papers Volume 12*. Clementsport: Canadian Peacekeeping Press, 91–114.
Green, J., 2001. 'Canaries in the Mines of Citizenship: Indian Women in Canada'. *Canadian Journal of Political Science* 34(4) (December), 715–38.
Hampson, F. O., J. Daudelin, J. Hay, H. Reid and T. Martin, 2002. *Madness in the Multitude: Human Security and World Disorder*. Don Mills: Oxford University Press.
Harring, S. L., 1998. *White Man's Law: Native People in Nineteenth-Century Canadian Jurisprudence*. Toronto: University of Toronto Press.

Hoogensen, G. and K. Stuvoy, 2006. 'Gender, Resistance, and Human Security'. *Security Dialogue*, 37(2) (June), 207–28.
Hoogensen, G. and S. V. Rottem, 2004. 'Gender Identity and the Subject of Security'. *Security Dialogue* 35(2) (June), 155–71.
Huliaris, A. and N. Tzifakis, 2007. 'Contextual Approaches to Human Security: Canada and Japan in the Balkans'. *International Journal* 62(3), 559–75.
ICISS, 2001. *The Responsibility to Protect: Report of the International Commission on Intervention and State Sovereignty*. Ottawa: International Development Research Centre.
IPCC, 2007. *Climate Change 2007: Synthesis Report*. Intergovernmental Panel on Climate Change Fourth Assessment Report Cambridge: Cambridge University Press.
Johansen, B. E., 2003. *Indigenous Peoples and Environmental Issues: An Encyclopaedia*. Westport: Greenwood Press.
Kirmayer, L. J., G. M. Brass, T. Holton, K. Paul, C. Simpson and C. Tait, 2007. *Suicide Among Aboriginal People in Canada*. Ottawa: Aboriginal Healing Foundation.
Krause, K. and M. C. Williams, 1997. 'From Strategy to Security: Foundations of Critical Security Studies'. In K. Krause and M. C. Williams, eds, *Critical Security Studies: Concepts and Cases*. London: UCL Press, 33–60.
Lowry, M., 2002. 'Creating Human Insecurity: The National Security Focus in Canada's Immigration System'. *Refuge* 21(1) (November), 28–39.
Mitura, V. and R. D. Bollman, 2003. 'The Health of Rural Canadians: A Rural-Urban Comparison of Health Indicators'. *Rural and Small Town Canada Analysis Bulletin* 4(6) (October). Ottawa: Statistics Canada, 1–23.
Nef, J., 1999. *Human Security and Mutual Vulnerability: The Global Political Economy of Development and Underdevelopment*, 2nd Edition. Ottawa: International Development Research Centre.
Newman, E., 2001. 'Human Security and Constructivism'. *International Studies Perspectives* 2(3), 239–51.
O'Brien, K. and R. Leichenko, 2007. *Human Security, Vulnerability, and Sustainable Adaptation*. Human Development Report Office Occasional Paper. New York: UNDP.
Peou, S., 2002. 'The UN, Peacekeeping, and Collective Human Security: From an Agenda for Peace to the Brahimi Report'. *International Peacekeeping* 9(2), 51–68.
Price-Smith, A. T., 1999. 'Ghosts of Kigali: Infectious Disease and Global Stability at the Turn of the Century'. *International Journal* 54(3) (Summer), 426–42.
Riddell-Dixon, E., 2005. 'Canada's Human Security Agenda'. *International Journal* 60(4), 1067–1092.
Roberts, D., 2008. *Human Insecurity: Global Structures of Violence*. London: Zed Books.
Shani, G., M. Sato and M. K. Pasha, eds, 2007. *Protecting Human Security in a Post 9/11 World: Critical and Global Insights*. New York: Palgrave Macmillan.
Singh, V., 2004. 'The Rural-Urban Income Gap within Provinces: An Update to 2000'. *Rural and Small Town Canada Analysis Bulletin*, 5(7) (December). Ottawa: Statistics Canada, 1–20.
Sjoberg, L., ed., 2009. *Gender and International Security: Feminist Perspectives*. New York: Routledge.
Smith, H., 2006. 'Diminishing Human Security: The Canadian Case'. In S. J. MacLean, D. R. Black and T. M. Shaw, eds, *A Decade of Human Security: Global Governance and the New Multilateralisms*. Burlington: Ashgate, 73–82.

Statistics Canada, 2005. *Projections of the Aboriginal populations, Canada, Provinces and Territories 2001 to 2017*. Ottawa: Statistics Canada.
Statistics Canada, 2006. 'Harvesting and Community Well-Being Among Inuit in the Canadian Arctic: Preliminary Findings From the 2001 Aboriginal People's Survey'. *Survey of Living Conditions in the Arctic*. Ottawa: Statistics Canada. Available at http://www.statcan.ca/english/freepub/89-619-XIE/2006001/part2.htm, Accessed on January 1 2012.
Thomas, C. and P. Wilkin, eds, 1999. *Globalization, Human Security, and the African Experience*. Boulder: Lynne Rienner.
Thomas, N. and W. T. Tow, 2002. 'The Utility of Human Security: Sovereignty and Humanitarian Intervention'. *Security Dialogue* 33(2) (June), 177–92.
Thompson, D., 2008. 'Is Race Political?' *Canadian Journal of Political Science* 41(3) (September), 525–47.
United Nations (UN), 2005. *Resolution Adopted by the General Assembly 60/1. 2005 World Summit*. UN Document A/RES/60/1. New York: United Nations.
United Nations Development Programme (UNDP), 1994. *Human Development Report 1994: New Dimensions of Human Security*. New York: United Nations.
United Nations Development Programme (UNDP), 2009. *Human Development Report 2007–2008. Fighting Climate Change: Human Solidarity in a Changing World*. New York: United Nations.
United Nations Office on Drugs and Crime (UNODC), 2010. *Homicide Statistics, Criminal Justice and Public Health Sources – Trends (2003–2008)*. Vienna: United Nations Office on Drugs and Crime. Available at http://www.unodc.org/unodc/en/data-and-analysis/homicide.html, Accessed on January 1 2012.
VanderZwaag, D., R. Huebert and S. Ferrara, 2002. 'The Arctic Environmental Protection Strategy, Arctic Council and Multilateral Environmental Initiatives: Tinkering while the Arctic Marine Environment Totters'. *Denver Journal of International Law and Policy* 30(2), 131–71.
Wæver, O., 1995. 'Securitization and Desecuritization'. In R. D. Lipschutz, ed., *On Security*. New York: Columbia University Press, 46–86.
Wæver, O., B. Buzan, M. Kelstrup and P. Lemaitre, 1993. *Identity, Migration and the New Security Order in Europe*. London: Pinter.
Wisner, B. et al., 2007. 'Climate Change and Human Security'. *Radix – Climate Change and Human Security*. Available at http://www.radixonline.org/cchs, Accessed on January 1 2012.
Young, I. M., 2003. 'The Logic of Masculinist Protection: Reflections on the Current Security State'. *Signs: Journal of Women in Culture and Society* 29(1), 1–25.

5
Water and Security in Africa: State-Centric Narratives, Human Insecurities

Larry A. Swatuk

Introduction

Africa has long been a battleground of underdevelopment, described by UNICEF (1994: 25) as being locked in a downward spiral of population increase, environmental degradation and poverty. Homer-Dixon (1999) drew many of his case studies from Africa in explication of the role of renewable resource degradation in 'acute conflict'. Collier and Hoeffler (2004) centred attention on African states' dependence upon resource extraction and its link to civil war, spawning a vast literature on the so-called resource curse (see chapters by Arthur and Whitman in this volume). Case studies of West African conflicts highlighted the role of lootable resources (diamonds, timber) in political instability (Richards, 1996; Reno, 1998; Ellis, 1999; also, see Le Billon, 2001 for an overview). Others have speculated on the role of unemployed youth in gang violence, as child soldiers, and as ready conscripts into Africa's many rebel movements. This 'youth bulge' is thought to be a key contributor to peri-urban instability, including inter-ethnic and gender-based violence, which is funded by trade in drugs, small arms and endangered species (Goldstone, 2001; Urdal, 2006). Based on such analysis, former US Assistant Secretary of State for Africa Affairs, Susan Rice (quoted in Black and Adibe, 1998: 59), declared in 1998 that it was the goal of the Clinton Administration to

> Protect the U.S. and its citizens from the threats to our national security that emanate from Africa ... [including] weapons proliferation ... state-sponsored terrorism, narcotics flows, the growing influence of rogue states, international crime, environmental degradation and disease.

Most recently, worries about the lack of adaptive capacity of African states to climate change have been added to the mix (Busby et al., 2010). Water resources have figured centrally in debates regarding the ways and means of avoiding 'the coming anarchy' (Kaplan, 1994) described previously, and achieving human/state/regional security in Africa (Green Cross International, 2000; Faeth, 2011). The non-substitutability of water as a necessary resource for life, combined with its shared nature across many of Africa's states, leads some scholars to suggest that water cooperation can have tangible peace and development effects 'beyond the river' (Conca and Dabelko, 2002; Sadoff and Grey, 2002; Wolf et al., 2005).

This chapter focuses on water issues in Africa. It interrogates the assumption that interstate approaches to and cooperation for 'water security' will result in enhanced peace and development across the continent. It argues that discourses of 'crisis' and 'conflict' privilege high-level interstate planning and action, to the exclusion of those most seriously affected by water insecurity, such as the rural and peri-urban poor. Moreover, it leads state-makers towards high-modern 'solutions' to water insecurity – that is, expensive infrastructure development – that appear to benefit sections of African states and societies that already enjoy a high degree of water security, namely urban industry and commercial agriculture.

The chapter is organized into seven sections, including the introduction. The second section engages the 'water wars' and 'water and conflict' narrative. It suggests that structural violence is far more problematic than interstate conflict, but that the dominant narrative tends to elide state and human security discourses around water. Section three describes some of the efforts being made to effect 'structural change' in African political economies, while section four highlights the perceived role of cooperation on shared rivers (including harmonization of national policies, laws and institutions) therein. Section five reflects on the fact that decades of 'structural change' have failed to alter the facts of 'structural violence'. Yet as material and physical conditions worsen for the poor and marginalized, elites enjoy a high level of water security and continue to cooperate on large-scale infrastructure projects that will in all likelihood be to their further benefit.

Section six presents a short case study of the Nile River Basin, arguing that Egypt and Ethiopia are trapped in an argument about the suitability of infrastructure – an argument that neither side can 'win' so long as it continues to be framed in terms of 'national security'. Given that elites in all riparian states enjoy relative water security, the Nile Basin states are unlikely to undertake water works that will threaten their neighbours to the extent that it threatens their own positions in power. A modified form of the *status quo* is therefore most likely, with Ethiopia erecting several dams, Egypt transferring water out of the basin into the Sinai, and all states engaging in dialogue through the Nile Basin Initiative. None of these activities will help redress the deeply abiding social inequalities in the basin; indeed, some of these activities will no doubt exacerbate them. Structural violence born of environmental injustice will therefore persist within the context of interstate approaches to 'water security'. Section seven presents a short conclusion.

Water and violence

> There is no precedent for a country developing without harnessing its rivers and utilizing its water resources.
>
> World Bank Senior Water Advisor (quoted in Yohannes, 2008: 87)

Much has been said about the potential for twenty-first century 'water wars', particularly in 'basins at risk' (Wolf, Yoffe and Giordano, 2003) or 'hydropolitical hotspots' (Zeitoun and Warner, 2006), several of which – the Nile, Zambezi, Inkomati, Cunene – are said to be located in Africa. While the water wars hypothesis is consistently challenged (Wolf et al., 2005), it persists partly due to recent studies speculating on the impact of climate change on the stability of African states and societies (Schnellnhuber et al., 2007). Even the 'environmental peacemaking' community of scholars highlights the central importance of a changing or unpredictable hydrological cycle as a driver of conflict. Almost all of these studies take as their baseline assumption some form of existing or impending physical water scarcity, due to either one or a combination of (i) absolute limits of hydrology, (ii) technical boundaries or (iii) demographically driven 'water crowding' (Falkenmark and Rockstrom, 2004). Given that many states in Africa share transboundary rivers, these scholars argue, there is real possibility of large-scale violent conflict in the near future (Toset et al., 2000). In the recent words of US Secretary of State Hilary Clinton (2010), 'As water becomes increasingly scarce, it may become a potential catalyst for conflict among – and within – nations.'

While the spectre of 'agential violence' (see Stoett, this volume) animates the world's media and state-houses, the lack of access to potable water for households or economic water for small-scale industry and smallholder farming reveals the depth and character of structural violence as it manifests across Africa. According to the UN World Water Development Report 3, 'Africa faces the toughest challenges of any continent. While most of the developing world has managed to reduce poverty, the rate in Sub-Saharan Africa has not changed much since the 1980s. With 40% living below the extreme poverty line of US$1 per day and 73% of the population below US$2 a day, according to World Bank figures, this continues to be the world's poorest region' (UN, 2009: ix). The intimate link between water, human security and economic development is well known (World Bank, 2004: 2; UN, 2006). At a national level, water consumption varies directly with GDP/capita with the world's richest states using the most water. Those countries with the highest Human Development Index (HDI) values are also the heaviest users of freshwater. Countries playing 'catch-up', such as China and India, are engaged in a massive exercise to harness their water resources primarily for industrial and agricultural development. To paraphrase Tony Allan (2003), these countries are engaged in a late modern hydraulic mission, a process through which the developed countries already have passed as exemplified by the many large dams and extensive water works (from urban supply to inter-basin transfer schemes) that dot the landscapes of the global North.

In contrast, according to a World Health Organisation-UNICEF report (2005: 5), '1.1 billion people lack access to safe drinking water. 2.6 billion people lack adequate sanitation. 1.8 million people die every year from diarrhoeal diseases,' the vast majority of whom are children under five years of age, most in Sub-Saharan Africa (SSA). Gleick (2002) estimates that by 2020 'as many as 135 million people will die from preventable water-related diseases' if appropriate actions are not taken. In the words of the World Water Council, 'the situation is no longer bearable'. For the UN, the right to water is 'indispensible for leading a life in human dignity' and 'a prerequisite for the realization of other human rights' (UNESCO, 2002).

In Africa, those most likely to suffer extreme poverty live in rural areas. According to the African Development Bank (2007: x),

> Eighty-five percent of sub-Saharan Africa's poor live in the rural areas and depend largely on agriculture for their livelihoods. Agricultural growth is therefore clearly key to poverty reduction; it can also help drive national economic growth. Yet agriculture in the region remains a largely subsistence activity, production has not kept pace with population growth, food self-sufficiency has declined, the household income required to afford bought-in food has not been generated and the numbers of malnourished people are consequently rising.

These extreme difficulties have led to a rush to the cities. Africa's early modern settlements were relatively small, neo-European enclaves designed to serve the interests of a limited number of European traders, settlers and administrators. During the post-WWII rush to 'prepare' Africans for independence, various 'big push' projects, in particular large dam building for hydropower and water supply to the newly created capital cities were undertaken. Yet no one could anticipate the scale of the influx into these small towns. Kinshasa and Brazzaville, which sit across from each other on the Congo River, began life as small trading posts in the 1880s. Today they constitute a cross-border conurbation of more than 12 million people. The number of people living in African cities increased 13-fold between 1950 and 2000, from 33 million to 417 million urbanites. An estimated 42.4% of Africans lived in cities in 2000, in contrast to only 14.9% 50 years earlier (UN, 2006: 90).

In 1900, Africa had no cities with a population of one million. In 1950, there were two, and by 2000 the number of million cities had increased to 35 (see Rakodi, 1997; Biswas, 2006; UNFPA, 2007 for details). Africa's primary cities have extensive ecological footprints. They draw resources, capital and people from not only their own hinterlands, but from around the world. Africa's capital cities account for between 33% (e.g. Accra, Lagos) and 100% (e.g. Banjul, Monrovia) of all manufacturing in their countries (O'Connor quoted in Rakodi, 1997). Many obtain their water and energy resources over long distances via complex systems of hydraulic infrastructure (Conley, 1996). These hydraulic works can dramatically alter social and environmental systems, as has happened in and around Africa's large dams. The general inability of cities to supply citizens with many basic services and the corresponding demand for fuel wood has led to localized deforestation, soil erosion, the siltation and pollution of surface and groundwater bodies and enhanced vulnerability to flooding (Chenje and Johnson, 1996). As rural areas are deprived of the young and able-bodied, urban areas groan under the weight of their needs, thus turning assets into potential liabilities if only in terms of their everyday production of waste.

The dominant narrative of water and conflict in Africa tends to elide these factors: that is, a difficult hydrology made more so by climate change, combined with watercourses shared by two or more states, each of which is interested in harnessing more water for agriculture, industry and cities ineluctably leads to competition for an increasingly scarce resource. In this view, 'structural violence' is not really recognized as such; rather, poverty is thought to be largely accidental or situational, a consequence of African states' abiding general conditions of underdevelopment. Thus, to avoid agential interstate/tribal/communal violence and to overcome poverty, water resources must be harnessed for mutually beneficial development: state security and human security are one and the same.

Seeking 'structural change'

The wide array of development interventions that have and continue to emerge from such an analysis take as axiomatic the need to 'restructure' African political economies (World Bank, 1997; Moss, 2007).[1] As highlighted by Duffield (2007), this narrative collapses securities (state, human, international) with development. The 'crisis' aspects of this narrative are broadly applied (to development, water, climate change, HIV/AIDS) so leading to multiple entry points. The consequent economic (e.g. less state, more private sector) and political (e.g. increased role for civil society, better 'governance') cross-conditionalities for external investment and participation create a landscape well-suited to multiple actors (i.e. public-private partnerships), all of which are engaged in a reinvigorated attempt to modernize 'the African state' (World Bank, 1997; Mengisteab and Daddieh, 1998). With regard to water, this revolves around extensive infrastructure development: large dams, canals, groundwater-based irrigation systems, urban water supply and sanitation.

African state and civil-society leaders participate actively in both practical and policy related events at every conceivable scale of human endeavour: from the village water-point to various government departments and Ministries, to regional networks (e.g. Global Water Partnership-Africa; Nile Basin Initiative) and organizations (e.g. African Ministers' Council on Water),[2] and global forums (e.g. World Water Forum). Meshing these activities together is a dense network of extra-African international donor states, consortia, private sector actors and non-governmental organizations.[3] Numerous coordinating documents (e.g. Millennium Development Goals, Paris Declaration on Aid Effectiveness, Accra Agenda for Action, NEPAD) and bodies (e.g. African Union, G8) exist to ensure that all of these activities 'add up' to sustainable, equitable, efficient resource use for mutually beneficial economic and social development.

Shared rivers

Water has emerged at the centre of Africa's security and development agenda for three reasons: (i) all economic activities require water as an input (the development agenda), (ii) most of Africa's surface and groundwater is shared between two or more states (the security agenda), and (iii) decades of uncoordinated activity has led to widespread degradation of the resource base (the security and development agenda). For Conca (2006), 'One of the entry points for institution-building in defence of the world's watersheds is the fact that nearly all of the world's largest rivers cross national borders.' According to data from Oregon State University, as of 2004 there were 61 shared river basins in Africa. Cooperative management initiatives were in existence or underway in only 15 of these shared basins, leaving 46 without any formal initiatives.[4] In Africa, international river basins (IRB) constitute 62% of the continent, with 47 African states having territory in one or more IRB. Globally, shared waters have induced many states to sign agreements with each other. The Food and Agricultural Organisation (FAO) 'identified more than 2000 agreements that deal with some aspect of transboundary water issues (most of them bilateral agreements focused on navigation)' (Conca, 2006). Wolf and colleagues identify 145 international treaties since 1814 that deal with some non-navigational aspect of international waters. In Africa, many of the agreements that do exist were treaties made by and for colonial powers, most involving large-scale infrastructure development on major African rivers such as the Zambezi and the Nile. Driving cooperation on international rivers is a general belief that '[i]n many river basins use of water for human purposes through investments in water infrastructure for urban, industrial, and agricultural growth is approaching or exceeding the amount of renewable water available' (Svendsen, Wester and Molle, 2004: 585). Globally, there is general agreement that sustainable water management requires a combination of basin-level management structures and an integrated resource management approach. Thus, integrated water resources management (IWRM) places great emphasis on the creation of a well-structured enabling environment to address these issues. In particular, there is significant emphasis on legal, institutional and policy frameworks at the basin scale for sustainable resource use and management (Jonker, 2007).

Across the continent, numerous steps towards integrated planning and decision-making are underway. Transboundary river basins commissions and initiatives have been or are in the process of being established. Most African states are undertaking water reforms that include *inter alia* national water master plans, revised and rewritten water laws, institutional reforms including significant roles for stakeholder participation, and more transparent and inclusive forms of governance.

Significant amounts of donor funding have been made available for all of these exercises. Meaningful progress has been made, especially where the interests of powerful actors intersect with those of donors and coincide with immediate need, for example, in the wake of widespread drought (Gumbo and Van der Zaag, 2002), and/or in the immediate post-revolutionary aftermath of shared nationalist struggle (Amakali and Swatuk, 2009). A significant degree of these activities may be understood merely as 'formalism', that is, good written laws and agreements with little or no implementation (Akiwumi, 2006). Even where intentions are good, African states vary in their human resource and financial capabilities.

Structural change and structural violence

Nearly five decades of modernization-informed attempts at changing the socio-economic structure of SSA countries attest to the persistence of structural violence afforded in the first instance by colonial social forms later becoming 'sovereign' states (Grovogui, 2001). Like African states' performance towards the MDGs (UN, 2011), 'progress' towards more equitable, sustainable and economically efficient water resources development, use and management is highly uneven at best.

As shown in Figure 5.1, the percentage of people using unimproved sources of drinking water varies directly by class. This includes a significant number of the 'richest 20%' of rural dwellers, the percentage of which is almost equal to the 'poorest 20%' in urban areas. In vastly unequal societies, where Gini Coefficients of income inequality range between 0.45 and 0.64, adequate quantities and qualities of water flow towards a fraction of the population. In a recent study, Cullis and Van Koppen (2009) demonstrate through the application of a Gini Coefficient for water inequality in the Olifants River Basin of South Africa that water inequality almost perfectly mirrors income inequality. In a study of the Rufiji Basin in Tanzania, Dungumaro (2007) shows the direct correlation between income and water access.

Access to water for agriculture is also highly skewed towards the wealthiest individuals. Whereas irrigation for export cash crops commands between 40% (Botswana) and 100% (Sudan) of water resource use across SSA, the vast majority of peasant farmers depend on rainfall for crop production and boreholes, seasonal streams and hand-dug wells for watering their households and livestock (Swatuk, Motsholapheko and Mazvimavi, 2011). In consequence, they live with a very high element of risk: late rains, unanticipated dry spells, occasional floods, recurrent

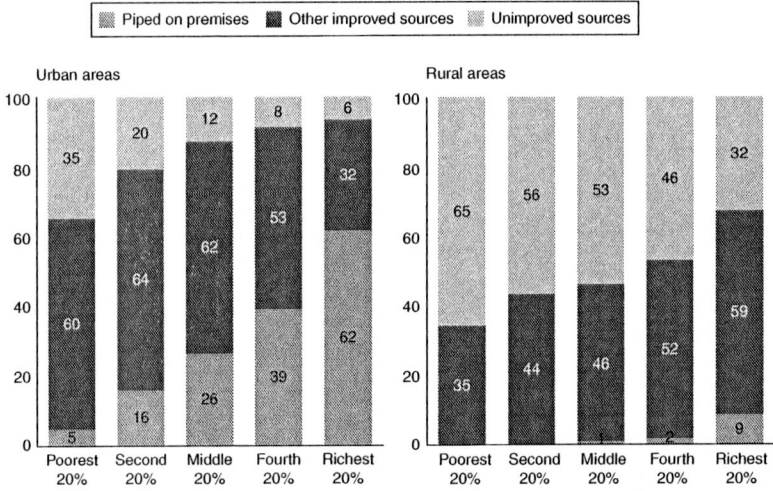

Figure 5.1 Poor, rural populations remain at a disadvantage in accessing clean drinking water
Source: UN (2011, p. 54).

and/or prolonged drought which can push Africa's peasant farmers and pastoralists beyond the brink of starvation with the 2011 drought crisis in the Horn of Africa being a fitting and distressing example.

Despite the extensive use of water in irrigation, 'in 2003, 850 million people in the world were food insecure, 60% of them living in South Asia and Sub-Saharan Africa, and 70% of the poor live in rural areas. In Sub-Saharan Africa the number of food-insecure people rose from 125 million in 1980 to 200 million in 2000' (UN, 2006). An estimated 51% of people living in SSA, subsist on less than US$ 1.25 per day (UN, 2011). Women account for two-thirds of all food production in developing countries, yet face gender-based discrimination in terms of access to land, water, labour, capital, technical and other services (CAWMA, 2007: 150). 'In developing countries rainfed grain yields are on average 1.5 t/ha, compared with 3.1 t/ha for irrigated yields, and increases in production from rainfed agriculture have originated mainly from land expansion. ... Sub-Saharan Africa, with 97 percent rainfed production of staple cereals such as maize, millet, and sorghum, has doubled cultivated cereal area since 1960, while yield per unit of land has barely changed' (CAWMA, 2007: 318).

Contrary to popular explanations regarding lack of capacity or poor governance, I believe that these limited achievements may be better explained by locating the African state form within its appropriate historical context (Herbst, 2000; for the South African case, see Swatuk, 2010). Created by imperial greed, the African state form is itself an instrument of structural violence. It was designed to facilitate the efficient extraction of resources from the continent, and to enhance the prosperity of European peoples. Plantation agriculture provides a good example of this.

Agriculture in Africa is dualistic in nature: a vast peasant sector characterized by low inputs of capital and technology, dependence on rainfall and/or simple irrigation technology, generally producing less than one tonne per hectare with only occasional surpluses that may be sold in local markets; and a large-scale, export-oriented, cash-crop producing sector dominated by private firms (some with strong government involvement) that generates significant revenues for private actors and African governments.

Across Africa, most of the water goes to cash crops grown plantation-style for export: cotton, tobacco, groundnuts, cocoa, tea, sugar, coffee and fruits of all kinds. Ali Mazrui (1986) aptly characterized African economies as 'beverage economies', growing the raw material that goes into beverages processed by and for the rest of the world. All of these products are readily substitutable; all have high elasticities of demand where a small rise in price will send buyers running in search of cheaper producers, and consumers turning to other products. Yet most African economies remain wedded to these practices, and indeed are in the process of expanding them. Irrigation has created a wealthy class of large-scale commercial farmers, many of whom are now turning to the production of biofuels (Cotula et al., 2009).

Most recently, a renewed 'land grab' is underway across the continent. This supplements the already extensive 'resource capture' and ecological marginalization (Homer-Dixon's terms; see Homer-Dixon, 1999) that occurred over the several centuries of colonial/imperial involvement with Africa, and survived the 'winds of change' independence of African countries from the late-1950s onward to today. 'Climate change is expected to exacerbate land degradation and water scarcity in many places and to increase the frequency of extreme weather events affecting harvests' (Cotula et al., 2009: 53; cf. Shongwe, Van Oldenborgh and Van den Hurk, 2009). This has led many Arab and Asian countries to seek out cultivable land in Africa. It is thought that of the 807 million hectares (m ha) of cultivable land across SSA, only 197 m ha is currently under cultivation (Cotula et al., 2009: 59), thus suggesting extensive 'under-utilization' of cultivable land across the continent. African elites, wishing to take advantage of Middle Eastern/Asian 'land hunger', have entered into numerous agreements with foreign private and state-owned firms to lease extensive tracts of land. For example, Cotula et al. (2009: 50), in a comprehensive study of five African states, show that by 2009, approximately 600,000 ha in Ethiopia, 500,000 ha in Sudan, and 640,000 ha in Tanzania (all of the latter devoted to biofuel production) have been leased to foreign companies, about half of which also includes 'national elites and urban middle classes' in the 'land grab'. While some of these processes are more equitable than others – involving systematic discussions with local communities and economic compensation where smallholder farmers are dispossessed of communal land – most lack transparency. Complementing many of these activities are extensive hydraulic infrastructure development projects (irrigation and hydropower) both proposed and underway across SSA, either funded by or/and built by the Chinese (see also, Van der Zaag et al., 2010).

Harnessing water resources has been a fundamental component of social development throughout history (Solomon, 2010). Typical of all societies, the extent and complexity of African social formations (villages, kingdoms, states) mirrors the availability of water resources – both blue (i.e. surface and accessible groundwater) and green (i.e. that in the soil available for transpiration by plants). Unlike the emergent hydraulic societies in the lower Nile and Tigris-Euphrates, however, African kingdoms were 'arable empires', rising and falling with rainfall patterns, rivers and water tables over time. There was little attempt or capacity to create extensive systems of water management prior to the arrival of European colonists who had already mastered several technologies (e.g. the water wheel) over the previous centuries (Solomon, 2010). Like much of African politics, water management was characterized by 'pervasive localism', bounded by the resource base and the capacity of people to draw their existence from it (Iliffe, 1995).

For much of the continent's known history, Africa's difficult hydrological cycles (bimodal, unimodal rainfall; high coefficients of variation; recurrent drought and flood) over varied landscapes (from tropical to semi-arid Savannah to arid desert) with limited soil fertility and numerous vectors of disease translated into short life expectancies (often less than 25 years of age) for a diffuse and often mobile population. People, as a scarce resource, therefore, rather than land or water was the most sought-after commodity on the continent prior to colonial rule. Significant African kingdoms arose along watercourses such as the Senegal, Niger and Limpopo rivers, and around major water bodies such as lakes Victoria, Tanganyika and Chad. But these kingdoms pale in comparison to those that arose in Egypt, the Middle East or China where a non-substitutable resource in an arid environment gave rise to highly centralized bureaucracies and socially differentiated societies. As Iliffe (1995) highlights, the availability of land combined with a limited population base often meant that any attempt to amalgamate people into a state-building enterprise resulted in their simply moving away beyond the reach of the proposed central 'authority'. Herbst (2000) describes this as ruling authorities' limited ability to 'broadcast power'.

Where extensive social formations under single-rulership did exist, such as the Ashanti Kingdom and Sokoto Empire in West Africa, 'rule' constituted a dense network of kinship relations among relatively autonomous groups. Under European rule, such networks were cross-cut by colonial boundaries demarcating 'British', 'French' or 'Belgian' sovereign territory. Rivers and watersheds became in some cases, boundaries of convenience; in other cases, these same rivers and watersheds were bisected by straight lines drawn up to satisfy European monarchs meeting in places such as Berlin, London and Paris. With the post-World War II move towards political independence, these boundaries were accepted by the budding new rulers of Africa.

Not only did Europe introduce a new political geography to the African continent, thereby disrupting (in the case of settler societies) or perverting (in the case of colonial enterprises) existing lines of authority, but also imperial and colonial powers undertook a highly specific hydraulic mission in service of 'empire' and intra-European competition. Commandeering African resources for the provision of services (water, sewerage, electricity) for European towns (e.g. Nairobi which began its life as a rail depot in 1899; Dar es Salaam which became the administrative centre of German East Africa in the late nineteenth century), mines, navigation, sporting activities, plantations and so on, embedded water resources within the landscape of historically derived structural violence. The discovery of precious minerals (diamonds, gold) at the top of watersheds in South Africa created the impetus for concerted state-building and water resource development, with the exploitation of land and African labour culminating in the most economically diversified state in Africa, but one where 'water apartheid' stubbornly persists (Ruiters and Macdonald, 2005).

The dominant modernization narrative of 1960s state-building in Africa argued that the 'new states' of Africa were weak because they lacked, in the first instance, modern infrastructure. In today's renewed climate of infrastructure development, many people are making the same case.[5] Yet, the African state, serving the few so well, seems particularly resilient (Clapham, 2001). Following the water – where it flows and how it is used by whom and for what – reveals not a 'crisis' based on absolute physical limits, but one based on historical lines of resource capture (both land and water) and ecological marginalization. Infrastructure development on the continent today enhances the power of African elites, and only in a very limited way benefits those with the least amount of water (and land) (UN, 2011). Moreover, eliding security and development through a 'potential conflict' narrative brings empowered elites to a bargaining table where resources are further 'captured', despite their being framed by a state-centric language of 'benefit sharing' (Daoudy, 2010). In explication of these ideas, the chapter now turns to a short case study of the Nile River Basin.

Case study: The Nile River

> The concern with the Nile waters [by Egypt] is not just a national security issue but rather a national survival obsession.
>
> Marawan Badr, Egyptian Ambassador to Ethiopia
> (1998 cited in Tafesse, 2001: 83)

The Nile River, at 6700 km, is the longest river in the world. With a basin area of 3 million km^2, it drains 10% of Africa, includes 11 countries (with South Sudan being the newest addition) and about 160 million people (Tafesse, 2001). Without doubt, the Nile constitutes a rich natural and environmental asset, whose natural capital formed the basis for a rich cultural heritage. Today, however, management of the waters of the Nile faces significant challenges.

As shown in Tables 5.1 and 5.2, Egypt alone among Nile River Basin states has achieved 'middle-human development' status, almost doubling its HDI value over the last 30 years. In contrast, the other ten basin states are among the poorest countries in the world. Egypt's GDP is roughly equivalent to that of all other basin states combined. Its status as a 'hydraulic society' stretches back five millennia and is evident in its current ability to deliver potable water and sanitation to its 85 million citizens.

Egypt's modern hydraulic capacities were developed over the latter half of the nineteenth century through to the middle of the twentieth century. Primarily under British colonial rule, Egypt's hydraulic mission was given a regional dimension. Various agreements were forged between 1902 and 1959 in order to secure the unimpeded flow of the Nile for Egypt (partly in service of cotton production for the factories of Manchester and Lancashire), so giving form to a long-held Egyptian goal of securing the 'unity of the Nile Valley' (see Tafesse, 2001 for a detailed discussion).

Table 5.1 Selected data on Nile Basin states highlighting HDI, population structure, access to water and sanitation

Country	HDI rank (n=169)	HDI 1980 (unless stated otherwise)	HDI 2010	Pop 1990 (mil)	Pop 2010 (mil)	Pop 2030 (mil)	Urban 1990 (%)	Urban 2010 (%)	% Pop w/o access to water (2008)	% Pop w/o access to sanitation (2008)
Burundi	166	0.181	0.282	5.7	8.5	11.9	6.3	11.0	28	54
DRC	168	0.267	0.267	37.0	67.8	108.6	27.8	35.2	54	77
Egypt	101	0.393	0.620	57.8	84.5	110.9	42.5	43.4	1	6
Eritrea	–	–	–	–	–	–	–	–	39	86
Ethiopia	157	0.250 (2000)	0.328	48.3	85.0	131.6	12.6	16.7	62	88
Kenya	128	0.404	0.470	23.4	40.9	63.2	18.2	22.2	41	69
Rwanda	152	0.249	0.385	7.2	10.3	16.1	5.4	18.9	35	46
S. Sudan	–	–	–	–	–	–	–	–	–	–
Sudan	154	0.250	0.379	27.1	43.2	61	26.6	40.1	43	66
Tanzania	148	0.329	0.398	25.5	45.0	75.5	18.9	26.4	46	76
Uganda	143	0.281	0.422	17.7	33.8	60.8	11.1	13.3	33	52

Source: UNDP (2010); World Bank (2010).

Table 5.2 Selected data on Nile Basin states highlighting GDP, project agricultural output and cities

Country	GDP ($ billions)	GDP (per cap $)	GDP growth 1970–2008	Arable land (mil ha)	Irrigated land (% of cropland)	Agric. Output (Revenue/ha) % change 2000–2080	Crop Yield % change 2000–50	Largest City (pop) (in basin= Y or N)
Burundi	1.2	144	−0.3	–	–	–	–	Bujumbura (240,000) (Y)
DRC	11.7	182	−3.0	6.7	0.1	−14.7	−7.0	Kinshasa 8.75 mil (N)
Egypt	162.3	1,991	2.5	3.0	100.0	+11.3	−27.9	Cairo 11 mil (Y)
Eritrea	1.7	336	0.9	–	–	–	–	Asmara 514,000 (N)
Ethiopia	25.6	317	1.3	13.1	2.5	−31.3	+0.5	Addis Abeba 2.93 mil (N)
Kenya	30.4	783	0.5	5.3	1.8	−5.5	+6.1	Nairobi 3.52 mil (N)
Rwanda	4.5	458	1.2	–	–	–	–	Kigali 965,398 (Y)
S. Sudan	–	–	–	–	–	–	–	Juba 163,455 (Y)
Sudan	55.9	1,353	1.9	19.4	10.2	−8.9	−1.3	Khartoum 4.38 mil (Y)
Tanzania	20.5	496	0.9	9.2	1.8	−24.2	−2.0	Dar es Salaam 3.34 mil (N)
Uganda	14.3	453	0.9	5.4	0.1	−16.8	−5.0	Kampala 1.59 mil (Y)

Source: World Bank (2010); city data from CIA Factbook available at https://www.cia.gov/library/publications/the-world-factbook/.

Particularly contentious to the upper riparian states are the 1929 and 1959 agreements signed between Egypt and Britain (on behalf of Sudan and its upper riparian colonies), and between Egypt and a newly independent Sudan for the 'full utilization of the Nile waters'. According to Tafesse (2001: 76–7), the 1959 'agreement apportioned the total annual discharge of the Main Nile, as measured at Aswan, i.e. 74 billion cubic metres, between Egypt and the Sudan. The division was made after deducting the anticipated net surface evaporation and seepage at the reservoir, which is estimated to be 10 billion cubic metres per year. Of this amount, Egypt was allotted 55.5 billion cubic metres, while the Sudan was allowed to use the remaining 18.5 billion cubic metres'. Ethiopia, which contributes approximately 86% of the water to the Nile, and the equatorial riparians, who contribute 14% to total flow, were allocated nothing. Ethiopia was not consulted on the agreement at all (Waterbury, 1979).

Contemporary dynamics

As shown in Tables 5.1 and 5.2, populations have increased significantly throughout the basin. Of the nine Nile Basin states for which there are data, five will see their populations triple in size between 1990 and 2030 (DRC, Ethiopia, Kenya, Tanzania, Uganda), and four will experience at least a doubling of their populations (Burundi, Egypt, Rwanda, Sudan) (UNDP, 2010). A significant proportion of this growth is urban, with two of the region's largest cities (Khartoum and Cairo) having no alternative to Nile River water.

Such dramatic population increases in poor states with limited financial and human resources raises concerns about their capability to ensure food security, jobs and economic opportunity, and to provide basic services. The popular uprising against Egypt's Mubarak, post-election riots in Kenya, South Sudanese secession, and persistent social instability and violence across much the rest of the region highlight the precariousness of early twenty-first century state-building in this part of Africa. Speculation about the impact of climate change on the flow of the Nile, combined with persistent drought further heightens anxieties.[6] 'Many poorer countries are not even able to manage their current variability', let alone deal with climate change (Muller, 2007: 103) Egypt faces additional questions regarding the extent and effects of climate-induced sea-level rise which, combined with decreased Nile River flow, could lead to destructive saltwater intrusion (Al-Marashi, 2011).

Given these various dynamics, it is understandable that state actors are interested in securing more water for, *inter alia*, income generation through hydropower production, irrigation for commercial agriculture, drought/flood mitigation, aquaculture, industry and urban household use. Whereas the waters of the White Nile are under little pressure from upstream riparians, Ethiopia is unilaterally engaging in a wide variety of water infrastructure projects within the Blue Nile basin that have raised the concern of downstream states (e.g. Kenya on Lake Turkana where Ethiopia is erecting a large hydropower dam upstream; Eritrea and Egypt on the Tekeze River where Ethiopia, assisted by Sinohydro constructed a 188-metre high hydropower dam generating 300 MW of energy). At the same time, Egypt is engaged in extensive extra-basin water transfer schemes in the Sinai, which Ethiopia claims contravenes international law.

A difficult geopolitical context

The Nile Basin constitutes a complex and difficult geopolitical setting. Aside from colonial British-initiated hydraulic infrastructure projects, upstream riparians have had little impact on the hydrology of the basin. As states such as Ethiopia, Uganda and South Sudan begin to demand access to the waters of the Nile, the number of international actors involved in the geopolitical/geoeconomic landscape has risen significantly: from Chinese construction companies such as Sinohydro to Chinese and Middle Eastern private/parastatal actors interested in land acquisition (and water rights) for commercial agriculture; from the UNDP and the World Bank to numerous other donor states and not-for-profit organizations involved in various aspects of water resources management at all levels of society. Some frame their interests as contributing to water security for national wealth creation; others argue that they are interested in furthering human security particularly among 'civil society' in the basin; and still others, such as International Rivers, claim to speak on behalf of the environment – for all of these developmental interventions consist of violent alterations to the natural environment, often negatively impacting smallholder farmers at the same time (Hoering, 2006).

At the core of recent interstate activities is the Nile Basin Initiative. The Nile Basin Initiative (NBI) was launched in 1999 by riparian states with assistance from the international donor community in an effort to offset the negative trends in resource use and the conflict potential of Egyptian hydro-hegemony (Earle, Jagerskog and Ojendal, 2010). It is governed by the Council of Ministers of Water Affairs of the Nile Basin (Nile-COM) and with Secretariat housed in Entebbe, Uganda (see Mekonnen, 2010 for details). The NBI is pursuing a multitrack strategy with a development focus.

In addition to developing a shared vision for the basin, four thematic projects are being undertaken: (i) transboundary environmental action,

(ii) regional power trade, (iii) efficient water use for agricultural production and (iv) water resources planning and management. Extra-basin actors are also facilitating a number of confidence- and capacity-building activities. In the Eastern (Blue) Nile, countries are engaged in a number of fast-track projects in order to realize mutual benefits, currently focusing on (i) flood preparedness, (ii) Ethiopia-Sudan power transmission interconnection, (iii) irrigation and drainage, (iv) sub-basin planning and (v) watershed management. The emphasis has been on benefit sharing, rather than the 'equitable and reasonable use of the Nile River waters', a vague statement whose focus on water allocation seems only to rub salt into existing wounds (see Swatuk, Mengistu and Jembere, 2008 for an extended case study of the NBI; also Van der Zaag, Seyam and Savenije, 2002; Goor et al., 2010).

Ethiopia's participation in the NBI was contingent on the organization moving towards a Cooperative Framework Agreement (CFA) designed to 'set up a permanent, inclusive legal and institutional framework' that would culminate in a Nile Basin Commission (Mekonnen, 2010). The CFA in draft form was submitted to Nile-COM at Entebbe, Uganda in 2007 and has gone through several iterations. Numerous sticking points remain, in particular the language surrounding Article 14(b) concerning 'water security' for basin riparians. According to Mekonnen (2010), Egypt and Sudan wish to insert a clause reaffirming their existing claims to the waters of the Nile (as codified in the 1929 and 1959 treaties). In the end, the Article was left out and the CFA was initially acceded to by five riparians (Ethiopia, Kenya, Rwanda, Tanzania and Uganda). The CFA requires a minimum of six signatories and subsequent legislative ratifications to come into legal effect. Burundi became the sixth signatory in early 2011. Whether newly independent South Sudan will also sign is unclear. Eritrea has thus far sided with Egypt, so reflecting the ongoing tensions between Ethiopia and Eritrea. As the NBI lurches forward with no end in sight to upstream-downstream interstate tensions, scholars and activists puzzle over the ways and means of moving riparians away from 'zero-sum' perspectives towards 'mutually beneficial outcomes' (see, for example, Whittington, Wu and Sadoff, 2005; Scheumann and Neubert, 2006; Salame and Van der Zaag, 2010).

Conclusion

The Nile Basin case illustrates the complexity and difficulty of arriving at mutually acceptable arrangements for managing 'transboundary' waters, particularly where the downstream state has captured the resource (for which it has no substitutes) and is considerably more powerful than all other state actors in the basin, while the upstream states lack significant human, financial and other resource capacities (Swain, 2011). State-makers in Egypt and Ethiopia, in particular, seem content to frame their water security interests in terms of 'national survival', thereby turning an international impasse into a means of building shared identity (i.e. Egyptians defending themselves against an aggressive upstream 'other'; Ethiopians held back by an equally aggressive downstream 'other'), but an identity that reinforces unwillingness to budge from present positions. Egyptian policymakers have attempted to steer the water resource availability discussion towards all forms of water in the basin (i.e. 1160 billion cubic metres/year) thereby downplaying the centrality of the Nile watercourse with its 84 billion cubic metres/year to upstream riparians. As reasonable as this may seem, upstream riparians remain unconvinced of Egypt's sincerity given its unwillingness to renegotiate patently unfair historical agreements, and Egyptian state-makers' unilateral actions on extra-basin transfers. While it is unclear how events of the so-called Arab Spring at Tahrir Square will impact Egyptian policy on the Nile, what is clear is a generally felt need to 'negotiate now' because five years down the road the situation may be more intractable.[7]

Movement is necessary. In the absence of change, water insecurity for the many persists. Discussions around sharing the waters of the Nile continually focus on large-scale multipurpose storage (Ethiopia) versus unfettered flow (Sudan, Egypt). Put simply, state actors are trapped in a 'dams/no dams' argument. Outside actors involved in the NBI press for 'stakeholder involvement' and an increased role for 'civil society' based on their own best practices. But at the moment, the conflict/security/ development discourse is set within interlocking contexts of 'climate crisis' and 'there is no alternative to Nile water' that privileges high-level state actors and crowds out other voices and concerns.

In this case, where grinding poverty is the norm, what would constitute environmental justice? Surely it would begin with 'some water for all forever'. But Egyptian intransigence simply pushes Ethiopian state-makers towards mega-projects (big dam-building, commercial irrigation) in the mythic hope that stored water will facilitate enhanced revenue generation and ultimately state security. To revisit the epigram near the outset of this chapter, while it is true that development requires a concerted hydraulic mission, it is not clear how the choices made by state actors in the Nile River Basin 'add up' to a well-considered means for getting out from underdevelopment. This reminds me of the African proverb, 'when elephants fight, it is the grass that suffers'. How to move forward, not only in the Nile Basin but across Africa? In my view, the 'crisis and conflict' narrative will be difficult to displace. As long as it persists, so will planning remain a 'high level' prerogative at the levels of the central state and interstate relations. Yet, water insecurity is most seriously felt among rural smallholders and the peri-urban poor. It is at this level that the population-resource degradation-poverty spiral is most acutely felt, and it is this section of African society that is most vulnerable to the negative effects of climate change. Therefore, every effort should be made by influential donors states and other actors to bring cities and small farms to the centre of the 'water security' narrative: while the feasibility of large-scale infrastructure projects should continue to be discussed, it is really standpipes, VIP latrines, small dams and tree planting that should be front and centre of African water security policy. It is interesting to note that African leaders lack for none of these things.

Notes

1. Yet, 'between the 1960s and 2000, SSA registered absolute declines on virtually all indices of socioeconomic development' (Ikome, 2007: 14). SSA's overall economic performance during the first decade of the twenty-first century has been fairly robust (i.e. between 3–6% per annum) buoyed by strong demand for raw materials particularly from China, but with only a few states exporting only a few commodities (e.g. oil) accounting for the vast majority of new private investment (World Bank, 2011).
2. According to its website, 'The African Ministers' Council on Water (AMCOW) was formed in 2002 in Abuja Nigeria, primarily to promote cooperation, security, social and economic development and poverty eradication among member states through the management of water resources and provision of water supply services. The Mission of AMCOW is to provide political leadership, policy direction and advocacy in the provision, use and management of water resources for sustainable social and economic development and maintenance of African ecosystems. AMCOW has become a Specialised Committee for water and sanitation in the African Union' (see http://www.amcow.net/index.php?Itemid=1).
3. Conca (2006) argues that there has arisen a global expert network arrayed around the twin notions of Integrated Water Resources Management (IWRM) and the river basin as the proper unit of administration. This network serves to diffuse particular norms regarding appropriate water use and management.
4. This is not unusual. As recently as 2002, worldwide '158 international river basins lack[ed] any type of cooperative management framework' (UN, 2006: 613).
5. According to the World Bank, 'Africa has a similar water endowment to other continents but captures much less for its development. Less than 5%

of agricultural land is irrigated, less than 10% of hydropower potential has been tapped, and only 58% of Africans have access to a clean water source' (see http://siteresources.worldbank.org/INTAFRICA/Resources/aicd_factsheet_water.pdf).

6. Not surprisingly, there is little agreement on the likely impact of climate change. Several models suggest decreased flows, while others suggest the opposite (see De Wit and Stankiewicz, 2006; Al-Marashi, 2011).

7. Interviews with a high ranking Egyptian official and a formerly high-ranking Ethiopian official, Washington, DC, July 2011.

References

African Development Bank, 2007. *African Development Report: Natural Resources for Sustainable Development in Africa*. Oxford: Oxford University Press for the African Development Bank.

Akiwumi, F. A., 2006. '"Indigenous People Participation": Conflict in Water Use in an African Mining Economy'. In T. Tvedt and T. Oestigaard, eds, *A History of Water Volume 3: The World of Water*. New York: I. B. Taurus, 49–77.

Allan, J. A., 2003. 'IWRM/IWRAM: A New Sanctioned Discourse?' *Discussion Paper No. 50*. Water Issues Study Group, University of London.

Al-Marashi, I., 2011. 'Egypt'. In D. Moran, ed., *Climate Change and National Security: A Country-Level Analysis*. Washington, DC: Georgetown University Press, 177–88.

Amakali, M. and L. A. Swatuk, 2009. 'Different Approaches to Local Level Participation in River Basin Management in Namibia: A Comparison Between the Kuiseb and Cuvelai Basins'. In L. A. Swatuk and L. Wirkus, eds, *Transboundary Water Governance in Southern Africa: Examining Underexplored Dimensions*. Bonn: Nomos Press, 111–32.

Biswas, A. K., 2006. 'Water Management for Major Urban Centres'. *Water Resources Development* 22(2): 183–97.

Black, D. R., C. Adibe, 1998. *The Clinton Administration and Africa: A View from Ottawa*, Canada. Issue: A Journal of Opinion, 26(2), 58–63.

Busby, J., T. G. Smith, K. L. White and S. M. Strange, 2010. *Locating Climate Insecurity: Where are the Most Vulnerable Places in Africa?* Austin, Texas: Robert S. Strauss Center for International Security and Law Working Paper Series.

Chenje, M. and P. Johnson, eds, 1996. *Water in Southern Africa*. Harare/Maseru: SADC/SARDC/IUCN.

Clapham, C., 2001. *Africa in International Relations*. Cambridge: Cambridge University Press.

Clinton, H. R., 2010. 'World Water Day'. *Remarks made by H.R Clinton, U.S. Secretary of State, at the National Geographic Society*, 22 March. Available at: www.state.gov/secretary/rm/2010/03/138737.htm, accessed 20 January 2012.

Collier, P. and A. Hoeffler, 2004. 'Greed and Grievance in Civil War'. *Oxford Economic Papers* 56: 563–95.

Comprehensive Assessment of Water Management in Agriculture (CAWMA), 2007. *Water for Food, Water for Life: A Comprehensive Assessment of Water Management in Agriculture*. London: Earthscan and Columbo: International Water Management Institute.

Conca, K., 2006. *Governing Water: Contentious Transnational Politics and Global Institution Building*. Cambridge, MA: MIT Press.

Conca, K. and G. D. Dabelko, eds, 2002. *Environmental Peacemaking*. Washington: Johns Hopkins University Press.
Conley, A., 1996. 'A Synoptic View of Water in Southern Africa'. In H. Solomon, ed., *Sink or Swim? Water, Resource Security and State Cooperation*. IDP Monograph Series No. 6. Pretoria: Institute for Defence Policy, 1–37.
Cotula, L., S. Vermeulen, R. Leonard and J. Keeley, 2009. *Land Grab or Development Opportunity? Agricultural Investment and International Land Deals in Africa*. London and Rome: IIED/FAO/IFAD.
Cullis, J. and B. van Koppen, 2009. 'Applying the Gini Coefficient to Measure Inequality of Water Use in the Olifants River Water Management Area, South Africa'. In L. A. Swatuk and L. Wirkus, eds, *Transboundary Water Governance in Southern Africa*. Bonn: Nomos Press, 91–110.
Daoudy, M., 2010. 'Getting Beyond the Environment-Conflict Trap: Benefit Sharing in International River Basins'. In A. Earle, A. Jagerskog and J. Ojendal, eds, *Transboundary Water Management: Principles and Practice*. London: Earthscan, 43–55.
De Wit, M. and J. Stankiewicz, 2006. 'Changes in Surface Water Supply Across Africa with Predicted Climate Change'. *Sciencexpress Report*. Available at www.sciencexpress.org/2March2006/Page1/10.1126/science.1119929, accessed 20 January 2012.
Duffield, M., 2007. *Development, Security and Unending War*. Cambridge: Polity Press.
Dungumaro, E. W., 2007. 'Socioeconomic Differentials and Availability of Domestic Water in South Africa'. *Physics and Chemistry of the Earth* 32: 1141–7.
Earle, A., A. Jagerskog and J. Ojendal, eds, 2010. *Transboundary Water Management: Principles and Practice*. London: Earthscan.
Ellis, S., 1999. *The Mask of Anarchy*. New York: New York University Press.
Faeth, P., 2011. *Water Vulnerabilities, Climate Change and Conflict in Poor Countries*. (Draft) Alexandria, VA: CNA.
Falkenmark, M. and J. Rockstrom, 2004. *Balancing Water for Humans and Nature: The New Approach in Ecohydrology*. London: Earthscan.
Gleick, P., 2002. 'Water and Human Health'. In R. M. Saleth, ed., *Water Resources and Economic Development*. Cheltenham, UK: Edward Elgar Publishers, 268–80.
Goldstone, J. A., 2001. 'Demography, Environment and Security'. In P. F. Diehl and N. P. Gleditsch, eds, *Environmental Conflict*, Boulder, CO: Westview Press, 38–61.
Goor, Q., C. Halleux, Y. Mohamed and A. Tilmant, 2010. 'Optimal Operation of a Multipurpose Multireservoir System in the Eastern Nile River Basin'. *Hydrology and Earth System Sciences* 14: 1895–908.
Green Cross International, 2000. *National Sovereignty and International Watercourses*. Lausanne: Green Cross International.
Grovogui, S. N., 2001. 'Sovereignty in Africa: Quasi-Statehood and Other Myths in International Relations'. In K. Dunn and T. M. Shaw, eds, *Africa's Challenge to International Relations Theory*. Basingstoke: Palgrave Macmillan, 29–45.
Gumbo, B. and P. Van der Zaag, 2002. 'Water Losses and the Political Constraints to Demand Management: The Case of the City of Mutare, Zimbabwe'. *Physics and Chemistry of the Earth* 27: 805–14.
Herbst, J., 2000. *States and Power in Africa: Comparative Lessons in Authority and Control*. Princeton: Princeton University Press.

Hoering, U., 2006. 'Ethiopia's Water Dilemma'. *International Rivers* website. Available at www.internationalrivers.org/en/node/2492 (accessed on 28 August 2011).
Homer-Dixon, T., 1999. *The Environment, Scarcity and Violence*. Princeton: Princeton University Press.
Ikome, F. N., 2007. *From the Lagos Plan of Action to the New Partnership for Africa's Development: The Political Economy of African Regional Initiatives*. Midrand, South Africa: Institute for Global Dialogue.
Iliffe, J., 1995. *Africans: The History of a Continent*. Cambridge: Cambridge University Press.
Jonker, L., 2007. 'Integrated Water Resources Management: The Theory-Praxis-Nexus, a South African Perspective'. *Physics and Chemistry of the Earth* 32: 1257–63.
Kaplan, R., 1994. 'The Coming Anarchy', *The Atlantic Monthly*, February, available at www.theatlantic.com/magazine/archive/1994/02/the-coming-anarchy/4670/, accessed 20 January 2012.
Le Billon, P., 2001. 'The Political Ecology of War: Natural Resources and Armed Conflicts'. *Political Geography* 20(5): 561–84.
Mazrui, A. A., 1986. *The Africans: A Triple Heritage*. Boston: Little, Brown.
Mekonnen, D. Z., 2010. 'The Nile Basin Cooperative Framework Agreement Negotiations and the Adoption of a "Water Security" Paradigm: Flight into Obscurity or a Logical Cul-de-sac?' *European Journal of International Law* 21(2): 421–40.
Mengisteab, K. and C. K. Daddieh, eds, 1998. *State Building and Democratisation in Africa: Faith, Hope and Realities*. Westport, CT: Greenwood Press.
Moss, T., 2007. *African Development: Making Sense of Issues and Actors*. Boulder, CO: Lynne Rienner.
Muller, M., 2007. 'Adapting to Climate Change: Water Management for Urban Resilience'. *Environment and Urbanization* 19: 99–113.
Rakodi , C., ed., 1997. *The Urban Challenge in Africa*. Tokyo: UNU Press. Available online at http://www.unu.edu/unupress/unupbooks/uu26ue/uu26ue0i.htm, accessed 20 January 2012.
Reno, W., 1998. *Warlord Politics and African States*. Boulder, CO: Lynne Rienner.
Richards, P., 1996. *Fighting for the Rainforest: War, Youth and Resources in Sierra Leone*. London: James Currey.
Ruiters, G. and D. Macdonald, eds, 2005. *The Age of Commodity: Water and Privatization in Southern Africa*. London: Earthscan.
Sadoff, C. and D. Grey, 2002. 'Beyond the River: The Benefits of Cooperation on International Rivers'. *Water Policy* 4: 389–403.
Salame, L. and P. Van der Zaag, 2010. 'Enhanced Knowledge and Education Systems for Strengthening the Capacity of Transboundary Water Management'. In A. Earle, A. Jagerskog and J. Ojendal, eds, *Transboundary Water Management: Principles and Practice*. London: Earthscan, 171–86.
Scheumann, W. and S. Neubert, eds, 2006. *Transboundary Water Management in Africa*. Bonn: German Development Institute.
Schnellnhuber, J., R. Schubert, N. Buchmann, 2007. *Climate Change as a Security Risk*. London: Earthscan for the German Advisory Council on Global Change.
Shongwe, M. E., G. J. van Oldenborgh and B. J. J. M. Van den Hurk, 2009. 'Projected Changes in Mean and Extreme Precipitation in Africa under Global Warming. Part I: Southern Africa'. *Journal of Climate* 22: 3819–37.

Solomon, S., 2010. *Water: The Epic Struggle for Wealth, Power and Civilization*. New York: HarperCollins.
Svendsen, M., P. Wester and F. Molle, 2004. 'Managing River Basins: An Institutional Perspective'. In M. Svendsen, ed., *Irrigation and River Basin Management: Options for Governance and Institutions*. Cambridge, MA: CABI, 1–18.
Swain, A., 2011. 'Challenges for Water Sharing in the Nile Basin: Changing Geo-Politics and Changing Climate. *Hydrological Sciences Journal* 56(4): 687–702.
Swatuk, L. A., 2010. 'The State and Water Resources Development through the Lens of History: A South African Case Study'. *Water Alternatives* 3(3): 521–36.
Swatuk, L. A., A. Mengistu and K. Jembere, 2008. *Conflict Resolution and Negotiation Skills for Integrated Water Resources Management*. Pretoria: Cap-Net.
Swatuk, L. A., M. Motsholapheko and D. Mazvimavi, 2011. 'A Political Ecology of Development in the Boteti River Basin of Botswana – Locating a Place for Sport'. *Third World Quarterly* 32(3): 453–76.
Tafesse, T., 2001. *The Nile Question: Hydropolitics, Legal Wrangling, Modus Vivendi and Perspectives*. Munster: Lit Verlag.
Toset, H., P. Wollebaek, N. P. Gleditsch and H. Hegre, 2000. 'Shared Rivers and Interstate Conflict'. *Political Geography* 19: 971–96.
UN, 2006. *Water a Shared Responsibility: The United Nations World Water Development Report 2*. Paris and New York: UNESCO and Berghahn Books.
UN, 2009. *Water in a Changing World: The United Nations World Water Development Report 3*. Paris and London: UNESCO and Earthscan.
UN, 2011. *Millennium Development Report 2011*. New York: United Nations.
UNDP, 2010. *Human Development Report*. New York: Oxford University Press.
UNICEF, 1994. *The State of the World's Children*. Oxford: Oxford University Press.
UNESCO, 2002. 'The Right to Water'. *General Comment 15*. Available at http://www.unhchr.ch/tbs/doc.nsf/0/a5458d1d1bbd713fc1256cc400389e94?Open document, accessed 20 January 2012.
UNFPA, 2007. *State of the World's Population 2007*. Available at http://www.unfpa.org/swp/2007/index.htm, accessed 20 January 2012.
Urdal, H., 2006. 'A Clash of Generations? Youth Bulges and Political Violence'. *International Studies Quarterly* 50: 607–29.
Van der Zaag, P., D. Juizo, A. Vilanculous, A. Bolding and N. Post Uiterweer, 2010. 'Does the Limpopo River Basin have Sufficient Water for Massive Irrigation Development in the Plains of Mozambique?' *Physics and Chemistry of the Earth* 35: 832–37.
Van der Zaag, P., I. M. Seyam and H. H. G. Savenije, 2002. 'Towards Measurable Criteria for the Equitable Sharing of International Water Resources'. *Water Policy* 4: 19–32.
Waterbury, J., 1979. *Hydropolitics of the Nile Valley*. New York: Syracuse University Press.
Whittington, D., X. Wu and C. Sadoff, 2005. 'Water Resources Management in the Nile Basin: The Economic Value of Cooperation'. *Water Policy* 7: 227–52.
Wolf, A., A. Kramer, A. Carius and G. D. Dabelko, 2005. 'Managing Water Conflict and Cooperation'. In Worldwatch Institute, *State of the World 2005: Redefining Global Security*. New York and London: W. W. Norton and Co, 80–95.
Wolf, A., S. B. Yoffe and M. Giordano, 2003. 'International Waters: Identifying Basins at Risk'. *Water Policy* 5: 29–60.

World Bank, 1997. *World Development Report*. New York: Oxford University Press.
World Bank, 2004. *Water Resources Sector Strategy: Strategic Directions for World Bank Engagement*. Washington: The World Bank.
World Bank, 2010. *World Development Report*. Washington: The World Bank.
World Bank, 2011. *World Development Report*. Washington: The World Bank.
Yohannes, O., 2008. *Water Resources and Inter-Riparian Relationships in the Nile Basin: The Search for an Integrative Discourse*. Albany: State University of New York.
Zeitoun, M. and J. Warner, 2006. 'Hydro-Hegemony – A Framework for Analysis of Trans-Boundary Water Conflicts'. *Water Policy* 8(5): 435–60.

6
Avoiding the Resource Curse in Ghana: Assessing the Options

Peter Arthur

Introduction

The finite supply of fossil fuels combined with increased demand is leading to an intensification of efforts by various states and multinational corporations (MNCs) to discover and control new sources of oil. This has become even more urgent in recent times with the Western world interested in reducing its reliance on oil from the Middle East, and the expanding economies of China and India interested in satisfying their demands irrespective of the origins of supply. Given the global importance of fossil fuels, control of these natural resources have the potential to confer great economic and strategic benefits to the countries where they are found.

Much scholarship has been devoted to the resource curse hypothesis particularly as it pertains to African primary commodities (e.g. Collier and Hoeffler, 2004; see also Swatuk, this volume). Significant oil deposits have been discovered recently along the west coast of Africa. Ghana, long dependent on minimally beneficiated cash crops such as cocoa, stands to benefit greatly from its offshore oil deposits. Ghanaians are hopeful that this oil will help fuel an era of sustainable and equitable socio-economic development. However, in looking at its nearby neighbours, a key question arises: why has the discovery and exploitation of oil not improved the overall socio-economic situation of a number of producer countries? Oil-rich African countries such as Nigeria and Angola have suffered decades of political instability and show very high levels of poverty. Far from a developmental blessing, people living in the Niger Delta region of Nigeria regard oil as a 'resource curse'. In light of these facts, this chapter assesses various suggestions and options proposed by international donors, academics and global civil society to ensure that Ghana avoids the 'resource curse'. Specifically, the chapter looks at the following six options: (i) establishment of an oil fund, (ii) economic diversification, (iii) participation in the Extractive Industries Transparency Initiative (EITI), (iv) transferring oil ownership to local private sector, (v) dealing with property rights issues and (vi) the promotion of good governance. The chapter argues that with the expected growth in oil exploration in Ghana, the need and importance of good governance as embodied in democratic structures, and the requisite regulatory structures and institutions, will be crucial if the country is to avoid what some scholars have called 'the paradox of the plenty'. Significantly, it will be argued that the use of an accountable and transparent system at all levels of government, coupled with a well-entrenched system of checks and balances, as well as ensuring that oil revenue improves the socio-economic conditions of all citizens as opposed to a few elites will be the basis on which Ghana can avoid the resource curse. Put differently, Ghana must avoid the rent-seeking behaviour that has characterized countries in Africa that have discovered oil. The new revenue that will accrue from oil activities will not help the poor and overall socio-economic development of the country if proper governance structures and measures are not put in place.

The resource curse

Studies show that developing countries with abundant natural resources generally experience less than impressive socio-economic growth and performance when compared to those with fewer natural resources. As Weinthal and Luong (2006: 36) point out, mineral-abundant countries in the developing world are more prone to poor economic performance, unbalanced growth, corruption and income inequality. Glyfason (2001: 848) also notes that of the 65 countries that can be classified as natural-resource rich, only four of them (Botswana, Indonesia, Malaysia and Thailand) managed to attaining long-term investment exceeding 25% of Gross Domestic Product (GDP) on average from 1970 to 1998, and per capita Gross National Product (GNP) exceeding 4% on average over the same period. According to Sachs and Warner (2001: 828–29), oil wealth has not helped generate sustainable and more equitable socio-economic development; rather, it has contributed to deep-seated corruption and other rent-seeking behaviour that retards development and growth.

Sachs and Warner (2001) argue that resources have the undesirable effect of worsening the plight of the poor for several reasons: (i) it is inevitable that uncontrolled political and social conflict, in a tribal conscious society, will worsen once resources are discovered; (ii) weak institutions, inherited from colonialism, do not have the necessary structures to effectively prevent rent-seeking and the misuse of revenue by government officials; (iii) there is a lack of transparency as to how the revenue is managed; and (iv) even though a country's GDP may increase, without the political will to fairly distribute resource revenue, inequality continues to deepen. Moreover, natural resources increases the risk of armed conflict by financing and motivating conflict, as well as increasing the vulnerability of countries to armed conflict by weakening the ability of political institutions to peacefully resolve conflict (LeBillon, 2001).

History of Ghana's oil discovery

Since attaining independence from Britain in 1957, not only has Ghana's economy been generally open and integrated into the world trading system, but also primary production accounts for almost half of the country's GDP. Moreover, Ghana is heavily dependent on mineral resources, notably gold, and agriculture, especially timber and cocoa, which typically provides about a third of all export revenues. In fact, at 40%, agriculture is the most important sector in Ghana's economy. The dominance of the agricultural sector not only ensures that nearly 40% of GDP are from that sector but that it also contributes to 50% of all employment in the country (Aryeetey and Kanbur, 2008: 9). Manufacturing on the other hand contributes some 10% of GDP. In the meantime, as much as half of the country's revenue from international trade and exports go into oil imports, thereby reducing the availability of scarce foreign exchange for other essential economic activities. It was to reduce the country's reliance on foreign oil that the Ghana government in 1983 established the Ghana National Petroleum Corporation (GNPC) to undertake the exploration, development, production and disposal of petroleum in the country (Gary, 2009).

Prior to the establishment of the GNPC, the Petroleum Department under the Ministry of Fuel and Power carried out the procurement of crude oil and petroleum products. The Technical Directorate of the Ministry of Fuel and Power and the Geological Survey Department coordinated petroleum exploration activity and received reports on operations. The GNPC was established to support the Ghana government's objective of providing adequate and reliable supply of petroleum products and reducing the country's dependence on crude oil imports through the development of the country's own petroleum resources. In addition to coordinating petroleum exploration activity, the GNPC took over the assets, liabilities and functions of the then Petroleum Department and assumed responsibility for the importation of crude oil and petroleum products to meet national demand (GNPC, n. d.). By holding exclusive rights to Ghana's onshore and offshore petroleum basins, GNPC became the channel through which any foreign oil company could gain access to petroleum exploration and production rights (Gary, 2009: 38).

Although the GNPC engaged in extensive offshore oil and gas exploration after it was created in 1983, this was met with modest to little success in terms of oil discovery. However, this changed in 2004 when Kosmos Energy, a Dallas firm founded in 2003, sent its oil exploration team to Ghana to search the deep waters off the shore of the country's west coast. The team had made major oil discoveries in Equatorial Guinea a few years earlier with a different company. Backed by two of the world's largest private equity firms, Blackstone Group and Warburg Pincus, Kosmos signed a petroleum agreement with the Ghanaian government, then headed by President John Kufuor. The deal opened up 483,600 acres for exploration and possible production. An additional 273,298 acres was added in late 2006. As part of the deal, Kosmos gave the GNPC 13.75% interest and promised to pay royalties and taxes on any oil that might be discovered. The agreements between Kosmos Energy were approved by the Ghanaian Parliament. A three-year hunt paid off in June 2007 when the Kosmos Energy team discovered oil at the Jubilee Field, named by the Ghana government because the discovery came the same year the country celebrated its 50th anniversary of independence (*The Washington Times*, 2010).

It is estimated that the Jubilee fields holds three billion barrels of recoverable oil, with a planned production rate of 120,000 per day, and an estimated 120–60 million cubic feet of gas per day (Kapela, 2009: 1). The Jubilee field straddles two oil blocks: the West Cape Three Points block led by Kosmos Energy and the neighbouring Deepwater Tano block, led by the Anglo/Irish Company Tullow Oil that has 34.7% ownership (Gary, 2009: 19). Kosmos and Tullow are joined by other companies in the ownership structures for the Jubilee blocks. Besides the US company Anadarko Petroleum Corporation which has a 23.49% stake in both blocks that cover the Jubilee field, there is also Sabre Oil and Gas with a 2.81% stake. Finally, the E. O. Group, which is owned by two Ghanaians, has a 1.75% ownership stake in the West Cape Three Points block (Gary, 2009: 21). The E. O. Group first got Kosmos

Energy interested in coming to Ghana and then introduced the firm to government officials (*The Washington Times*, 2010).

With the potential of producing in excess of 300 million barrels of recoverable oil in its first phase and a production capacity of 120,000 barrels of crude per day, the Ghanaian government is looking at as much as $1 billion a year in revenue once production starts, according to the International Monetary Fund (IMF). Some critics have charged that the deal between Kosmos and the Ghana government was too favourable to Kosmos, short-changing Ghana on potential revenue. But others in the oil industry defend the deal, saying Kosmos took a huge and expensive risk on a deep-water project that had no guarantee of success (*The Washington Times*, 2010). This is significant because prior to this discovery at the Jubilee oilfields, only smaller independent oil and gas companies showed any interest in Ghana's offshore oil prospects, while super majors like ExxonMobil and national oil companies like China National Offshore Oil Corporation (CNOOC) delayed interest until late 2009 (Kapela, 2009: 7).

Avoiding the resource curse

Ghana has been at the receiving end of numerous suggestions and recommendation on how to avoid the resource curse as typified by Nigeria, and rather follow in the footsteps of Botswana where revenue from the country's diamond industry has been utilized in a judicious manner for the benefit of the population as a whole (Kapela, 2009). In the immediate period following the discovery of oil, Ghana's then president, John Kufuor, declared that the country would avoid the resource curse and use its newfound oil wealth to transform the social and economic conditions in the country (Cavnar, 2008). How might this be achieved? This section examines some of the recommendations that are prevalent in the literature and assesses which approach offers the best prospect of avoiding the resource curse in Ghana.

Creation of oil fund and diversification of the economy

Within the literature on the resource curse, an important recommendation that is often offered relates to how the revenue derived from oil should be disbursed. For all intents and purposes, this has been one of the main areas of contention that has bedevilled many resource-rich countries. In instances, as is the case in Nigeria, where the general population feels it is not benefiting from the oil revenue, then it is likely to spark tensions in society. Indeed, dissatisfaction with the share of national petroleum revenue allocated to the Niger Delta region of Nigeria where much of the oil exploration takes place, and other communities directly affected by production operations and the overall benefits they derive from such operations has resulted in attacks and sabotage on key oil pipelines. Subsequently, there is often the cessation of oil and gas activities, destruction of property, violent protests, abductions, killings and loss of lives, illegal oil bunkering, as well as increased activities by armed local groups demanding more control of oil resources (Arthur, 2006: 362; Idemudia, 2009: 8).

Unsurprisingly, among the solutions most often suggested to properly manage oil resources and avoid a resource curse is the creation of a special oil fund. In the US state of Alaska, which has the Alaska Permanent Fund, there is the direct provision of money from the oil fund to state residents on grounds that individuals are the best possible judges of what is good for them, and will therefore use money distributed to them by the government in the way they deem best (Weinthal and Luong, 2006: 42). Moss and Young (2008) suggest that Ghana can adopt a policy similar to the Alaska Permanent Fund in its efforts to avoid the natural resource curse. They argue that direct cash distribution of oil receipts to Ghanaians will provide citizens with an immediate highly visible welfare benefit and a direct incentive to actively participate in monitoring revenue flow. In addition, it would create a sense of ownership among the entire population over the oil fund's revenue.

Similarly, there is the case in a country like Chad that limits government discretion in spending the money, and transfers the proceeds from oil directly to the people (Birdsall and Subramanian, 2004). The funds are used for social and economic infrastructure projects and expenditure, the provision of public goods such as schools, hospital and roads, as well as other income-generating investments to help protect the communities against some of the social and economic challenges and problems of the communities (Arthur, 2006). As Glyfason (2001: 851) rightly notes, the importance of investing in human capital and human resources from the revenue that accrues from natural resources cannot also be underestimated in the efforts to avert a resource curse. As he points out, education is a prerequisite for economic growth and development because it stimulates growth by improving labour efficiency and fostering democracy, as well as creating conditions for good governance, improving health and enhancing equality.

In particular, Norway, the world's third largest oil exporter behind Saudi Arabia and Russia, represents the best possible example of how a country like Ghana can conduct itself and manage its oil resources.

This is because Norway traditionally puts away a large share of its wealth from oil resources into a national pension fund, which continues to grow as a result of the funds being invested in non-Norwegian stocks and bonds. The idea behind is that such an approach will limit any attempt or effort by politicians to use the money for pork-barrel projects. It was therefore an encouraging sign that in the 2008 budget statement, the government promised to design a Stabilisation Fund to serve as a measure to insulate the economy from external shocks – specifically the unpredictability of export earnings from the country's main exports, that is, cocoa, gold, timber and oil, in the near future (Gary, 2009: 46). This was reaffirmed by Ghana's current Finance Minister, Dr Kwabena Duffuor, who stated in January 2010 that the government would set up a sovereign wealth fund for oil money which is estimated to have an upside of around $2 billion when production starts (Yeboah, 2010).

The creation of an oil fund, however, is not without its problems, and might therefore prove to be insufficient in stemming the resource curse. As Birdsall and Subramanian (2004) point out, oil funds are unable to insulate oil revenues from appropriation by weak or unaccountable governments. They are no substitute for public accountability or for the checks and balances provided by the press and a healthy democracy. For example, in Chad, the government promised to spend the revenue from oil activities on social programmes and projects such as health care and education, as well as put in place anti-corruption laws. Finally, it committed to publishing reports on how the funds were spent, create an independent oversight committee to ensure that it followed the rules, and also be subjected to checks and oversight from non-governmental organizations (NGOs). Despite all these undertakings as well as the oversight by NGOs, the country's president managed to use the first wave of revenue to buy a presidential airplane. Similarly, in countries such as Kazakhstan and Azerbaijan which have also established oil funds, they have been found to suffer governance flaws, including the lack of accountability and transparency. As a result of such developments, some economists and academics have argued that oil funds are no more effective than other measures and options for averting or mitigating the threats of a resource curse (Yeboah, 2010).

It is in this vein that besides the creation of an oil fund, directing revenue to improve the dilapidated nature of infrastructure in many parts of the country, especially the rural areas, diversifying the economy, improving the manufacturing base of the country as well as developing the agro-processing industry are equally important. This is essential to encourage economic activity and productions throughout Ghana, not just in the oil-producing areas, as well as continue keeping people in farming and avoiding a collapse of the rural farming sector, and ultimately prevent Ghana from suffering from the Dutch disease. Such a suggestion is important given the experience of a country like Nigeria that saw its agricultural sector and rural economy collapse as a result of a focus on the oil sector at the expense of others. While one of the largest exporters of oil palm in the post-independence period, contributing more than 82% of the country's total value of domestic exports, Nigeria now accounts for only 7% of world production from its high of 43% in the 1960s. This is due to the devastation in the rural economy and agriculture sector, and the migration of citizens from the rural to the urban areas in search of jobs in the oil sector (Oladipo, 2008: 76). In sum, it would be a mistake for Ghana to get a false sense of economic and financial security as a result of the oil discovery. This is because with oil unlikely to remain the only source of energy for the foreseeable future as well as given its finite nature, it becomes important to diversify the economy to shield the country from shocks and fluctuations that typically characterize oil prices on the international market.

EITI, CSOs and the oil and gas sector

Another important process by which the resource curse can be averted is for Ghana to become part of the Extractive Industries Transparency Initiative (EITI). The EITI, launched in 2002, basically aims at increasing transparency in financial transactions between governments and companies within the extractive industries. As an initiative that aims at improving oversight, and also preventing corrupt practices, such as the diversion of revenues from extractive industries intended for public government accounts into private accounts, the EITI involves the full publication and verification of company payments made to governments and of government revenues received from oil, gas and mining activities. The underlying assumption of this is that opacity that marks business-government relationship in the extractive industry facilitates greed, the mismanagement of natural resource revenue and the inability to hold governments accountable (Idemudia, 2009: 10). Hence, transparency over payments and revenues increases accountability as this information is publicly available, and it is easier to exert pressure on governments for better spending on key basic services such as education and health.

As of now, Ghana's participation in the EITI that it signed on to in 2003 is restricted to the mining industry, but Vice-President John Mahama recently stated in a speech that Ghana hopes this can be extended to the oil sector. The EITI process can be assisted by the activities of civil society organisations (CSOs). Domestic civil society groups have played critical roles in Ghana by being the channels for promoting and protecting the values of various groups, shaping public opinion, influencing public policy and reporting on political activities. They have broadened and stimulated political participation and supplemented the efforts of political parties by encouraging Ghanaians to be involved in the electoral and voting process. They have also mobilized the public through press conferences, aggregated the interests of various groups and communicated their demands to policymakers, as well as sent memoranda and delegations to the government (Arthur, 2010). Within the context of helping Ghana to avoid the resource curse, CSOs can play a watchdog function by ensuring that the government is transparent and accountable in the use of oil resources and funds. An active, independent and free civil society, combined with a strong independent media that serves as a check on government activities will be vital to helping Ghana survive the governance challenges posed by the coming oil boom (Gary, 2009: 48).

While the virtues of initiatives such as the EITI cannot be underestimated, it would at the same time be presumptuous to assume that they are the magic bullet or wands for all the challenges that a country like Ghana might face. This is because the EITI, for example, has its own unique challenges. A major weakness of the EITI approach is its voluntary nature. In addition, companies that participate in the initiative are only obliged to report payment in countries of operation that subscribe to EITI. Also, some countries may make progress on disclosure of information but not improve other aspects needed to address the resource curse, such as respect for human rights and independent media (Gary, 2009: 15). Moreover, while EITI can arm citizens with information about the finances of government, it cannot by itself create the constituencies or mechanisms of accountability that appear to be critical to avoiding the natural resource curse (Moss and Young, 2009: 12). Finally, EITI places enormous faith in civil society to demand accountability, yet pays little attention to the nature, character and capacity of civil society in Africa (Idemudia, 2009). In Ghana, many of the local CSOs currently lack funding and are more dependent on external support to boost their resource base, which shows a pattern of resource deficiency of civic organizations. Moreover, the lack of adequate funding partly accounts for low staffing and poor conditions of work experienced by CSOs. The staffs of many CSOs are therefore over-burdened with responsibility, which in turn affects their functioning and performance (AfriMAP,

Open Society Initiative for West Africa and Institute for Democratic Governance, 2007: 55). As a result of the limited institutional capacity and dearth of material resources among civil-society groups, it means that they rely solely on activism as a strategy for achieving their objectives. While activism may be effective on some issues, it is also crucial for CSOs to strengthen the institutional and technical capacities of civil-society groups in Africa, as well as diversify their strategy to include lobbying of governmental institutions and agencies in their engagement with the state (Idemudia, 2009: 16).

Privatization of GNPC's operations

Another suggestion to avert a resource curse relates to the idea of establishing an agency that will be independent of the GNPC, and accountable to the people's representative (Parliament), and be ultimately responsible for the commercial activities of the activities in the oil sector (Kapela, 2009). As it stands now, the GNPC stands as both a de facto regulator and a participant in a commercially viable field. It is in this regard that there have been calls by donors, including the World Bank and the German government aid agency, GTZ, and others to unbundle the GNPC and split the roles of regulator and commercial entity (Gary, 2009: 38). The new commercial agency, if established should not only be insulated from the executive arm of the government but also function largely as its own entity and with control over the nation's oil wealth. Ghana can learn from the situation in Sao Tome and Principe where the Oil Revenue Law created a new independent oversight body, the Petroleum Oversight Commission, made up of governmental and civil society members to be responsible for commercial and practical management of the oil sector. Besides overseeing and monitoring the disbursement of funds, the agency should solely be accountable to the Ghanaian parliament (Yeboah, 2010).

While Kapela (2009: 21) sees such an approach as a sound policy recommendation, he argues that the overall threat of succumbing to the resource curse may not be prevented because the ownership structure of the oil still is in the hands of the government where oil rents inevitably accrue to a government coffer. As a result, Weinthal and Luong (2006) as well as Kapela (2009) have called for private domestic ownership over state ownership in Ghana's oil sector. In particular, Weinthal and Luong (2006: 36) contend that some of the solutions proposed to deal with the resource curse need strong state institutions which are widely absent in the developing world. In addition, the solutions assume state ownership over mineral wealth and thus the need for external actors to constrain the state. Citing the case of the Russian gas sector, which is primarily dominated by the state-owned monopoly, Gazprom, Weinthal and Luong (2006: 43) suggest that under state ownership, the boundary and lines of demarcation between the main actors – state elites and bureaucrats – is blurred because there is no clearly identifiable principal. However, under private domestic ownership, the boundary between the state elites and private domestic owners becomes clear. This is because there is a clearly identifiable principle, as well as an increase in transactions and monitoring, which makes it difficult for state elites to extract and engage in rent-seeking behaviour and activities, and for private owners to hide their income (Weinthal and Luong, 2006: 45). Moreover, privatization leads to sustained improvements in performance and efficiency. Apart from the potential for increasing output, sale returns and capital investment and expenditure, privatization will also lead to a decrease in employment intensity. In sum, privatization and transfer of ownership to local companies will lead to the separation of commercial decisions in its administration from political authorities (Kapela, 2009).

Weinthal and Luong (2006), and Kapela's (2009) suggestion for the transfer of ownership to the local private sector is laudable and quite novel within the context of African countries. However, with an estimated 80% of the world's proven oil reserves currently held by national and state-owned oil companies, there is no reason why Ghana should embark on the privatization path suggested by Weinthal and Luong (2006), as well as Kapela (2009). It is important to remember that the experience of many developing countries with privatization in other areas of the economy, as was the case during the implementation of neo-liberal structural adjustment programmes (SAPs) in the 1980s and 1990s, has generally been negative. Not only did privatization concentrate wealth in the hands of a few, but also, it increased the prices of products and denied many people access to essential services. Moreover, the 50-50 partnership between De Beers and the Botswana government in Diamond Trading Company Botswana (DTCB) shows the benefits of having greater governmental stakes in a resource and extractive industry (Hagan, 2009: 30).

Thus, rather than the privatization of the activities of the GNPC advocated by Kapela (2009), what is needed in Ghana is for the country to create an appropriate regulatory and legal framework in the oil and gas sector that will enhance their performance and curb interference in commercial investment decisions by the national government. To do so, Ghana must first review its legal framework, specifically the

Petroleum Exploration and Production Law passed in 1984. With many of Ghana's oil laws written in the 1980s, it is a welcome development that the government wants to rewrite the oil laws to make it more suitable for an active and newly emerging oil sector. It can do so through an open legislative process that encourages public involvement and debate and also requires all oil production be made public (Cavnar, 2008). Another important aspect of this should be to ensure that there is a large local content in the oil sector by using a large fraction of domestic goods and services, employing and training internal staff and skills, and transferring technology to the domestic economy. The Ghana Petroleum Regulatory Authority (GPRA) Bill that was released in October 2008 in order to establish the correct framework for Ghana to be an oil-producing and exporting country was a step in the right direction (Hagan, 2009).

As Hagan (2009) points out, the Bill makes provision for the promotion of local content, the sale of local goods and services, the employment and training of Ghanaians and the state oil company involvement in the industry. Owing to the high risk and capital-intensive nature of the oil industry, producing countries usually struggle to fully benefit from their resources because substantial amounts of profits are paid to shareholders and foreign creditors instead of investing the revenue into the local economy. The GPRA seeks to promote local content and the supervision of the upstream petroleum industry which includes the exploration and production of natural gas and crude oil. Section 100 of the Bill allows for governmental involvement in petroleum activity but its involvement will be determined by the Parliament. Section 103 gives priority to competent national entities. This will enable Ghana to provide goods and services to the petroleum industry which will also give priority to the purchase of local content and if a foreign company provides the goods and services, the company 'must operate from Ghana and team up with a company owned by a citizen of Ghana'. Finally, Section 105 that deals with the employment and training of Ghanaian citizens states that the company granted exploration licence by the GNPC will need to present a detailed programme on its plans of recruiting and training Ghanaian citizens. The licensee is also compelled to first advertise positions to competent Ghanaians who have the requisite qualifications and experience.

If the Bill can be successfully implemented then it will provide an excellent framework in which Ghana can develop its oil industry and translate oil revenue into development (Hagan, 2009). While there are strategic concerns involved in successfully implementing the policy that provides grounds for effective local participation and benefits, the promotion of a local content in the oil and gas sector would also help Ghana's economy in terms of job creation, income generation, business expansion and industrialization drive.

Dealing with property rights issues

Despite the importance of a local content, it also needs to be pointed out that there are other stakeholders that are often involved in the exploration of oil. Besides the Ghanaian government that is expected to represent the citizens of the country, there are also the oil companies that render the intellectual and menial labour to exploit the oil as well as the workers and people in the oil-producing area whose way of life could be affected by the exploration of the oil (Cavnar, 2009). As Gary (2009: 52) points out, expectations are already rising in the Western region, where the oil exploration is taking place, among the youth that the emerging oil industry will provide jobs and other benefits. In addition, the local business class is eager to provide the goods and services to add to the 'local content' of the industry. Also, local district chiefs and politicians are jockeying for the 'right' to any earmarked benefits. Thus, another recommendation on how to avoid the resource curse relates to the issue of property rights and 'ownership of oil resources'. According to Ross (1999: 320), where property rights are weakly enforced, firms face difficulty operating. This is because the risks associated with investments being lost will not necessarily be offset by the profits that might accrue to the firm. Although resource extraction can still proceed, the firms earning resource rents will have to pay criminal gangs, private armies or nascent rebel armies for the private enforcement of property rights. The varying interests and challenges with property rights and ownership can sometimes lead to misunderstanding among stakeholders. That is exactly what is going on as of now between the Ghanaian government and Kosmos, which is interested in selling its stake in the Jubilee oilfields for $4 billion to ExxonMobil. The government of Ghana is opposed to Kosmos selling its stake to ExxonMobil on the grounds that Kosmos' contract includes a clause giving the GNPC a right of first refusal should they decide to sell. Thus, by agreeing to sell to ExxonMobil, the Ghanaian government believes that Kosmos is in breach of the first-refusal clause.

However, for critics, there is no clause in the contractual deal that ensures that Kosmos gives preferential treatment or first refusal to Ghana. For them, since taking office in January 2009, the John Atta Mills-led National Democratic Congress (NDC) government has repeatedly sought to interfere with Kosmos' business. While it is not unusual for foreign companies to have local partners, the new Ghanaian government in 2009, for example, asked the US Department of Justice to determine whether the E. O. Group or Kosmos violated the Foreign Corrupt Practices Act (FCPA), which prohibits payments of foreign officials to obtain or keep a business (*The Washington Times*, 2010). Besides the disagreement with Kosmos, the NDC government in January 2010 revoked a petroleum licence for a Norwegian firm, Aker ASA, which had been approved in November 2008 by Ghana's previous parliament. Aker ASA was informed by Ghana's Minister of Energy, Joe Oteng-Adjei, that its offshore exploration and development licence that was negotiated with the prior Ghanaian administration was invalid because the company's agreement failed to meet the legal requirements of registering a subsidiary in Ghana.

It has been suggested by the main opposition party, the New Patriotic Party (NPP), that the reason behind the NDC government's opposition to the proposed Kosmos/ExxonMobil deal is its belief that associates of former President Kufuor wilfully caused financial loss to Ghana by corruptly getting shares in Kosmos. This is explained by the fact that the E. O. Group's two Ghanaian partners, George Owusu and Dr Kwame Bawuah-Edusei, had close ties to the Ghanaian government under John Kufuor. While George Owusu served as Kosmos' representative in Ghana, Dr Bawuah-Edusei who practiced medicine in the United States was later appointed as Ghana's ambassador to the US by the Kufuor administration (Gary, 2009; *The Washington Times*, 2010). Whatever their intentions, the NDC government is seen by the NPP as engaging in a 'political witch-hunt' and harassing the local private businesses involved in the oil and gas sector, especially those affiliated with the NPP. Indeed, this should not come as a surprise since, as Opoku (2010) argues, while having a long history of stifling businesses associated with the NPP, the NDC at the same time helps to secure the meteoric rise of a new crop of capitalists that are linked to the NDC.

In addition, the NDC government, it is believed, is trying to stop the Kosmos and ExxonMobil deal so the CNOOC can buy the Kosmos stake. It is an open secret that China is actively expanding into Africa as part of its broad economic and foreign policy of influencing African governments at the expense of the West and gaining access to resources and markets (Anshan, 2007; Kragelund, 2009: 479). China's interest in buying the Kosmos shares is seen as part of this attempt at gaining increasing influence in Africa. While there are many Chinese-run infrastructure projects under way across the African continent (Gadzala,

2010: 41), there is however, concern about China's operations in Ghana and other parts of the developing world. There is particular concern that Chinese companies, especially in the construction industry import Chinese labour, including convict labour, while unemployed Africans are ignored (Anshan, 2007: 81; Alden, 2007). Adopting a similar approach in the oil sector will obviously be incongruent with the local content provision stipulated in the new GPRA Bill. What would be equally worrying is that Ghana will become dependent on foreign companies for such a strategic resource. Thus, rather than selling to the Chinese or the privatization model that is advocated by Weinthal and Luong (2006), as well as Kapela (2009), a better route will be for the GNPC to raise funds from private international banks to acquire the Kosmos shares.

Fostering democracy and promoting accountability and transparency

In light of the foregoing, this chapter's main argument is that state ownership of the oil industry and the fostering of the democratic process are important to averting a resource curse in Ghana. This is because democratic institutions have the ability to constrain officials and also the potential to limit the excessive nature of corruption that has generally been a bane of many resource-rich countries in Africa. According to Ite (2004: 5), the absence of political transparency and accountability, coupled with the high incidence of corruption, have all combined to undermine the ability of the various levels of government in a country like Nigeria from putting in place policies and programmes that would contribute to the overall socio-economic development of the oil-producing areas. Since countries that are rich in resources generally rank at the lowest end of not only the World Bank's Governance Research Indicators but also Transparency International's Corruption Perception Index (Weinthal and Luong, 2006: 36), having a system of governance and government that is transparent and accountable in nature as embodied in a democracy can address some of the challenges associated with a resource curse. This is because it is not just the presence of natural resources that leads to the resource curse: rather, it is the 'governance structures' around extracting and processing resources and managing generated revenues that determines whether natural resources will turn out to be either a curse or blessing (Idemudia, 2009: 4). Having in place a democratic system of governance prevents a situation where authoritarian and corrupt government officials will use the revenue accruing from the oil and other resources to consolidate their power and stifle the activities of civil society (Kapela, 2009). It also makes it possible to better analyse the activities of the state and hold them accountable for their actions. More importantly, it ensures that not only are important social and environmental issues addressed but also public institutions and structures are transparent since there is often a political costs associated with acting in a corrupt and rent-seeking manner. In countries like Nigeria and Chad, it was the institutional vacuum and the absence of democratic structures that enabled their governments to misuse oil revenue (Moss and Young, 2009).

The existence of a democratic system of governance is one area where, compared with Nigeria and other countries characterized by the resource curse, Ghana has a distinct advantage. This is because Ghana has been able to relatively consolidate the democratic process which began around 1992. For example, in December of 2008, it undertook its fifth successive presidential and parliamentary elections that were by all intents and purposes very peaceful. In fact, in the country's political history, the election in December 2008 represented only the second time that a democratically elected incumbent president uninterruptedly handed over power to the opposition political party (Gyimah-Boadi, 2009: 138). What is equally significant is that in the past decade, the Ghanaian electorate has freely and effectively engaged in a turnover of government between the two main parties, the NPP and NDC, without much violence. The foregoing suggests that the Ghanaian electorate is now more in tune with democratic goals, so much so that they are generally seen as being against military presence in the political sphere. The days when governments were changed by military coups and bullets rather than ballots seem to be a phenomenon of the past (Arthur, 2010: 221). It is not surprising that on the issue of governance, Ghana scores above the 50th percentile in the World Bank Institute's Governance Indicator rankings and has been making steady progress in these rankings over the past decade (Gary, 2009: 7).

In sum, a democratic government that owns the national oil company, which is the situation in Ghana as of now, has better prospects of promoting social equality and equity with the oil money than leaving it to the private sector and generating revenue from tax and royalties from oil production alone, as well as from the economic activity generated by offshore oil production and downstream industry. State-owned oil companies can provide resources to finance various social programmes and projects in the country. These can include medical clinics to provide health care, as well as primary, secondary and tertiary education programmes, and job-creation programmes outside of the oil industry.

Aside from that, state-owned oil companies can serve the interests of the general public by generating revenue streams that can contribute to energy security, wealth creation, industrialization and socio-economic development, and supply essential energy fuels and associated services. In addition, with state ownership, domestic demands are expected to take precedence over international demands. Often, the oil companies will not be preoccupied with exporting their oil, as foreign companies would. In the process, the state-owned oil companies will recognize the demands of the domestic market, resulting in fuel supplies reaching all the parts of the country at reasonable prices (Falola and Genova, 2005: 56-7). Moreover, if the management of the revenue derived from oil activities is based on a system that is fair, transparent and accountable, then oil revenue will become a blessing that will facilitate socio-economic development rather than becoming a curse (Gary and Karl, 2003).

Conclusion

This chapter examined and assessed the various options available to Ghana in its attempt to avoid the resource curse that has plagued a number of countries that have recently discovered oil and gas. The mere existence of oil and gas does not necessarily lead to conflict. Rather, it is the unequal distribution of rents from oil activities that are at the root of much of the instability that bedevil countries that experience the resource curse. Moreover, the problem of unclear and ill-defined property rights as well as the inability to enforce property rights poses severe challenges to the political stability of a country. In addition, widespread corruption, the inability to earn income from assets and resources, which is a crucial element of property rights, as well as a weak or non-existent state apparatus, and the inability to hold a government accountable are serious problems. The existence of one or more of these problems and their interrelationships are masked by generic claims of 'resource curse'. For Ghana to ensure maximum benefit sharing from oil and gas exploitation, there is need for transparency and accountability so that political elites do not take advantage of their position to enrich themselves and family members through corrupt sub-contracts and oil-trading practices, while the rest of society is marginalized and impoverished. Across resource-dependent political economies, rent-seeking provides ruling elites with the means of maintaining their hegemony. It is crucial that oil revenue is not controlled by ruling cliques and government officials who enter into convenient negotiations with the oil companies. Such an approach is bound to divide the country between a privileged and wealthy ruling minority, while the rest of society remains impoverished.

Moreover, how revenues will be disbursed across Ghana's socio-economic landscape is a key factor if oil and gas are to act as drivers of sustainable and equitable socio-economic development in Ghana. This, as argued previously, can be realized with structures and strong institutions that guarantee transparency and financial accountability and by promoting, sustaining and consolidating the democratic process that is currently taking place in Ghana. Without it, then, rent-seeking behaviour among the elites will be rife, and in the process lead to tensions and possible conflict in the country. An accountable and transparent system of government, together with good political leadership will ensure that the rents from natural resources are not squandered. With well-entrenched checks and balances, the chances of oil revenues being wasted or siphoned off can be minimized (Birdsall and Subramanian, 2004: 87–9). In the absence of political transparency and accountability at all levels of government in the country, policymakers will continue to engage in corrupt practices to the overall detriment of the socio-economic development of the country. This is because the problems of underdevelopment in many developing nations are due to the lack of accountability and a transparent legal framework, failure to enforce property and contractual rights, corruption, dictatorship, and the mismanagement of public funds (Arthur, 2006).

References

AfriMAP, Open Society Initiative for West Africa and Institute for Democratic Governance, 2007. *Ghana: Democracy and Political Participation*. Dakar: Open Society for West Africa.
Alden, C., 2007. *China in Africa: Partner, Competition or Hegemon*. London: Zed Books.
Anshan, L., 2007. 'China and Africa: Policy and Challenges'. *China Security* 3(3): 69–93.
Arthur, P., 2006. 'The Problem of "Resource Curse" and the Distribution of Oil Revenue in Nigeria'. In A. Griffiths, ed., *Global Perspectives on Oil and Security*. Halifax: Centre for Foreign Policy, Dalhousie University, 352–75.
Arthur, P., 2010. 'Democratic Consolidation in Ghana: The Role and Contribution of the Media, Civil Society and State Institutions'. *Commonwealth and Comparative Politics* 48(2): 203–26.
Aryeetey, E. and R. Kanbur, 2008. 'Ghana's Economy at Half Century: An Overview of Stability, Growth and Poverty'. In E. Aryeete and R. Kanbur, eds, *The Economy of Ghana: Analytical Perspectives on Stability, Growth and Poverty*. Accra: Woeli Publishers, 1–19.

Birdsall, N. and A. Subramanian, 2004. 'Saving Iraq from its Oil'. *Foreign Affairs* 83(4): 77–89.
Cavnar, A. 2008. 'Averting the Resource Curse in Ghana: The Need for Accountability'. *Ghana Centre for Democratic Development* 9(3): 1–8.
Collier, P. and A. Hoeffler, 2004. 'Greed and Grievance in Civil War'. *Oxford Economic Papers* 56: 563–95.
Falola, T. and A. Genova, 2005. *The Politics of the Global Oil Industry: An Introduction*. Westport, CT: Praeger Publishers.
Gadzala, A., 2010. 'From Formal to Informal-Sector Employment: Examining Chinese Presence in Zambia'. *Review of African Political Economy* 37(123): 41–59.
Gary, I., 2009. *Ghana's Big Test: Oil's Challenge to Democratic Development*. Oxfam America and the Integrated Social Development Centre. Available at http://www.oxfamamerica.org/files/ghanas-big-test.pdf, accessed July 2, 2010.
Gary, I. and T. L. Karl, 2003. *Bottom of the Barrel: Africa's Oil Boom and the Poor*. New York: Catholic Relief Services.
Ghana National Petroleum Corporation (GNPC), n. d. *About GNPC*. Available at http://www.gnpcghana.com/aboutus/ (accessed on 17 May 2010).
Glyfason, T., 2001. 'Natural Resources, Education and Socioeconomic Development'. *European Economic Review* 45(4–6): 847–59.
Gyimah-Boadi, E., 2009. 'Another Step Forward for Ghana'. *Journal of Democracy* 20(2): 138–52.
Hagan, A., 2009. *Can Ghana Successfully Avoid Oil-Induced Instability? A Comparative Analysis of Nigeria and Botswana*, B.A. Honours Thesis, submitted to the Department of International Relations, University of the Witwatersrand, South Africa.
Idemudia, U., 2009. 'The Quest for the Effective Use of Natural Resource Revenue in Africa: Beyond Transparency and the Need for Cultural Compatibility in Nigeria'. *Africa Today* 56(2): 1–24.
Ite, U., 2004. 'Multinationals and Corporate Social Responsibility in Developing Countries: A Case Study of Nigeria'. *Corporate Social Responsibility and Environmental Management* 11(1): 1–11.
Kapela, J., 2009. *Ghana's New Oil: Cause for Jubilation or Prelude to the Resource Curse*, M.A. Thesis submitted to Duke University, USA.
Kragelund, P., 2009. 'Knocking on a Wide-Open Door: Chinese Investments in Africa'. *Review of African Political Economy* 36(122): 479–97.
LeBillon, P., 2001. 'The Political Ecology of War: Natural Resources and Armed Conflict'. *Political Geography* 20(1): 561–84.
Moss, T. and L. Young, 2009. *Saving Ghana from its Oil: The Case for Direct Cash Distribution*, Working Paper 186. Washington: Centre for Global Development.
Oladipo, J. A., 2008. 'Agro-Industry as Strategy for Rural Development: An Impact Assessment of Oil Palm Industry'. *European Journal of Social Sciences* 7(1): 75–87.
Opoku, D. K., 2010. 'From Quasi-Revolutionaries to Capitalist Entrepreneurs: How the P/NDC Changed the Face of Ghanaian Entrepreneurs'. *Commonwealth and Comparative Politics* 48(2): 227–56.
Ross, M. L., 1999. 'The Political Economy of the Resource Curse'. *World Politics*, 51: 297–322.
Sachs, J. and A. Warner, 2001. 'The Curse of Natural Resources'. *European Economic Review* 45(4–6): 827–38.

The Washington Times, 2010. 'Ghana Discovery Sparks Fight Over Oil: Partnership with US-based Firm Collapses', 26 March. http://www.washingtontimes.com/news/2010/mar/26/ghana-discovery-sparks-fight-over-oil/?page=all, accessed December 31, 2011.

Weinthal, E. and P. J. Luong, 2006. 'Combating the Resource Curse: An Alternative Solution to Managing Mineral Wealth'. *Perspectives on Politics* 4(1): 35–53.

Yeboah, S., 2010. 'Ghana: Is Oil Fund all Country Needs to Defeat the Resource Curse?' Available at http://allafrica.com/stories/201002011494.html (accessed on 17 May 2010).

7
Sexual Violence, Coltan and the Democratic Republic of Congo

Shelly Whitman

Introduction

While it is often stated that women and children are the most vulnerable during armed conflict, the Democratic Republic of the Congo (DRC) exemplifies the ultimate lack of protection and deliberate targeting of civilians that has come to characterize modern warfare. The DRC held their first democratic election in 2006 following a series of peace talks that led to the installation of a transitional government, and now the 'New National Government'. Despite such movements towards democracy and peace, the DRC is still struggling with the conflict in the Eastern section of the country, the Kivus. This conflict continues under the eye of MONUSCO, the United Nations Peacekeeping Mission for the DRC and the rest of the world.

The conflict in the DRC is largely fuelled and sustained by the drive for economic resources that are essential to our global economy. One of the most important resources to be extracted from the DRC is coltan. Coltan is an essential mineral used in the production of such day-to-day products as computers and cell phones. International companies take large security risks to fly directly into the DRC in the middle of conflict zones to obtain the mineral from local armed groups.

The focus of this chapter is be on the extremely high levels of sexual violence in the Democratic Republic of the Congo and how this weapon of war is being utilized to benefit those extracting minerals. Unspeakable horrors are the order of the day for many women in the Eastern DRC, despite age or ethnicity. The United Nations estimates that 7000 women and girls have been raped in the past year alone in the Eastern DRC.

Chris Coulter, who recently published *Bush Wives and Girl Soldiers: Women's Lives through War and Peace in Sierra Leone* (2009), discusses the connection between sexual violence used as a tactic or weapon of war and the global economy. In Sierra Leone the commodity was diamonds. Coulter and others such as Cynthia Enloe (2000), Susan McKay and Dyan Mazurana (2004) argue that the use of sexual violence as a military tactic is a product of the global economic system, which drives the need for mineral resources. Many similarities can be drawn between Sierra Leone and the DRC, in particular patterns of sexual violence used as war tactics.

A local Kiswahili saying holds, 'Congo is a big country – you will eat it until you tire away!' This is precisely what many armed groups, neighbouring countries, Western nations and multinational companies have done over the past one hundred years to the Democratic Republic of the Congo (Herbst and Mills, 2009). The raping of the country's natural resources has precipitated the increased levels of sexual violence endured by the women of the DRC. I contend that it is not the abundance or scarcity of resources per se that determines conflict and violence, but the way they are governed, who has access to them and for what purposes are they used (Global Witness, 2010).

Theories related to the resource curse have focused on the paradox that countries with abundant natural resources tend to have less economic growth than countries without these natural resources. Some of the reasons highlighted as to why this paradox exists are (i) reliance on exports of raw resources, (ii) Dutch disease (an economic theory which causes revenues from natural resource exports to damage a nation's productive economic sectors by causing an increase of the real exchange rate and wage increase (Ross, 1999), (iii) excessive borrowing, (iv) revenue volatility, (v) conflict, (vi) corruption and (vii) resource taxation. Scholars such as Albert Hirschman and Robert Baldwin have argued that resource industries were unlikely to stimulate growth in the rest of the economy, particularly if foreign multinationals dominated resource extraction and were allowed to repatriate their profits instead of investing them locally (Hirschman, 1958; Baldwin, 1966). The external interest and competition or conflict that may ensue from resource extraction industries combined with corruption and poor governance structures have characterized the situation in the DRC throughout its history. Local investment and taxation of resource extraction industries in the DRC have never occurred. Instead, political leaders from the local to the national level within the DRC have benefitted from individual contracts and back-door dealings with resource extraction companies.

It is my hope that an examination of the coltan industry and conflict in the DRC and how the phenomenon of sexual violence relates to this

Conflict in the DRC

The DRC is one of the poorest countries in the world, with an unemployment rate of 85%, and at the same time 79% of the population lives on less than $2 per day (Mukenge, Kady and Stanton, 2010). The DRC's formal economy is dominated by the mining sector, with minerals as the main export, representing the single largest source for foreign direct investment. The conflict in the DRC is directly linked to a struggle for power and resources which involves the Government of the DRC, non-state armed groups backed by external nations such as Uganda, Rwanda, Burundi and local defence units. While its resource wealth should easily support development and the proper functioning of the state apparatus, neither the population nor the state benefit from the country's natural resource endowments (Kok, Lotze and Van Jaarsveld, 2009). The DRC is currently ranked 176th on the 2009 UNDP Human Development Index (UNDP, 2009).

In 1994, the arrival of hundreds of thousands of refugees fleeing from or being perpetrators of the Rwanda genocide into Eastern DRC contributed to political instability in the Congo. While the 1994 genocide 1994 did not necessarily cause the conflict in the DRC, it is viewed as one of the major precipitating factors for the conflict that began in 1996. Laurent Kabila led a rebel movement in 1996, with the support of Rwandan and Ugandan troops to overthrow Mobutu Sese Seko, the then President of the DRC. He succeeded in taking the capital in May of 1997 and transformed what was then Zaire into the Democratic Republic of the Congo. One year later, in 1998, war broke out again in the east when the Rwandan and Ugandan governments were unhappy with Kabila's broken promises to them which led to the development of the RCD – *Rassemblement Congolais pour la Democratie*, an armed group that emerged in the Eastern DRC backed by Uganda and Rwanda. In the meantime, the DRC government called upon its Southern African Development Community neighbours – Zimbabwe, Angola and Namibia – to send its armies to protect the sovereign DRC. In addition, another rebel group, the *Mouvement pour la Liberation du Congo* (MLC), backed by Uganda, emerged in the northwest of the DRC. The second war officially ended in 2003 with the culmination of the inter-Congolese dialogue and the Sun City negotiations in 2002, and then the All-inclusive Pretoria Peace Agreement of 2003.

In addition, there is another set of armed actors called the Mayi-Mayi.[1] They originally began as local armed groups that emerged as a response to the violence in the Eastern DRC to protect their villages. However, as the conflict continued, the Mayi-Mayi groups became manipulated and bribed by the larger armed groups. The Mayi-Mayi have now become an armed group less concerned with just defence and protection of their communities and focused instead on promoting conflict. This is in large part due to the fact that the Mayi-Mayi have become accustomed to the economy created by the conflict and the fact that integration processes have marginalized the Mayi-Mayi. It has been estimated that 5.4 million people lost their lives as a result of the war in the DRC (International Rescue Committee (IRC), 2008). Many of the violations committed against civilians, including sexual violence, have amounted to war crimes and crimes against humanity. The women of the Congo began a campaign in 2000 where they argued the war was being fought on their bodies (Réseau des Femmes, 2005).

In 2006, the DRC experienced its first set of democratic elections. This was an extremely difficult operation to launch given the lack of infrastructure, civic education needs, high levels of illiteracy and the possibilities of insecurity and corruption. Joseph Kabila remained the President following the election results and international observers such as the SADC Election Observer Mission, the UN Observer Mission and the Carter Centre Election Observation Delegation declared the election to be free and fair. However, despite these elections, unifying both the country and the new national army – *Forces armées de la République démocratique du Congo* (FARDC) – has proven to be extremely problematic. This is in large part due the magnitude of the underdevelopment in the DRC, the large population and the lack of roads and infrastructure. The Eastern DRC, or the North and South Kivu provinces, remains outside the effective control of the government in Kinshasa.

The FARDC was formed after the installation of the transitional government in 2003 and was designed to bring together elements of all of the main armed groups and the government under its umbrella. New brigades were formed of soldiers from each of the main groups who undertook three months basic training and instruction across the country. Overall, 18 brigades were integrated. The FARDC is effectively the new national army and has continued to integrate and consolidate its control over the east with the assistance of MONUSCO and the Amani Leo operations. As of March 2011, the FARDC has been reconfiguring its units in the Kivus and dispersing battalions into regiments, which are the size of brigades. Some of these regiments are in the process of being deployed outside of the Kivus to try to avoid the alliance building between Hutu (PARECO) and Tutsi (CNDP) brigades (Stearns, 2011). Conflict in the Eastern DRC persisted after the 2006 elections. In the east there existed the Mayi-Mayi local defence units, the CNDP (*Congres National pour le Defense de les Peuples*), the FARDC and the FDLR (*Forces Democratique pour la Liberation du Rwanda*). General Laurent Nkunda led the CNDP, who had the backing of neighbouring Rwanda. In January 2008, Nkunda agreed to sign a peace pact aimed at ending years of conflict. But by August 2008, heavy clashes erupted between the FARDC and CNDP. In October 2008, the Congolese government accused Rwanda of backing General Nkunda, and therefore having a direct role in the raping and killing of thousands of Congolese civilians. Rwanda denied this support and UN peacekeepers engaged the CNDP in an attempt to support the FARDC troops.

By January 2009, there was the launch of a joint DR Congo-Rwanda military operation against Tutsi rebels led by Nkunda that lasted five weeks. Laurent Nkunda was arrested and taken to Rwanda. No formal charges either by the International Criminal Court, the DRC government or Rwanda have been laid as of yet against Nkunda. Rwanda's about face with regards to support for Nkunda was clearly linked to the international outcry from donors to Rwanda, who threatened to pull their support if Rwanda did not stop supporting Nkunda (Shepherd, n. d.).

In 2009, during a rapid reintegration process in Eastern Congo, an estimated 12,000 combatants from rebel groups joined the Congolese army ranks, swelling the army's numbers in the east to 60,000 soldiers (Human Rights Watch, 2009). The haste with which this process occurred created more difficulties as issues related to pay, discipline and command and control led to further widespread abuses. Armed groups such as the CNDP now had increased control over a wider territory in the country, making it difficult to distinguish between protection and belligerent forces.

In April 2009, the Hutu militia (FDLR) re-emerged after the end of the joint DR Congo-Rwanda campaign. By May 2009, President Kabila approved a law giving amnesty to armed groups as part of a deal meant to end fighting in the east. In December of 2009, the UN Security Council decided to extend the mandate of MONUC, the largest peacekeeping mission in operation with the aim of beginning withdrawal in 2010. As of July 2010, the peacekeeping mission has now been renamed MONUSCO, the United Nations Organisation Stabilization Mission in the DRC. Its current authorization emanates from UN SC Res. 1925 of May 2010 and has authorization until 30 June 2011. At present MONUSCO has 22,016 total uniformed personnel (MONUSCO, n. d.). The peacekeeping mission in the DRC has a Chapter VII mandate, emphasizing that the protection of civilians must be a priority.

What is coltan?

'Coltan', a term unique to Central Africa, is an abbreviation of columbotantalite, the name given to an ore containing both niobium and tantalum (Hayes and Burge, 2003: 33). It is a black metallic grit that occurs in alluvial or riverine deposits and is obtained by panning, much like gold. Through refining, the two elements are separated from one another and converted into a metallic powder. Tantalum is valuable as a metallic element that is twice as dense as steel and highly resistant to heat and corrosion. It can store and release an electrical charge, a property that has made it a vital material for capacitors in miniaturized and portable electronic equipment, including mobile phones. Other applications include its use in surgical equipment, turbine blades for jet engines and lining chemical reactors (Hayes and Burge, 2003: 11).

There are four types of capacitors: ceramic, aluminium, tantalum and film (Hayes and Burges, 2003: 24). Tantalum, however, is the most expensive option, has the highest capacitance, greatest stability, can be used to make significantly smaller units and is the most reliable in a broad range of temperatures. Coltan passes through numerous hands, some of which are legal, some illegal and some covered in blood. Local miners dig, pan and bag the coltan. The local miners are forced to pay spoonfuls of coltan to the military forces that control the land and another to the local authorities (Hayes and Burges, 2003: 33). Coltan from different mining sites is initially collected by local traders (*comptoirs*), who often mix illegally and legally mined ores. This coltan is then tested for the percentage of tantalum and purchased by *negotiateurs*, or traders (Hayes and Burges, 2003: 33). Many *negotiateurs* operate without a licence, which can cost up to US$40,000 per year, and smuggle coltan across borders by road and air. It is estimated that the DRC contains 80% of the world's coltan reserves (Vesperini, 2001).

The coltan is then shipped to Europe and Asia where few refiner companies transform the coltan extracted in several countries into tantalum, which is then used for microchips in electronic devices (Totolo, 2009). Shipping of the coltan is done directly by the various armed groups and local companies to international companies such as Thiarsco (Thailand Smelting and Refining), Malaysia Smelting Corporation, African Ventures Ltd (Hong Kong), Afrimex (UK), Amalgamated Metal Corporation (UK),

Clepad Experts (Belgium) and Mineral Supply Africa (Rwanda-based but owned by UK owner) (United Nations, 2008). In this chain, corporations do not have any effective policies for distinguishing 'clean' and 'dirty' coltan. Australia is responsible for 60% of the current world production (United Nations, 2008). All of the production of the largest mines is sold in advance, on fixed price contracts to key tantalum processors. There is no central market for tantalum and prices are most often determined by dealers on an individual transaction basis.

In 2000, increased demand for new electronic products such as laptops and Sony's PlayStation 2 caused a tantalum supply shortfall, which caused a rush of panic and a massive price increase. In the DRC this led to a rush to mine coltan from citizens and armed groups of the DRC. The price increased from US$30 per pound in 1999 to US$380 per pound in 2000 (United Nations, 2008). At this time, the RCD-Goma, then in control of the North and South Kivu region, granted a monopoly on the coltan trade to the Great Lakes Mining Company, Société Minière des Grands Lacs (SOMIGL), in an effort to maximize their profits. SOMIGL was created by the RCD in November 2000 and had four official shareholders: Ms Gulamali and two unnamed directors, as well as RCD that owned 75% of the company. The other parties to SOMIGL were Africom, Promeco and Cogecom – the names of the individuals behind these companies remain a mystery (Tegera, 2002). According to former RCD-Goma leader, Dr Adolphe Onusumba, in 2000 his rebel movement raised only US$200,000 per month from diamonds compared to US$1 million from exporting 100–50 tons of coltan per month (Vick, 2001).

The primary companies involved in the extraction and refinement of tantalum from ore, which produces the metal as a powder, are the American firm Cabot Corporation, German firm H. C. Stark and Chinese government-owned firms (Hayes and Burge, 2003: 22). The telecommunications industry is an important consumer of tantalum capacitors, accounting for approximately 18% of demand units (Hayes and Burge, 2003). Ericsson pioneered handsets that do not use any tantalum and the actual number of capacitors used per handset by other manufacturers, including Motorola and Nokia, is decreasing, though this is offset by the increase in global volume of handset production. In addition, GSM and 3G phones, which require the high capacitance of tantalum, have triggered a resurgence in the demand, as have. Increases in the demand for LCD monitors and PDAs.

While the various foreign armies that have been involved in the DRC claimed security as their main justification for their presence, all have been accused by the United Nations Expert Panel on the Illegal Exploitation of Natural Resources of illegal exploitation of the natural resources of the DRC by the ... UN Expert Panel. ... In April 2001, the UN Expert Panel reported widespread exploitation of natural resources by foreign troops.

Congolese armed groups earn an estimated $8 million per year from trading in tantalum (Pendergast, 2009). CNDP, FDLR, Rwanda, Uganda, the Mayi-Mayi groups and FARDC are all benefitting from the extraction of resources from the DRC and especially from coltan. Each group controls a different area of the Kivus and based on their location, their access to particular mines and minerals will differ. This control is also very difficult to monitor as armed groups' movements are fluid and change continuously. With this in mind, the UN Expert Panel on the Illegal Exploitation of Resources from the DRC's 2008 and 2009 reports do highlight the scope of the particular armed groups involvement and it is here that I would like to summarize some of these key findings. The FDLR has access to considerable reserves of cassiterite, coltan and wolframite in the Mwenga and Uvira areas of South Kivu as well as the Walikale area of North Kivu. It was calculated by the UN Expert Panel that the FDLR could earn at least several hundred thousand dollars up to a few million dollars a year from this trade (United Nations Expert Panel, 2009: 42). The CNDP had controlled the Bibatama coltan mine in Rubaya in 2008 in Masisi territory. The coltan obtained is sold to MUNSAD *comptoir* in Goma and it is estimated that Bibatama mine produces hundreds of kilograms of coltan ore per week (Group of Experts, 2008: 15). Trademet, a Belgian company, finances MUNSAD. In addition, an FDLR and FARDC collaboration in joint operations against the CNDP have led to collusion with arms trades and mineral concessions. The FARDC is heavily involved in the minerals trade, particularly with the control of the Bisie Mine (Group of Experts, 2008: 31).

It should be noted that the mining areas are often heavily taxed by the FDLR, PARECO, CNDP and Mayi-Mayi groups – whoever is in control of that territory. The Expert Group has attempted to develop a list of principal mining sites in North and South Kivu under the control of the armed groups, but the information is incomplete due to the lack of cooperation with the *comptoirs* (Group of Experts, 2008: 32). This is understandable due to the high level of insecurity that is pervasive.

Sexual violence as a weapon of war

Sexual violence during armed conflict is often associated with rape; however, this is only one form of sexual violence during war. Sexual mutilation, forced prostitution and forced pregnancy are other forms of sexual violence that are equally damaging (Reynolds, 1998: 601) Women are raped in all forms of armed conflict, international and internal, whether the conflict is fought primarily on religious, ethnic, political or nationalist grounds, or a combination of all of these.

> They are most often raped by men from all sides to the conflict. The reality is that rape and violent sexual abuse of women in armed conflict has a long history ... Rape in War is not merely a matter of chance, of women victims being in the wrong place at the wrong time. Nor is it a question of sex. It is rather a question of power and control which is structured by male soldiers' notions of their masculine privilege, by the strength of the military's lines of command and by class and ethnic inequalities among women.
>
> Chinkin (1994: 326)

Throughout the world, sexual violence is routinely directed against females during situations of armed conflict. This violence may take gender-specific forms, like sexual mutilation, forced pregnancy or sexual slavery. Being female is a risk factor and rape in conflict is used as a weapon of war to terrorize and degrade a particular community to achieve a political end (Chinkin, 1994). In these situations, gender intersects with other aspects of a woman's identity such as ethnicity, religion, social class or political affiliation. The humiliation, pain and terror inflicted by the rapist are meant to degrade not just the individual woman but also to strip the humanity from the larger group of which she is a part. The rape of one person is translated into an assault upon the community through the emphasis laced in every culture on women's sexual virtue: the shame of a rape humiliates the family and all those associated with the survivor (Nowrojee, 1996).

Sexual violence is not just an unfortunate aspect of war, but a deliberate tactic used as a weapon of war. It is a serious crime that finally received international criminal accountability following the wars in the Former Yugoslavia and the genocide of Rwanda. The Geneva Conventions of 1949 and their Additional Protocols do deal with sexual violence; however, even when the Conventions are addressing sexual violence, they fail to list it as a 'grave breach'. As a result, it was not given the priority and attention that it deserved as a serious war crime. The 1995 UN Beijing Declaration and Platform for Action helped to bring to the forefront the need to identify and act upon sexual violence in war particularly through Section E of the Platform for Action, which identified women and armed conflict. By 1996, the UN Special Rapporteur for Rwanda (Special Rapporteur, 1996) had reported that sexual violence was both systematic and employed as a weapon of war:

> Rape was the rule and its absence the exception ... Under-age children and elderly women were not spared ... Pregnant women were not spared. Women about to give birth or who had just given birth were also the victims of rape in hospitals ... women who were 'untouchable' according to custom were also involved and even corpses.

The International Criminal Tribunal for Rwanda was the first international court to convict those responsible for rape as a form of genocide.

Chris Coulter makes the important point that rape is not only a deliberate weapon of war but also reflects the low status of rights for women in society, which was magnified by the war (Coulter, 2009: 127). The reactions of families and communities to women who had been raped also reflected local understandings of morality. In detailing any account of war and sexual violence, the details and extent of the rapes and sexual violence are rarely discussed. As Coulter points out (2009: 128), however, to shy away from explicit descriptions of sexual violence is also a way of silencing and censoring women's experiences. Coulter's work and research on Sierra Leone is helpful in understanding the sexual violence in the DRC for a number of reasons. First, her research details the accounts of sexual violence from the perspective of the girl soldiers or 'bush wives', a common phenomenon in the DRC. Second, she challenges assumptions about victimization by addressing questions related to agency and survival techniques, which are completely under-researched. Third, it is an account of the tactics employed by armed groups to control and manipulate a population through the use of rape as a weapon of war. Fourth, it coincides with the illegal exploitation of natural resources – diamonds.

While there may be nothing new about the use of rape as a weapon of war, there certainly are new forms of sexual violence combined with extreme violence that have emerged over the last ten years in the DRC. It is my belief that failing to understand the tactics, degree of violence and effects of the sexual violence in the DRC not only silences the women, but allows the attackers to continue their brutality as the international community turns a blind eye. If, however, we recognize that the sexual violence is not a 'normal part' of Congolese society and the causal factors that contribute to the extreme levels of violence, then we have a much better chance of ending this abuse.

Sexual violence in the Eastern DRC

Although rape has long existed in the past in the DRC and the Kivu region, it has been regarded as a deeply reprehensible act and an extreme humiliation for the victim, her family and her husband especially. Therefore, a woman who had been raped would not return immediately to her home; she would send a message to her husband to warn him of what had occurred. He would then arm himself with a spear and go in search of the rapist, whom he absolutely had to kill to avenge the insult. The woman would have to wash herself at the edge of the village to purify herself and change her clothes before returning home (Réseau des Femmes, 2005: 27). The humiliation aspect of rape is still very much alive today in the DRC; most communities stigmatize women who have been raped and hold them accountable for the shame and humiliation that they have suffered. This leads to many women not reporting rape or seeking medical assistance. In a study conducted by International Alert, *Reséau des Femmes pour un Dévelopment Associatif* and *Reséau des Femmespour la Défense des Droits et la Paix* from 1996 to 2003, 70% of the rape victims they interviewed had received no medical treatment at all. Some had decided not to go to a health centre, preferring not to reveal what had happened for fear of being stigmatized (Réseau des Femmes, 2005: 41).

It has been suggested that the impact of the sexual violence against women in the Great Lakes region and its use as a weapon of war has heightened the use of such tactics in the DRC. Particularly, if you assess that the *genocidaires* from Rwanda escaped into the DRC, the support of armed groups in DRC by Burundi and Rwanda have increased the levels of violence against the overall population in the DRC. Many women were subjected to widespread sexual violence during the Rwandan genocide. The UN Special Rapporteur for Rwanda reported in 1996 that approximately 250,000 women had been raped during the genocide in Rwanda (Human Rights Watch, 2004). Many women were raped in front of their families and then killed. Similarly in Burundi, all the fighting forces committed acts of sexual violence against the most vulnerable in society. Despite the end of the conflict in Burundi, sexual violence against women remains one of the main problems to resolve.

The impact of these conflicts and the influx of armed groups from Burundi and Rwanda into the DRC has certainly had an impact on the levels of sexual violence in the DRC. When the wars in the DRC broke out in 1996 and 1998, this led to displacing people, and many women and girls were forced to turn to 'survival sex' from relatively wealthy foreign soldiers and UN peacekeepers. Targeted rape as a means to torture, humiliate and control became the order of the day in the Eastern DRC. In one study conducted in South Kivu alone, out of 492 Rape with Extreme Violence cases between 1996 and 2003, 57.3% of the women were convinced that the extreme violence and cruelty inflicted on them by armed forces was 'proof that there was a plan to destroy and exterminate the Congolese people or in any case the communities that the women belonged to' (Réseau des Femmes, 2005: 48).

The rapes and sexual violence committed in the DRC are conducted with unprecedented cruelty, perpetrators having devised the most humiliating treatment they can inflict on the victims. Many rapes occur in public places and in the presence of witnesses. Public rapes have also been given a name in the Eastern DRC and one particular rape is called *la reign*. In these cases, women are publicly stripped, tied upside down and gang raped in the middle of a village. The types of rape that have been identified include individual rape, gang rape, rape in which victims are forced to rape each other, rape that involves intentional transmission of HIV (Mukengere Mukwege and Nangini, 2009) and rape involving objects being inserted into the victim's genitals (Réseau des Femmes, 2005: 27). Attackers often throw acid in the vaginas of the women they have raped, or cut off their breasts. In many cases the rape victims are tortured and murdered. These acts of sexual violence leave victims with profound physical, psychological and emotional trauma.

Most of the rapes and sexual violence that occur seem to have been planned in advance by the attackers. Rape and pillage of villages seem to go hand in hand (Réseau des Femmes, 2005: 35). One such example is the attack on Walikale area, North Kivu that took place on 2 August 2010. In this attack, FDLR and Mayi-Mayi fighters took over ten villages in the area and systematically raped women and baby boys over a period of four days. During these four days they looted villages, raped 179 women and babies and killed three MONUSCO peacekeepers (Rwanda News Agency, 2010). In other instances, women are also kept as sex slaves and cooks by the armed groups. The permission to invade and rape a village is often given as a reward to the armed group by the commanders, as payment of the armed groups rarely occurs.

It is important to note that all sides to the conflict have committed sexual violence. For the victims it is often difficult for them to identify the attackers because of fear or because they are often left unconscious. According to Human Rights Watch, the government army – the FARDC – due to its size is the single largest perpetrator of the sexual violence against women and girls (Human Rights Watch, 2009: 21).

The 14th Brigade of the FARDC was created in 2006 and is supposed to control the North and South Kivu region. Without sufficient pay or food, soldiers have attacked civilians to loot and extort goods. The violence against women and girls peaked between January and August 2008, when the brigade had almost no provisions to sustain itself (Human Rights Watch, 2009). In March 2009, the 14th brigade officially ceased to exist when it was combined with the other armed groups in the process of 'mixage'. However, this integration process required very little vetting or training and many of the armed groups now have greater access to resources and territory to commit sexual violence as a result of this process. A UN official in North Kivu warned that the number of reported rapes by FARDC soldiers was on the rise in early 2009 (Human Rights Watch, 2009: 21).

Age is not a barrier to become a victim of sexual violence. Girls as young as toddlers and women as old as grandmothers are targeted equally.[2] The United Nations Population Fund (UNFPA) has reported that more than 65% of the victims of sexual violence during 2008 were children, the majority adolescent girls. In addition, 10% were children under ten years (Human Rights Watch, 2009: 14). The targeting of young girls can be attributed to a few different factors: (i) young girls are often performing chores that may leave them vulnerable to attack, such as gathering water and wood; (ii) young girls are most likely virgins and the belief is that they would therefore be less likely to be HIV positive and (iii) it is also a means to destroying the fabric of a community as a 'raped girl' is ostracized and therefore viewed as unmarriageable.

Denis Mukwege, a Congolese gynaecologist in Bukavu, states 'that everyday at least 10 new women and girls that have been raped show up at his hospital' (Gettleman, 2007). Many have been so sadistically attacked from the inside out, butchered by bayonets and assaulted, that their reproductive and digestive systems are beyond repair. According to the UN, 27,000 sexual assaults were reported in 2006 in South Kivu province alone. The latest figures estimate 1100 rapes per month as assessed between November 2008 and March 2009 (United Nations Security Council, 2009). 'The sexual violence in the Congo is the worst in the world,' said John Holmes, UN Under Secretary General for Humanitarian Affairs (Gettleman, 2007). Malteser International, a European aid organization that runs health clinics in Eastern DRC, said that in Shabunda village, 70% of the women reported being sexually brutalized (Gettleman, 2007).

Traditional ways of coping with the rapes in the past involved husbands avenging the wrong by physically harming the attacker, but the current insecurity has left men unable to 'avenge' these wrongs as they would be overpowered and killed by the armed groups. This has meant that men instead take out their frustration and humiliation on the women who have been raped, and often results in the men abandoning their wives.

One man explained that if one's wife is raped men feel ill at ease; they believe they have lost their dignity and self-esteem. If your wife belongs only to you, you feel proud and you think you have something that others don't have. But if she is raped, you lose your pride and you are worth nothing in the community.

Harvard Humanitarian Initiative (2009: 26)

The Harvard Humanitarian Initiative compiled a research report that was released in 2010, in which a comparison of the types of perpetrators in 2004 and 2008 was revealed. In 2008, there was a 17-fold increase in the reported number of civilian perpetrators and a 77% decrease in the number of reported cases by armed combatants. Yet, it should be kept in mind that armed combatants were still the predominant perpetrators in 2008 (Harvard Humanitarian and Oxfam, 2010: 19). The point made by this report was that the pervasive use of rape as a weapon of war, combined with the impunity for such perpetrators, has meant that rape is becoming more prevalent among civilian attackers. As Stephen Lewis, the former UN Special Envoy for HIV/AIDS in Africa has said, 'the capacity for brutality by so many perpetrators – and on the flip side, the capacity for indifference by so many witnesses – is the ugly apex of a trend gone unchecked' (Lewis, 2007). The long-term outcomes translate into the slow death of a population. The breakdown of society and identity in the Eastern DRC is a disturbing trend that will have repercussions for many years to come. Relationships between men and women have been altered in the most negative manner possible. Children born of rape are a common phenomenon.

Coltan and sexual violence

Sexual violence in the DRC is often fuelled by militias and armies fighting over control of minerals. Available data on the extent of sexual violence in the DRC, and especially the Eastern region, is very difficult to obtain for many obvious reasons: lack of infrastructure, insecurity, ethical considerations and lack of political will. Despite this, the deadly nexus between the worst violence against women in the world and the demand for electronics containing conflict minerals from the Congo is undeniable (Pendergrast, 2009: 3).

The publicly available data on the extreme sexual violence in South Kivu reveals some connections between the location of the coltan mining areas and incidents of sexual violence. The Walungu region is rich in both gold and coltan and is one of the administrative territories of the FDLR. Kabare also has deposits of coltan, and is controlled by the FDLR. Shabunda is another mining town that contains coltan and is surrounded by jungle; it has been largely besieged by the Mayi-Mayi who kidnapped townswomen for use as sex slaves. Armed groups have set up their own mining company in Shabunda called the Great Lakes Mining Company, which monopolizes the exploitation of natural resources (Mampasu, 2002). However, a comprehensive mapping and analysis of all sexual violence cases that have been reported and their proximity to the mining areas has not been conducted to this date. At the same time, the location of the armed groups does correlate to mining areas and the data available also reveals that armed groups are responsible for the majority of the sexual violence attacks.

In 2000 we saw the rise of the price of coltan coincide with the demand for the new Sony PlayStation 2 and laptops. This meant the price of coltan went from US$30 per pound to US$380 per pound between 1999 and 2000. The coltan rush led many to stake their claim on the territory of the Eastern DRC. At the same time, reports of sexual violence and village attacks took a dramatic surge upwards. The Harvard Humanitarian Initiative's April 2010 Report, *Now, the World is Without Me*, investigated the rape epidemic and the region's militarization. The report concludes that several spikes in sexual assault numbers could be explained by a military strike or an intensification of military activity. The Report studied the number of sexual assaults by month and year, and was compared to documented military offensives for the South Kivu area. As an example, the number of reported rapes for June 2004 indicates a significant spike in sexual assault, 160 cases alone, as compared to a monthly average of 65 per month. At this same time, Laurent Nkunda and his troops seized control of Bukavu. Such evidence is also witnessed in an April 2004 clash between FARDC troops and FDLR, and in 2009 when the joint Rwandan-Congolese military offensive against the FDLR took place (Harvard Humanitarian and Oxfam, 2010: 34).

Similarly in the latter half of 2008, there was a prediction of a shortage of coltan from Australia, which led speculators to seek more coltan from the DRC. From August 2008 to November 2009, we witnessed the bloodiest attacks yet, resulting in refugee flows and high levels of sexual violence that surged once again.

Since January 2008 there were an estimated 875,000 internally displaced persons in North Kivu province, which included 155,000 new internally displaced since January 2008. This represents an increase of 45% from the previous year. The recurrent armed clashes in 2008 have led to continuous waves of population displacement, which have affected approximately 150,000–180,000 persons since late August 2008. In South Kivu, the number of internally displaced also increased and as of September 2008, internally displaced persons from North Kivu were estimated at 65,000.

UN Secretary-General (2008)

Each time we hear the announcement of a new electronic product, we also need to consider the potential impact this has on the price and availability of coltan. The numbers of personal computers used worldwide were estimated to double from 2004 to 2010 to 1.3 billion machines. Forrester Research has predicted that the growth will be driven by emerging markets such as China, India and Russia (Mattocks, 2004). How does this demand increase relate to increased levels of conflict and violence? It is also well documented that pornography, sex trafficking and prostitution are linked to the illicit economies of war, and seeing as other aspects of the war in Sierra Leone and the DRC are connected to the global economy, it should be no surprise that pornography could also have been distributed and consumed by the combatants of the wars (Coulter, 2009: 128). As I will discuss the link between the global greed for coltan and the increased levels of extreme sexual violence, we may certainly require further research into the origin of tactics of sexual violence as a weapon of war in the DRC.

Addressing the use of sexual violence in the Eastern DRC

The Panzi Hospital is located in Bukavu, South Kivu. This hospital is renowned for its treatment of victims of sexual violence and is the best-funded hospital in South Kivu, primarily receiving funds from Communaute des Eglises de Pentecote en Afrique Centrale (CEPAC) (Mukengere Mukwege and Nangini, 2009: 3). Because it is a referral hospital, it receives the most severe cases of sexual violence from smaller centres in the region. However, the hospital runs far beyond its capacity and continually faces a shortage of resources and personnel

(Mukengere Mukwege and Nangini, 2009: 4). Treatment is offered for free and in-hospital care is provided for those needing surgical treatment. Psychological treatment is also provided and husbands are counselled not to blame their wives for their traumas, as well as being counselled on forgiveness to overcome their anger (Mukengere Mukwege and Nangini, 2009: 4). Between August 1999 to August 2006, Panzi Hospital treated 9778 patients, of which 76% were confirmed as rape survivors (Mukengere Mukwege and Nangini, 2009: 4).

According to MONUC, only 11% of donor funds for sexual violence have been allocated for the physical protection of women and girls (Human Rights Watch, 2009: 4). There is heavy criticism that much donor funding is focused on the after effects of the sexual violence and not the prevention. The difficulty with this approach is that very little is done to halt the high levels of violence against women and the psychosocial impacts that accompany such violence cannot be erased. It also fails to send a strong message to the perpetrators of the violence as well as the women victims as money is not spent on apprehending or preventing their access to the women.

UN Secretary-General Ban Ki-moon recently announced a new Special Representative, Margot Wallstrom, who is tasked with combating sexual violence against women and children in conflicts. The Secretary-General stated, 'I am horrified and outraged by the use of rape as a weapon of war' (Agence France-Presse, 2010). It is hoped that the alarm bells of the DRC will prompt attention and action on sexual violence in conflict zones. Potential action that is required could include the following: foot patrols conducted by UN peacekeepers to ensure women are escorted safely to and from their villages, patrols to protect known areas of vulnerability, lighting that could be provided in villages to help protect women, and the apprehension of perpetrators of rape and the subsequent effective prosecution of such perpetrators. In February 2011, a positive step has been taken towards the ending of impunity for such crimes in the DRC. Nine soldiers, including a commanding officer, Lt Col Kibibi Mutware, of the FARDC have been sentenced to between 10 and 20 years imprisonment for an attack on the town of Fizi in South Kivu that took place on 1 January 2011. Over 50 women were viciously and systematically raped in that attack (Fominyen, 2011). A military court that sentenced the men was part of a mobile gender justice court that has been travelling around remote areas of South Kivu to provide justice to victims of sexual violence and is a project by the Open Society Initiative and the American Bar Association.

Since the International Criminal Court (ICC) came into being, Congolese women and girls assisted and supported by civil society organizations have been waiting and hoping for concrete action on sexual violence by the highest international criminal authority. They stress that women and girls are the first victims of armed conflict, that violence against women is particularly serious and that it should be prosecuted to the full extent of the law. An historic march took place in South Kivu in November 2010 where over 4000 women were demanding peace and justice. However, the ICC has also been plagued by its ineptitude with collecting testimony and evidence related to sexual violence in the DRC. Such instances include the lack of protection afforded to women who give testimony. White UN vehicles arrive in villages and take Congolese women to their offices to hear their stories; when this occurs all the people in the village are aware that the reason she is with the UN is because she is reporting a rape. Many women endure backlashes for giving testimony and others fear repercussions. In a country where the stigmatization of those that are raped is the norm, the ICC has failed to protect the best interests of the women victims. Alternatives to 'Western style' justice must be sought when it comes to the burden of proof and the collection of evidence.

In November 2007, Olive Lemba, Joseph Kabila's wife, opened a countrywide campaign to raise awareness and push for an end to impunity to combat sexual violence (Human Rights Watch, 2009: 6). In 2006, a landmark sexual violence law came into force, providing a much-improved legal framework to try those responsible. Penalties for rape range from five to 25 years imprisonment but are doubled when committed by a public official, by a group or with the use or threat of a weapon. In 2008, the ICC launched an investigation into crimes committed in the Kivus, including sexual violence. The military justice system is a weak institution in the DRC and to date only a fraction of the acts of sexual violence committed have been prosecuted. In 2008, 27 soldiers were convicted of crimes of sexual violence in North and South Kivu; at the same time the UN registered 7703 new cases of sexual violence in the same area (Human Rights Watch 2009: 6).

In April 2001, Electronic Business News asked several companies involved in purchasing coltan or tantalum capacitors for their reactions about the conflict in the DRC and the links to coltan. The responses included the following:

- 'You hope your suppliers are doing things legally but beyond that what can you do?'
- 'We don't view the source of tantalum as an issue for us, but more for the capacitor suppliers.'

- They were surprised to learn of the situation, they purchased tantalum solely on the quality, they did not trace its origin, and they trusted their suppliers to provide tantalum from 'appropriate' sources.
- The situation was inexcusable, but it was too difficult to trace the origin of ores, so it was up to the Congolese government to control the mining.

Hayes and Burge (2003: 35)

Tracing coltan and holding corporations that are end users accountable for the source of the coltan is a difficult task. In part this is due to the nature of the conflict and the various armed groups that are involved, hence there is no central authority to be held accountable. Additionally, it is also the nature of the extraction and export of the coltan. Since, coltan is extracted manually, then melted down before being exported, there are no specific markings that can be placed on the product itself, which is much different from the diamond mining industry and the Kimberley process. 'In many cases, tracing back to the origins of a particular supply of coltan is pretty difficult, even impossible,' explains Michael Petricone, senior vice-president of government affairs at the Arlington, Virginia-based Consumer Electronics Association. 'We're concerned about the entire mine operation, but right now it's very challenging to figure out how we trace this' (Lehrer, 2010).

In August 2009, US Secretary of State Hillary Clinton visited the DRC. Many hoped that this visit would help to focus attention on the sexual violence in the DRC and thereby influence action. After visiting Goma, Ms Clinton promised $17 million in aid for victims of sexual violence. On the one hand this could be viewed as a positive contribution from the United States, on the other her visit failed to highlight the direct link to resource extraction. Additionally, the most remembered event of her trip was the 'misquote' from a journalist which was interpreted to ask her 'what does her husband think should be done?' Attention to the issue is important, but understanding how to address root causes is far more necessary.

Conclusions

We need to link economic governance approaches with international peace and security, which includes human rights protection. During the inter-Congolese dialogue, economic questions were always treated as peripheral to the key issues of democratic governance, peace and stability. Getting agreement on the formation of the transitional government and the New National Army were prioritized as key stumbling blocks. But taking the gun out of economics is the prerequisite for taking the gun out of politics (Global Witness, 2010: 8).

In December 2008, the UN Security Council extended existing targeted sanctions to cover individuals or entities supporting the illegal armed groups in the Eastern DRC through illicit trade of natural resources. The Security Council simultaneously mandated MONUC to use its monitoring and inspection capacities to curtail the provision of support to illegal armed groups derived from the illicit trade in natural resources. In November 2009, the Council instructed the Group of Experts to produce recommendations to the Sanctions Committee for guidelines for the exercise of due diligence by the importers, processing industries and consumers of mineral products regarding the purchase, sourcing (including steps to be taken to ascertain the origin of the mineral products), acquisition and processing of mineral products from the DRC. It also recommended that importers and processing industries adopt policies and practices, as well as codes of conduct, to prevent indirect support to armed groups in the DRC (Global Witness, 2010: 12).

There are clearly numerous impediments to the regulation of coltan and to the implementation of SC Resolution 1896. To date, none of the companies that support armed groups in the DRC through illicit natural resource transactions have been placed on the targeted sanctions list (Global Witness, 2010: 14). In addition, MONUC's capabilities have proven time and time again to be inadequate and adding one more task of such a monumental nature will clearly be difficult. Lastly, monitoring information flow and sanctions implementation requires a political will and internal capacity that has been non-existent over the history of the DRC.

It is also important to note that merely advocating for banning of purchasing and mining of coltan from the DRC will not produce the magic cure. Given the extreme levels of poverty, people need to be able to use their resources to create employment and contribute to development. Instead we need to find ways to regulate the coltan extraction industry, put pressure on the armed groups and their backers to end the abuse of the DRC, and protect the women of the DRC.

Recommendations

The international community must design strategies to stop the direct and indirect financing of armed groups by Western corporations. Even though the trade chain of coltan is extremely complex, a proper certification scheme for 'conflict-free' coltan could promote its legal extraction while fighting its role in fuelling conflict. Germany financed a pilot study for this project, and the Congolese finance minister announced that a 'fingerprint' programme for Congolese coltan will be finalized in 2009 (Society for Geology Applied to Mineral Deposits, 2008).

> Without doubt, there are regional and local variations in the composition of coltan. These are due to differences in geological age and mineralogical and chemical composition of host pegmatites and their derivative heavy mineral concentrates. Zoned CGM crystals perfectly mimic the chemical evolution of pegmatitic melts (Lahti, 1987) and thus can be used as monitors of the fractionation stage of the source rocks. This allows distinction of locations even in districts and provinces of similar geological ages, similar host rocks or similar parent melt compositions. Each tantalum deposit has its unique characteristics. Therefore, a fingerprint of samples of suspect or unknown origin should be possible when a large and high-quality analytical data base is created.
>
> Society for Geology Applied to Mineral Deposits (2008)

A certification scheme for legally mined Coltan might be a first step for an effective contribution of the international community to a solution of the conflict. However, there is a risk that the international community and the conflicting parties will make decisions only in order to please the Western donors, without seeking long-term solutions for regional hostilities (Totolo, 2009).

High-level officials must be held accountable for sexual violence and this includes the President of the DRC. The International Criminal Court must employ innovative methods in the collection of evidence that would include locally relevant and contextually specific methods that do not necessarily adhere to 'Western evidentiary legal standards' and bring light to the connections between the use of sexual violence as a weapon of war and the resource extraction. MONUC troops must be equipped, trained and given the resources to physically protect women in the DRC as well as to assist with the monitoring and reporting of violations. The international community has for far too long declared that the DRC is the 'heart of darkness' and is therefore doomed for eternity, incapable of mending and too complex to understand. Given the magnitude of the human rights violations and the global economic connections, it is imperative that we work towards realistic, long-term and incremental solutions for peace and stability in the DRC.

Notes

1. Mayi-Mayi is Kiswahili for water, as it is believed that this group obtains its 'magical' powers and strength from water.
2. In the author's visit to Panzi Hospital, Bukavu in July 2010, the hospital statistician showed me statistics that indicated 66 girls under the age of three and 50 women above the age of 65 had been admitted to the hospital from January 2010 to July 2010 for sexual violence.

References

Agence France-Presse, 2010. 'UN Chief Appoints Envoy to Curb Rape in Wars'. Available at http://www.google.com/hostednews/afp/article/ALeqM5gGV5g7Y pslxtNtkqxCrTTqb65dAQ (accessed on 1 September 2011).
Baldwin, R. E., 1966. *Economic Development and Export Growth: A Study of Northern Rhodesia, 1920–1960*. Berkeley: University of California Press.
Chinkin, C., 1994. 'Rape and Sexual Abuse of Women in International Law'. *European Journal of International Law* 5, pp. 326–41.
Coulter, C., 2009. *Bush Wives and Girl Soldiers: Women's Lives Through War and Peace in Sierra Leone*. Ithaca and London: Cornell University Press.
Enloe, C., 2000. *Maneuvers: The International Politics of Militarizing Women's Lives*. Berkeley: University of California Press.
Fominyen, G., 2011. 'Alertnet, Rights Groups Welcome Jail Terms for Congo Mass Rape', 22 February. Available at http://www.trust.org/alertnet/news/rights-groups-welcome-jail-terms-for-congo-mass-rape/ (accessed on 1 September 2011).
Gettleman, J., 2007. 'Rape Epidemic Raises Trauma of Congo War'. *The New York Times*, 10 July. Available at www.nytimes.com/2007/10/07/world/africa/07congo.html (accessed on 8 February 2010).
Global Witness, 2010. *Lessons Unlearned: How the UN and Member States must do more to End Natural Resource-Fuelled Conflicts*. Available at http://reliefweb.int/node/343314 (accessed on 1 September 2011).
Group of Experts, 2008. *Final Report of the Group of Experts on the Democratic Republic of the Congo*, 12 December, S/2008/773.
Harvard Humanitarian Initiative, 2009. *Report for the Open Society Institute, Characterizing Sexual Violence in the Democratic Republic of the Congo: Profiles of Violence, Community Responses, and Implications for the Protection of Women*, August. Available at http://www.un.org/en/peacekeeping/missions/monuc/reports.shtml (accessed on 1 September 2011).
Harvard Humanitarian Initiative and Oxfam America, 2010. *Now the World is Without Me: An Investigation of Sexual Violence in Eastern Democratic Republic of the Congo*, Available at http://www.oxfam.org/sites/www.oxfam.org/files/DRC-sexual-violence-2010-04.pdf (accessed on 4 January 2012).
Hayes, K. and R. Burge, 2003. *Coltan Mining in the Democratic Republic of Congo: How Tantalum-using Industries can Commit to the Reconstruction of the DRC*. Flora and Fauna International Conservation Report, Cambridge, UK.
Herbst, J. and G. Mills, 2009. 'There is No Congo'. *Foreign Policy*. Available at http://www.foreignpolicy.com/story.cms.php?story_id=4763 (accessed on 31 March, 2009).

Hirschman, A. O., 1958. *The Strategy of Economic Development*. New Haven: Yale University Press.
Human Rights Watch, 2004. *Struggling to Survive: Barriers to Justice for Rape Victims in Rwanda*, September, 16(10).
Human Rights Watch, 2009. *Soldiers who Rape, Commanders who Condone: Sexual Violence and Military Reform in the Democratic Republic of Congo*. Available at http://reliefweb.int/node/317258 (accessed on 1 September 2011).
International Rescue Committee (IRC), 2008. 'IRC Study Shows Congo's Neglected Crisis Leaves 5.4 Million Dead: Peace Deal in North Kivu increased Aid Critical to Reducing the Death Toll'. Available at http://www.rescue.org/news/irc-study-shows-congos-neglected-crisis-leaves-54-million-dead-peace-deal-n-kivu-increased-aid--4331 (accessed on 1 September 2011).
Kok, A., W. Lotze and S. Van Jaarsveld, 2009. *Natural Resources, the Environment and Conflict*, ACCORD. Available at http://www.accord.org.za/downloads/reports/Natural_Resources_Conflict.pdf (accessed on 1 September 2011).
Lehrer, E., 2010. 'Industry and Congress Work to Block Congolese Coltan'. Available at http://www.heartland.org/infotech-news.org/article/27173/Industry_Congress_Work_to_Block_Congolese_Coltan.html (accessed on 21 March 2011).
Lewis, S., 2007. 'Calls for a New UN Initiative to End Sexual Violence in the Eastern Region of the DRC, Nairobi'. Press release. Available at http://www.aidsfreeworld.org/Publications-Multimedia/Reports/Call-for-a-new-UN-initiative-to-end-sexual-violence-in-the-eastern-region-of-the-DRC.aspx (accessed on 21 August 2011).
Mampasu, C., 2002. 'Shabunda: The Forgotten Kosovo'. *Humanitarian Exchange Magazine*. Available at http://fex.ennonline.net/16/shabunda.aspx (accessed on 1 September 2011).
Mattocks, J., 2004. 'Number of PCs Worldwide to Double by 2010: Over a Third of New PCs to Come from China, Russia and India'. Available at http://www.newsfox.com/pte.mc?pte=041216011 (accessed on 31 August 2011).
McKay, S. and D. Mazurana, 2004. *Where are the Girls? Girls in Fighting Forces in Northern Uganda, Sierra Leone and Mozambique: Their Lives During and After War*. Montreal: Rights and Democracy.
MONUSCO, n. d. Facts and Figures at www.un.org/en/peacekeeping/missions/monusco/facts.html, accessed on 30 March 2011.
Mukenge, M., A. M. Kady and C. Stanton, 2010. *Global Fund for Women, Funding a Women's Movement Against Sexual Violence in the Democratic Republic of the Congo: 2004–2009*. Available at www.globalfundforwomen.org (accessed on 1 September 2011).
Mukengere Mukwege, D. and C. Nangini, 2009. 'Health in Action. Rape with Extreme Violence: The New Pathology in South Kivu, Democratic Republic of Congo'. *PLoS Med* 6(12). Available at http://www.plosmedicine.org/article/info%3Adoi%2F10.1371%2Fjournal.pmed.1000204 (accessed on 31 August, 2011).
Nowrojee, B., 1996. *Shattered Lives: Sexual Violence during the Rwanda Genocide and its Aftermath*. London: Human Rights Watch.
Pendergast, J., 2009. *Can You Hear Congo Now? Cell Phones, Conflict Minerals and the Worst Sexual Violence in the World*. The Enough Project. Available at www.enoughproject.org (accessed on 15 January 2010).
Rwanda News Agency, 2010. 'Belgium Shocked at the FDLR Mass Rape of Women, Baby-Boys'. Available at http://www.rnanews.com/regional/4068-belgium-shocked-at-fdlr-mass-rape-of-woman-baby-boys- (accessed on 1 September 2011).

Réseau des Femmes (Réseau des Femmes pour la Défense des Droits et la Paix et International Alert), 2005. *Women's Bodies as a Battleground: Sexual Violence Against Women and Girls during the War in the Democratic Republic of Congo, South Kivu (1996–2003)*. Available at http://www.grandslacs.net/doc/4053.pdf (accessed on 31 August 2010).

Reynolds, S, 1998. 'Deterring and Preventing Rape and Sexual Slavery during Periods of Armed Conflict'. *Law and Inequality* 16, pp. 601–32.

Ross, M. L., 1999. 'The Political Economy of the Resource Curse'. *World Politics* 51: 2.

Shepherd, B., n. d. *Congo, Rwanda and the National Congress for the Defence of the People, Conciliation and Reconciliation*. Available at http:www.c-r.org/our-work/accord/cross-border-project/national-congress.php (accessed on 17 March 2011).

Society for Geology Applied to Mineral Deposits, 2008. *Finger-Printing of Conflict Minerals: Coltan Ores*. Available at http://e-sga.org/fileadmin/sga/newsletter/news23/SGANews23.pdf (accessed on 3 May 2010).

Special Rapporteur, 1996. UN Secretary-General's Special Rapporteur for Rwanda, Report 29. 29 January.

Stearns, J., 2011. 'Military Changes Come to the Kivus, Slowly'. *Congo Siasa Blogspot*. Available at http://congosiasa.blogspot.com/2011/03/military-changes-come-to-kivus-slowly.html (accessed on 4 March 2011).

Tegera, A., 2002. 'The Coltan Phenomenon: How a Rare Mineral has Changed the Life of the Population of War-Torn North Kivu Province in the East of the DRC'. Available at http://www.kongo-kinshasa.de/dokumente/ngo/polinst_coltan.pdf (accessed on 1 September 2011).

Totolo, E., 2009. 'Coltan and the Conflict in the DRC'. *ISN Security Watch*. Available at http://www.isn.ethz.ch/isn/Current-Affairs/Security-Watch/Detail/?lng=en&id=96390 (accessed on 1 September 2011).

United Nations, 2008. *Expert Panel on the Illegal Exploitation of Resources in the DRC* (December).

UNDP, 2009. *Human Development Report*. Available at http://hdr.undp.org/en/reports/global/hdr2009/ (accessed on 1 September 2011).

United Nations Expert Panel, 2009. *Expert Panel on the Illegal Exploitation of Resources from the DRC*, S/2009/603.

UN Secretary-General, 2008. *Report of the Secretary-General on Children and Armed Conflict in the DRC*, 10 November, S/2008/693.

United Nations Security Council, 2009. *Twenty-Seventh Report of the Secretary-General on the United Nations Organization Mission in the Democratic Republic of the Congo*. Available at http://www.un.org/en/peacekeeping/missions/monuc/reports.shtml (accessed on 1 September 2011).

Vesperini, H., 2001. 'Congo's Coltan Rush'. *BBC World Service*. Available at http://news.bbc.co.uk/2/hi/africa/1468772.stm (accessed on 8 May 2009).

Vick, K., 2001. 'Vital Ore Funds Congo's War'. *The Washington Post*, 19 March, accessed on 21 September 2011.

8
Official Secrets and Popular Delusions: Security at the End of the Fossil Fuel Age?

Shane Mulligan

Introduction

> Can I tell you the truth? I mean this isn't like TV news, is it? Here's what I think the truth is: We are all addicts of fossil fuels in a state of denial, about to face cold turkey.
>
> Kurt Vonnegut (2004)

Peak oil is an awkward topic to broach. While there is strong evidence that world oil production levels are near their maximum, and while a growing chorus warns of the challenges and threats this poses to economic growth and political stability, there is virtually no public policy discourse directed to the issue, and only a handful of academics seem prepared to investigate the phenomenon and its implications for economies, societies and state (as well as human) security. It is as if there is a tacit agreement to avoid the topic, an agreement in which we are all, to some extent, participating, through our avoidance of this 'elephant in the room'. The evidence for peak oil is often received with reticence, or even hostility towards the speaker. Indeed, breaching the silence of an open secret – 'something of which everyone is aware yet no one is willing to publicly acknowledge' – is akin to 'breach[ing] some implicit social contract, and groups indeed treat those who violate their norms of attention and discourse just as they do any other social deviants who defy their authority and disregard their rules' (Zerubavel, 2006: 77–8). This chapter aims to go further, however, to talk about the very fact that we don't want to discuss it, even though 'the very act of avoiding the elephant is itself an elephant!' (Zerubavel, 2006: 53) The latter, too, is something we don't generally talk about.

Why are governments, and most of the rest of us, ignoring (or at least avoiding discussion of) peak oil? This chapter examines a range of answers to that question, with a focus on the lack of policy discourse on the issue. It then looks to a number of contemporary issues in international politics – the geopolitics of oil and gas, responses to the global financial meltdown, and global 'climate' policies – to see if peak oil adds to or illuminates the rationale behind states' and other actors' actions. It concludes with some reflections on secrecy and security in an age of ecological decline.

Peak oil: An emerging consensus?

The discourse of energy security has long centred on questions of supply and price, but has also generally attributed energy security conditions to human agency: threats to importing states' energy supplies and prices may arise from hostile state actions, terrorist attacks on infrastructure, inadequate investment (and unfriendly investment environments), price gouging companies and market speculators. Thus the price spike of 2007–8 was widely blamed on 'speculators', while most analysts ignore that global production was flat from late 2004 to mid-2008 – even while rising prices spurred significant investments in oil sands, biofuels and deep-water production. Others argued that supply constraints were primarily due to inadequate investment and other 'above-ground factors', including violence and vandalism/terrorism in Nigeria, Iraq and elsewhere. Yet a growing chorus argued that supply constraints and price volatility were the foreseeable consequence of the approaching peak in oil production.

The expectation of peak oil is based on two simple facts: one, oil must be discovered before it can be 'produced'; and two, production in *any* field tends to rise to a maximum and thereafter decline. Global discoveries in fact peaked in 1965 (Campbell and Laherrère, 1998: 78–83), and since the early 1980s global consumption has consistently exceeded discoveries, and by a growing margin: in the first decade of this century, the ratio of discoveries to consumption may have been as high as 1:5, that is, for every barrel found, five barrels were burned (Heinberg, 2003). M. King Hubbert developed the peak oil model in the 1950s, and he used it to predict – correctly, as it turned out – that production in the contiguous 48 US states would peak around 1970. He also predicted that world production would peak around the year 2000; many analysts believe that the oil crises of the 1970s delayed the global peak, but that it looms large, and may already be behind us.

While there remains a debate over peak oil, it is not really a debate over whether a peak will occur, but when it will occur, what it will look like and how serious a problem it will be. As former US Energy Secretary James Schlesinger said to ASPO in 2007, 'we are all peakists now. Conceptually the battle is over, the peakists have won' (Hopkins, 2007). Nevertheless, expectations of the peak date vary from 2005 to 2030, and optimists (popularly known as 'cornucopians') argue that technology and new supplies are likely to produce an 'undulating plateau', rather than a peak, which some say we could remain on for decades before production falls.[1] Many peak oilers, however, see the production curve from 2004 to 2008 as just such a plateau. Figure 8.1 shows global crude oil production for the last decade: the image of an undulating plateau is clear, though a peak is not.[2] As Matt Simmons has pointed out in the film The End of Suburbia, however, 'we will probably only be able to see peak oil in the rear view mirror' (2004): if the production level achieved in July 2008 is indeed the highest we will ever see, it may be years before it is recognized that that *was* the peak. Indeed, if this economic downturn continues, along with falling *demand*, peak oil may not be recognized for decades among the events that surround it (Bardi, 2009: 323–6).

An imminent peak would seem to pose a serious threat to military, economic and even social stability, yet peak oil is surprisingly absent from current policy debates, and it seems that to date not a single national government has openly addressed the prospect. Yet a number

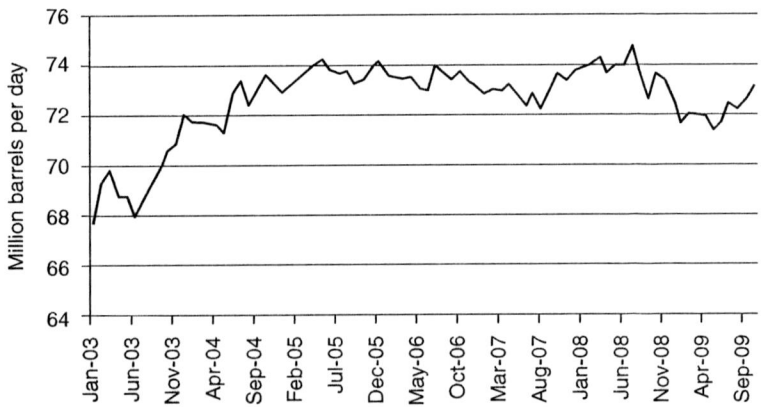

Figure 8.1 World crude oil production – EIA
Source: www.theoildrum.com.

of important reports have shown that the concern is very real. The 'Hirsch Report', commissioned by the US Department of Energy in 2005, pointed out that, while the date of the peak was uncertain, 'without timely mitigation' (by which the authors meant *decades* in advance), 'the economic, social and political costs will be unprecedented' (Hirsch, Bezdek and Wendling, 2005: 4). The Energy Watch Group (2007: 71), initiated by a German MP, concluded that oil likely peaked in 2006, and that by 2030 production will be 'dramatically lower': 'The world is at the beginning of a structural change of its economic system. This change will be triggered by declining fossil fuel supplies and will influence almost all aspects of our daily life.' A 2007 report by the US Government Accountability Office (GAO, 2007) admitted its concern that 'there is no co-ordinated federal strategy for reducing uncertainty about the peak's timing or mitigating its consequences'. In the US a 'peak oil caucus' has been running for a number of years, while the UK's 'All-Party Parliamentary Group on Peak Oil' includes 32 elected officials, and ASPO Switzerland currently counts 23 Parliamentarians among its members.[3]

Despite this, there is little public discourse on the threat posed by peak oil, and no educational campaigns, policy initiatives or even parliamentary debates seem to have arisen at the level of nation states, let alone at the global level. The relative obscurity of the voices on peak oil, the general lack of media attention and the range of uncertainties associated with it leave 'more room than is healthy for politicians to dodge, procrastinate or back-pedal on the policies needed' to deal with peak oil (Gavin, 2007). On the one hand, this is hardly surprising: democratic politics thrive on the rhetoric of hope, of 'energy independence' and the aspirations of the next 'energy superpower' (McQuaig, 2007). Voters don't tend to support the bearers of bad news, as the career of former US President Jimmy Carter, who consistently drew attention to the energy crisis, attests. On the other hand, the silence is rather shocking, given the centrality of energy in economic and industrial health, as well as the growing discussion of peak 'theory'. 'The growing popular debate on "peak oil" has had relatively little influence on conventional policy discourse. For example, the UK government rarely mentions the issue in official publications and ... does not feel the need to hold contingency plans specifically for the eventuality of crude oil supplies peaking between now and 2020' (UKERC, 2009: 1). The UK is far from alone in 'failing to give serious consideration to this risk' (UKERC, 2009: 164). Indeed, Canada does not appear to even *have* an official position on peak oil: Natural Resources Canada – the lead agency responsible for energy supply questions – looks to the reserves in the Alberta tar sands and argues that humanity has enough oil for the next 200 years (National Farmers Union (Canada), 2009). Canada is also a member of the International Energy Agency (IEA), and is thus bound to production-sharing agreements in the event of an energy shortage; however, as a net energy exporter, Canada has not deemed it necessary to hold strategic reserves, despite that Eastern Canada is largely dependent upon imported oil products and is thus highly vulnerable to shortages on the global market (Laxer, 2008).

The possible reasons for governments' silence on peak oil range from ignorance ('we don't know') to disbelief ('we don't buy it'), to helplessness ('yes, but what can we do?'), to conspiratorial silence ('we're working on it').[4] The most sympathetic perspective would accept that governments – that is, the people who perform the various offices, from resource bureaucrats to elected heads – generally don't know about peak oil, or don't understand its implications. One *Oil Drum* editor recently suggested that even 'the [US] Secretary [of Energy] seems woefully unaware of the underlying fragility of the energy supply situation' (Heading Out, 2009). However, such a claim seems dubious, and UK MP Michael Meacher laughs at the suggestion: 'It's not as though the leaders are not briefed [about peak oil] – *of course* they are' (original emphasis).[5] Indeed, it seems highly improbable that the Energy Secretary of the world's largest energy-consuming state would not be all too familiar with peak oil – especially given that the US peak is a frequently cited proof of the concept. More likely, politicians and bureaucrats (among others) may be committed to a way of thinking that assures them that peak oil is not a problem. The principal grounds for complacency seem to lie in the faith that the market mechanism is effectively infallible: the price mechanism, alongside technological advances, will provide the best way through. The market perspective is of course widely shared among the citizens of Western states, but it has also become deeply entrenched in policy circles, and no doubt many enjoy an infallible optimism about the market's ability to deliver.

According to Hughes (2009: 60), 'One of the reasons politicians, television news anchors and newspaper columnists are so reassuring about our energy future is that the people they get their information from are just as bullish ... [The EIA and IEA] invariably paint a view of the future that is barely distinguishable from the past', and a resumption of growth is believed to be merely a matter of time. The International Energy Agency's (IEA) flagship publication, the *World Energy Outlook*, has consistently claimed that, given sufficient investment, a peak in production is unlikely prior to 2030. However, the WEO is also a source of some alarming statistics, noting, for instance, that in order to meet demand projections (in the face of declines from existing fields), 'some 64 mb/d of additional gross capacity – the equivalent of almost six times that of Saudi Arabia today – needs to be brought on stream between 2007 and 2030' (WEO, 2008: 7).[6] The *WEO 2009* also notes that the investment required to meet projected energy demand is daunting: some $26 trillion between now and 2030. However, the high oil prices needed to attract sufficient investments may actually constrain economic activity and the availability of the capital. Indeed, the IEA estimates that investment in energy production had declined from 2008 to 2009 by some 20% in certain sectors: 'Energy companies are drilling fewer oil and gas wells, and cutting back on refineries, pipelines and power stations ... The financial crisis has cast a shadow over whether all the energy investment needed to meet growing energy needs can be mobilized' (WEO, 2009: 5). The IEA, then, is not all optimism, and in fact seems to suggest that production constraints are likely.

If we presume that government agencies actually pay attention to the fine print in the IEA's publications, and that they have noted the inevitability of a peak in conventional oil production, we have to approach the view of policymakers as fully aware of peak oil, and simply not willing (or able) to discuss the issue. Returning to US Energy Secretary Steven Chu, one former colleague has been quoted as saying the Secretary 'knows all about peak oil, but he can't talk about it. If the government announced that peak oil was threatening our economy, Wall Street would crash. He just can't say anything about it' (Bland, 2009). That a public acknowledgement, let alone an information campaign, could negatively impact markets, certainly suggests one reason for avoiding the issue. Voters are unlikely to respond well to falling markets, especially if these can be traced to politicians' ill-considered announcements regarding declining energy. Again, former US President Carter's fate is well recalled.

Yet the notion that governments are aware of a threat to societal well-being and political stability, and are not discussing it openly in order to protect themselves, is hardly comforting. Indeed, even when some have tried to discuss the issue, governments have resisted it. Jeremy Leggett, who edited the 2008 UK Industry Taskforce Report, says the Taskforce had initially invited the Department of Trade and Industry to conduct a joint industry-government study. The DTI replied, 'and this is the exact words used: "it would be too risky to do that". Their argument was ... basically, there isn't any risk, so why do a risk assessment, because if you do that you might scare the horses unnecessarily.' On the other hand, the UK government has widely embraced the Wicks (2009) review,[7] which Leggett notes 'dismisses peak oil out of hand'. Though the Taskforce had met with the authors of the review, including Wicks himself, neither the Taskforce nor its principal arguments are discussed in the report. Says Leggett, '[t]his is gross irresponsibility, and a form of betrayal of national interests, and I think the people involved in this will really live to regret it' (Leggett, n.d.).

Leggett's appeal to national interests, however, may be missing the point: the official silence may well be a policy choice informed, in some manner, by national interests. Peak oil is hardly a secret, but if governments are aware – as seems likely – and are taking steps to address it – as seems prudent – then the awareness and these steps are, in some sense, state secrets. We might look at this in terms of an 'open secret', an issue over which a silence is tacitly understood as appropriate or necessary to maintain social and group cohesion. Open secrets – or 'elephants in the room' – are characterized by an understanding that such silences are 'far less threatening than the efforts to end them' (Zerubavel, 2006: 78). Yet whatever actions are being taken to deal with peak oil are doubly guarded. To the extent they are motivated by peak oil concerns, not only is this motivation disguised (in favour of more palatable motives), but the very existence of a threat that might motivate such actions is not admitted (and is thus 'inadmissible' as evidence, even in scholarly work). Hence, it may well be as Mike Ruppert (2005) suggests:

> Most people have ... a serious misconception: ... that there is an urgent need to somehow make key decision makers and leaders of American and global life aware of the immediate problems of Peak Oil and Natural Gas. Nothing could be more off base. The world's key decision makers have been aware of and planning for this crisis for years.

But in the absence of a discourse that reveals such awareness, or that which discusses policy efforts to address it, how are researchers to approach this hypothesis? Clearly, we need to look not at what actors say about peak oil – because they do not say much – but at what they do. In this spirit, this chapter turns to interpret a number of current issues in international politics in light of an impending peak in oil global production.

Actions speak louder than words...

Blood for oil?

> I'm glad you asked. It has nothing to do with oil, literally nothing to do with oil.
>
> Donald Rumsfeld, quoted in CBS Radio (2002)

Surely the first area to look for policies and practices informed by peak oil is in terms of resource wars. Assumptions of self-interested states motivated by relative power differentials suggests that increasing scarcity of essential resources is likely to lead to interstate conflict. While it is widely recognized that the First Gulf War was driven by concerns about oil supplies, there was serious opposition to tying the 2003 invasion to oil. Donald Rumsfeld denied it, perhaps too loudly, but at least he then had the decency to retire: Tony Blair (2007) made the same assertion in *Foreign Affairs*, and then (briefly) considered seeking the EU Presidency. Alan Greenspan raised the ire of many in suggesting 'that it is politically inconvenient to acknowledge what everyone knows: the Iraq war was largely about oil.'[8]

As David Strahan (2007) writes, 'Iraq was indeed all about oil, but in a sense that transcends the interests of individual corporations, however large. The elephant in the drawing room was the fact that global oil production is likely to peak within about a decade.' The view that the War on Terror is effectively a pretext for actions motivated by other reasons, oil high among them, is widespread not only in the peak oil community, but also among academic scholars (Harvey, 2003; Klare, 2003). Even some who do not see peak oil recognize that the War has provided 'a cover that has enabled the Bush administration to do what it wanted to do anyway' (Waltz, 2002).

Not surprisingly, the US has been flagged for 'covert awareness' of peak oil. In 1999, former Vice-President Dick Cheney told an audience that by 2020 the world would need the equivalent of five Saudi Arabias to meet projected demand, and that the likely source, and thus 'the prize', was the Middle East oilfields (Aleklett, 2004). In 2008, President Bush himself noted that the Saudis could not very well be asked to pump more oil if they didn't have the capacity, suggesting that he might have actually been listening to his energy advisor Matt Simmons (ABC News, 2008). The representation of resource wars as a 'response to terrorists', or as part of a noble project of 'spreading democracy/freedom', offer seemingly useful justifications for these interventions. Seen through the lens of peak oil, however, they emerge as a strong statement of global power politics in its crudest form.

'Climate' policy

Energy security and climate change are closely tied in both political rhetoric, and in the policy response, especially in terms of renewable energy supplies. The IEA's *WEO 2009* outlines a '450 scenario' for future energy production, shaped by the aim of maintaining carbon dioxide concentrations below 450 ppm. Many of its policy recommendations to address emissions also promote the goals of energy security, and the IEA's Chief Economist, Fatih Birol, told the US Council on Foreign Relations (in response to a question) that even if global warming were not at issue, he would advocate 'ninety percent' of the 450 scenario policies for energy security reasons. He also told the group of his certainty that developing states are interested in climate negotiations – and in reducing emissions – far more for energy security reasons than for climate ones (WEO, 2007). Diplomatically, he did not point out that major industrial states might be acting for much the same reasons.

To be sure, developments in renewable energy are welcome in terms of both climate concerns and energy security, and the global push towards renewables is promising. It seems the threat of global warming is being taken seriously: the economic implications, the potential for widespread scarcities (of food and water) and conflict within and among states are significant. Yet there remains some tension between most energy/emissions projections and the demands of climate change mitigation. For instance, the IEA reference scenario has, for many years running, projected fossil fuels will continue to make up about 80% of growing consumption in coming decades – a scenario that is almost sure to bring about catastrophic climate change. However, many believe that climate change is already proceeding rapidly towards 'tipping points', after which anthropogenic emissions will have a negligible effect. In that case – one that is looking increasingly likely – the push for renewables will mean little for climate or its security implications. On the other hand, the observation that carbon supplies may be insufficient to fulfil the worst-case emissions scenarios – and thus that peak fossil fuels may be 'good news for climate change' – suggests a considerable challenge for the maintenance of electricity generation and manufacturing capacity (Madrigal, 2008). In either case, the future is not particularly bright.

The policies that would address energy security and climate change are largely complementary, in particular the diversification of energy supplies and the development of renewable sources of electricity. Yet the global warming agenda is a voluntary one, and this allows politicians and others to maintain that we have a choice in switching our power sources. Thus as fossil fuel scarcity begins to bite, declining supply ('bad') can be made to look like reduced emissions ('good'?). Whether due to peak oil or climate change concerns, our reliance upon fossil fuels seems sure to decline in the future, and even the semblance of normalcy will depend on a massive effort to develop alternative energy and fuel supplies. Solar, wind and geothermal energy hold a lot of promise, and may stem electricity supply concerns (thus enabling natural gas to be directed to other uses), and many states are developing enhanced grids for low-carbon electricity. In the absence of a technological breakthrough with second-generation biofuels, however, we appear to have few options to assist with liquid fuel supplies (Heinberg, 2009a, 2009b).

Responding to the economic crisis

A third policy area that might be examined in light of peak oil is the handling of the global economic crisis that, despite talk of 'green shoots', remains precarious in terms of employment figures, production and especially sovereign debt. While many deny that the recession/collapse was in part instigated by peak oil and high prices, there is a strong historical correlation between oil price shocks and subsequent recessions, and the spike of 2007–8 was 'one of the biggest shocks to oil prices on record' (Hamilton, 2009). Those who have been watching peak oil coming have long warned of the economic consequences: Kenneth Deffeyes, in *The End of Suburbia* (2004), suggested the peak would result in 'ten trillion dollars wiped from the stock market; two million jobs gone; state and municipal budget surpluses gone'. Leggett (2005) subtitled his major book with a prediction of *The Coming Global Financial Catastrophe*, painting a picture not unlike what many economies have seen since 2008 (2008–09), with declining real estate values and credit availability, along with rising unemployment. Lester Brown projected that 'when [oil] production turns downward, it will be a seismic economic event, creating a world unlike any we have known during our lifetimes' (Brown 2006: 21). If these trends represent the beginnings of a global energy descent, 'historians writing about this period may routinely distinguish between before peak oil (BPO) and after peak oil (APO)' (Brown 2008).

That peak analysts foresaw that an economic downturn is interesting, but hardly serves as proof that the current downturn is the result of peak oil. Nevertheless, many would argue that, for a number of reasons, peak oil marks something like the end of economic growth as we know it (Hall and Klitgaard, 2006: 4–22; Heinberg, 2009b; Aleklett et al., 2010). A principal reason is the historical link between energy (and oil) consumption and GDP growth. Despite efficiency gains, there is still very near a 1:1 correlation between declining oil supply and declining GDP; and as production stalled from late 2004, a halt to GDP growth could not be far behind (Hirsch, 2008). In consumption-based economies (like that of the US), oil prices inevitably impact on disposable incomes and take away from consumptive opportunities: that this could drive heavily indebted consumers into insolvency, leading to a housing market crash, was noted by the IEA (2004) itself as prices climbed through 2004. While it is easy in hindsight to recognize the bubble of real estate and financial innovation was destined to pop, it may be unfair to suggest that the expectation of a crash was widely shared. Some analysts clearly saw it coming, but there was also a good deal of genuine 'irrational exuberance' over the economy among consumers, investors and in policy circles.

Yet to the extent governments have been aware of peak oil, they have no doubt also been aware of the threat it poses to economic growth and the possibility, if not the certainty, of a financial meltdown. Was such foreknowledge part of the reasoning behind the infamous repeal of the Glass-Steagal Act (which enabled commercial banks to act as investment banks, and vice versa)? Did oil awareness help drive authorities to maintain low interest rates and 'growth' grounded in accumulating debt? The ongoing borrowing binge that has followed the onset of the crisis, while dressed up as Keynesianism, seems to many an utterly unsustainable shift of future wealth to the corporate sector. 'Everyone seems to know the current path of federal fiscal policy is a deathtrap over the long term ... [Yet] precisely because the size of the problem precludes easy answers, it lies beneath the surface of the public dialogue' (Kramer, 2010). In Europe, the noise about Greece's debt problems has evolved into a contest over who holds the distinction of being Europe's worst basket case, and whether they might go down together (Evans-Pritchard, 2010; Thomas, 2010).

The current crisis may well represent a rule-changing event, especially if peak oil affects opportunities for growth as severely as many expect. But how wide is such an expectation? Is it possible that governments (along with many banks, traders and analysts) realize that the old game of capitalism as played today cannot be sustained under conditions of declining energy? If so, has the future health of capitalism become irrelevant? Indeed, it may be in that case that the rational thing to do is seek to gain whatever can be withdrawn from the system prior to the major rule-changes that will be necessary to adapt to a declining energy order (even while the state upholds a requisite public discourse of recovery). Whether the advantages gained will still hold under whatever new rules emerge remains an open question.

Of elephants and silence

There are three major crises facing international order: the initiation of (energy) resource wars, a near certainty of continued climate change and an economic crisis that has no evident solution. I have presented these problems as 'elephants', issues of which we are well aware but the discussion of which is socially unwelcome, even subject to a tacit agreement of silence, obfuscation and the wide use of euphemism. Though only a few scholars and critical journalists – in the mainstream at least – give voice to the belief, is it not widely known that Iraq and Afghanistan are conflicts oriented towards the capture or control of energy resources? Have we not all pretty much accepted that there is little the world's governments can do to alleviate climate change (and an even lower likelihood that they *will* do anything)? Similarly, is it not evident that the global economy has entered a crisis phase of debt accumulation that will radically change the rules that govern that economy?

Of course, it is not by any means clear – to all respondents – that the answer to all these questions is yes. Over the last two centuries of fairly continuous growth, we have earned a reputation for, and perhaps a right to, a degree of optimism, including in human nature and liberal politics. Thus there are competing arguments for the Western occupations of Afghanistan and Iraq which are still widely accepted, and which some surely hold as genuine justifications for their own participation in these actions. The powerful images associated with climate change have generated a great deal of popular will to try to stop the damage caused by human activities, and no doubt some decision-makers share these sentiments and have internalized them. And of course economic downturns are not unusual (even if the current one is), and thus the expectation of recovery is justified by historical experience. That there is in fact widespread disagreement and arguments over all of these issues points to two central flaws with the claim that they represent 'elephants': a common realization which we all agree to not discuss. First, there seems to be a great deal of uncertainty and disagreement over the conclusions presented, which is to say we do not all know or realize the elephant is present; second, the degree of 'dissenting' discourse suggests that we have not all agreed to keep silent about it (them).

The question, then, might be a matter of the genuineness or sincerity of the reasons given by governments for their decisions. It *may* be that, while many are aware of peak oil, the policies outlined before are duly sought as remedies for *other* genuine problems, which happen to be (in some ways) resoluble through peak-friendly policies. Maybe, as some argue, leaders are avoiding the issue because they sincerely believe people will be better off – economically and psychologically – if they are not presented with the case for peak oil. When dealing with elephants, we tend to see 'silence as far less threatening than the efforts to end [it]' (Zerubavel, 2006: 78). Thus Sadad al-Husseini, former Vice-President of Saudi Aramco, suggests that those 'who are not expressing a concern [publicly] ... are doing that with a good intention: they feel like somehow this is a reality that the public at large can't handle ... [that] being in ignorance of these realities is better than knowing them ... and that somehow they will be solved. But in reality, if you don't have a public understanding of the issues you will never have the public support for the solutions ... So it's important to actually talk about the facts' (ASPO. TV News, 2009).

On the other hand, if 'solutions' can be represented as answers to other problems – terrorists, climate change, unemployment – public support may be easier to gain than under an honest presentation of the situation. It is difficult to gauge the degree to which peak oil is seen as a threat (i.e. as a genuine energy-security issue), but the issues discussed previously are all themselves generally presented in terms of security: terrorism, climate security and economic security. Alternative explanations, based on linking these issues to peak oil, suggest that the latter 'elephant' has given birth, in a sense, to these others. Ultimately, however, the crises discussed earlier can all be linked more broadly to a 'limits to growth' argument, the implications of which are, at the very least, frightening. As Meadows et al. argued in 1972, business as usual would seem to be bringing humanity towards a collapse scenario, entailing 'a sudden and uncontrollable decline in both population and industrial capacity' within a century (Meadows et al., 1972). The ecological limits of the human project are surely the mother of all elephants: neither can we hide the possibility that we have reached these limits, nor can we discuss it seriously (or not much). Our need to focus on hopeful outcomes makes talk of limits, let alone decline, collapse or 'die-off', an unwelcome topic in political conversation.

Conclusions: Energy, ecology and security in the twenty-first century

If the future, starting now, is to reveal these limits to us in increasingly discomfiting forms, the challenges facing us and our children are nevertheless in many ways unimaginable. Is it best to leave them unspeakable, as well? Is there anything to be gained by a more open public discussion of peak oil as a turning point in our history? Does holding off public acknowledgement hinder our chances of preparing for a future beyond oil, or is it likely that such preparations will be disastrous in themselves? 'Calculating what we ultimately gain and lose by opting to see, hear, and speak no evil is largely a matter of weighing short-term against long-term benefits ... [M]uch of what seems to benefit us in the short run often comes to haunt us in the long run' (Zerubavel, 2006: 79). Yet the image of ecological/energetic collapse does not suggest much we could do to prepare, even if we were discussing it. Ecology shows patterns to which humans too are subject: maybe we can't be helped; maybe we are simply doing what dumb organisms do.[9]

The arguments presented here suggest that there is a general silence on peak oil not because governments and others are unaware of it, but because that silence is itself a protective measure, indeed a security imperative. Among the systems upheld by surplus energy is a system of faith in those systems, a faith that then helps support those same systems. Such faith is not readily abandoned: for the state to be perceived to be doing something, *even if the illusion is obvious*, is still better than admitting the state's impotence in upholding human security in the face of ecological limits. 'A kingdom, after all, needs a king, even a naked one' (Zerubavel, 2006: 77). However, the critical analysis of domestic and international politics would surely profit from such a discussion: political correctness, analytical euphemisms and a heads-in-the-sand approach are encumbrances to analytical rigour, and promise failure for any efforts to secure our collective future.

Notes

1. The notion of an undulating plateau may be attributed to Daniel Yergin of Cambridge Energy Research Associates. CERA is somewhat notorious among peak oilers for its 'cornucopian' views.
2. Figure 8.1, based on EIA (Energy Information Administration) data to October 2009, is from Heading Out (2010). World liquids production (which includes natural gas liquids, ethanol, syncrude and other substitutes) shows a similar plateau.

3. See Roscoe Bartlett, Representative of 6th District, Maryland, 'Peak Oil'. Available at http://bartlett.house.gov/Issues/Issue/?IssueID=2057; http://www.appgopo.org.uk; http://www.peakoil.ch/new/e/peakoilparlament.php, accessed April 20, 2010. The Association for the Study of Peak Oil and Gas (ASPO), founded by Colin Campbell has national branches throughout the world (see http://www.aspo.org).
4. For an extended analysis on this point, with a wealth of commentary from readers, see Mulligan (2010).
5. In *Oil, Smoke and Mirrors*, Part 2 of 5 (available on www.youtube.com, accessed April 20, 2010).
6. All WEO publications can be found at www.worldenergyoutlook.org, April 20, 2010.
7. See www.decc.gov.uk/en/content/cms/what_we_do/change_energy/int_energy/security/security.aspx for the UK government response (accessed April 20, 2010).
8. The statement is from Greenspan's memoir *The Age of Turbulence: Adventures in a New World* (2007), and was reported by the *Times* of London 16 September 2007 ('Alan Greenspan Claims Iraq War Was really for Oil'). The following day Greenspan 'clarified' his statement in *The Washington Post* (Bob Woodward, 'Greenspan: Ouster of Hussein Crucial for Oil Security', 17 September 2007), denying that oil was the 'motive' for the war. He also noted in the same interview that one official told him in response to his concerns about oil security, 'Well, unfortunately, we can't talk about oil.'
9. Totoneila has long signed off *The Oil Drum* with the burning question: 'Are humans smarter than yeast?'

References

ABC News, 2008. 'Exclusive Presidential Interview: President Bush sits down in Saudi Arabia with Terry Moran', 16 January. Available at http://abcnews.go.com/Video/playerIndex?id=4140859, accessed on 20 April 2010.
Aleklett, K., 2004. 'Dick Cheney, Peak Oil and the Final Count Down', 12 May. Available at http://www.peakoil.net/Publications/Cheney_PeakOil_FCD.pdf, accessed on 20 April 2010.
Aleklett, K., M. Hook, K. Jakobsson, M. Lardelli, S. Snowden and B. Soderbergh, 2010. 'The Peak of the Oil Age'. *Energy Policy* 38(3) (March): 1398–414. Available at http://www.tsl.uu.se/uhdsg/Publications/PeakOilAge.pdf, accessed on 20 April 2010.
ASPO.TV News, 2009. 'Acknowledging the Reality of Peak Oil', 10 December. Available at http://www.youtube.com/watch?v=cd7QGbNKxoQ, accessed on 20 April 2010.
Bardi, U., 2009. 'Peak Oil: The Four Stages of a New Idea'. *Energy* 34: 323–6.
Blair, T., 2007. 'The Battle for Global Values'. *Foreign Affairs* (January/February).
Bland, A., 2009. 'Cheer Up, It's Going to Get Worse'. Available at http://www.bohemian.com/bohemian/06.17.09/feature-0924.html, accessed on 20 April 2010.
Brown, L. R., 2006. *Plan B 2.0: Rescuing a Planet Under Stress and a Civilization in Trouble*. New York: W. W. Norton & Co.

Brown, L. R., 2008. *Plan B 3.0: Mobilizing to Save Civilization*. London and New York: W. W. Norton & Co.
Campbell, C. J. and J. H. Laherrère, 1998. 'The End of Cheap Oil'. *Scientific American* (March): 78–83.
CBS Radio, 2002. 'Secretary Rumsfeld Live Interview with Infinity CBS Radio', 14 November. Available at http://www.defense.gov/Transcripts/Transcript.aspx?TranscriptID=3283 (accessed on 25 January 2010).
Energy Watch Group (EWG), 2007. *Crude Oil: The Supply Outlook*, EWG-Series No. 3/2007.
Evans-Pritchard, A., 2010. 'Fears of "Lehman-Style" Tsunami as Crisis Hits Spain and Portugal'. *The Daily Telegraph*, 4 February. Available at http://www.telegraph.co.uk/finance/financetopics/financialcrisis/7159456/Fears-of-Lehman-style-tsunami-as-crisis-hits-Spain-and-Portugal.html, accessed 20 April 2010.
Gavin, N., 2007. 'Global Warming and Peak Oil in the British Media: The Limits of Policy Development'. Paper presented at the *Energy Security in Europe* Conference, Lund University, Sweden, September. On file with the author.
Government Accountability Office (GAO), 2007. 'Crude Oil – Uncertainty about Future Oil Supply Makes it Important to Develop a Strategy for Addressing a Peak and Decline in Oil Production'. GAO-07-283, 28 February.
Greenspan, A., 2007. *The Age of Turbulence: Adventures in a New World*. London: Penguin.
Hall, C. A. S. and K. A. Klitgaard, 2006. 'The Need for a New, Biophysical-Based Paradigm in Economics for the Second Half of the Age of Oil'. *International Journal of Transdisciplinary Research* 1(1): 4–22.
Hamilton, J., 2009. 'Causes and Consequences of the Oil Price Shock of 2008–09'. Brookings Papers on Economic Activity. Available at www.brookings.edu, accessed on 20 April 2010.
Harvey, D., 2003. *The New Imperialism*. Oxford: Oxford University Press.
Heading Out (Editorial Board, *The Oil Drum*), 2009. 'Dr Chu, Dr Aleklett, and the Price of Oil', 22 November. Available at http://www.theoildrum.com/pdf/theoildrum_5893.pdf, accessed on 20 April 2010.
Heading Out (Editorial Board, *The Oil Drum*), 2010. 'Oil Demand Seems to be Moving Up – Are Higher Prices Around the Corner?' 13 January. Available at http://www.theoildrum.com/node/6122, accessed on 20 April 2010.
Heinberg, R., 2003. *The Party's Over. Oil, War and the Fate of Industrial Societies*. Gabriola Island, BC: New Society Publishers.
Heinberg, R., 2009a. *Searching for a Miracle: 'Net Energy' Limits and the Fate of Industrial Society*. Santa Rosa, CA: Post Carbon Institute.
Heinberg, R., 2009b. 'Temporary Recession or the End of Growth?' *Museletter #208*, August Available at http://heinberg.wordpress.com/2009/08/06/208-the-end-of-growth, accessed on 20 April 2010.
Hirsch, R., 2008. 'Mitigation of Maximum World Oil Production: Shortage Scenarios'. *Energy Policy* 36(2) (February): 881–9.
Hirsch, R. L., R. H. Bezdek and R. M. Wendling, 2005. *Peaking of World Oil Production: Impacts, Mitigation and Risk Management*. Washington: US Department of Energy, (February).
Hopkins, R., 2007. 'ASPO 6. In Praise of ... #2. "We Are All Peakists Now"', *Transition Culture*, 24 September. Available at http://transitionculture.org/2007/

09/24/aspo-6-in-praise-of-2-we-are-all-peakists-now/ (accessed on 25 August 2009).
Hughes, J. D., 2009. 'The Energy Issue: A More Urgent Problem than Climate Change?' In T. Homer-Dixon, ed., *Carbon Shift: How the Twin Crises of Oil Depletion and Climate Change Will Determine the Future.* New York: Random House, 59–96.
Hughes, L. 'Eastern Canadian Crude Oil Supply and its Implications for Regional Energy Security'. *Energy Policy* 38(6): 2692–2699.
IEA, 2004. *Analysis of the Impact of High Oil Prices on the Global Economy.* Paris: IEA.
Klare, M., 2003. *Rising Powers Shrinking Planet: The New Geopolitics of Energy.* New York: Holt.
Kramer, O. S., 2010. 'Unfunded Benefits Dig States' $3 Trillion Hole'. *Bloomberg*, 20 January.
Laxer, G., 2008. 'Freezing in the Dark: Why Canada Needs Strategic Petroleum Reserves'. 31 January. Available at http://www.ualberta.ca/PARKLAND/research/studies/SPR Report.pdf, accessed on 20 April 2010.
Leggett, J., 2005. *The Empty Tank: Oil, Gas, Hot Air, and the Coming Global Financial Catastrophe.* New York: Random House.
Leggett, J., n. d., Discussing the UK Industry Taskforce on Peak Oil and Energy Security. Available at http://www.aspo.tv/discussing-the-uk-industry-taskforce-on-peak-oil-and-energy-security.html, accessed on 20 April 2010.
Madrigal, A., 2008. 'World Coal Reserves could be a Fraction of Previous Estimates'. *Wired*, 17 December. Available at http://blog.wired.com/wiredscience/2008/12/world-coal-rese.html, accessed on 20 April 2010.
McQuaig, L., 2007. 'Canada: Energy Pussycat'. *Toronto Star*, 24 July, online at http://www.thestar.com/printArticle/238985, accessed on 20 April 2010.
Meadows, D. H., D. L. Meadows, J. Randers and W. W. Behrens III, 1972, *The Limits to Growth.* New York: Universe Books.
Mulligan, S., 2010. 'Heads in the Sand? Or, Why Don't Governments Talk About Peak Oil?' *The Oil Drum*, 5 January. Available at http://www.theoildrum.com/node/6100, accessed on 20 April 2010.
National Farmers Union (Canada), 2009. 'Canada's House of Commons must Convene Inquiry into Fossil Fuel Supply', 16 November. Available at http://www.energybulletin.net/node/50736, accessed on 20 April 2010.
Ruppert, M. C., 2005. 'Government, Financial, and Political Awareness of Peak Oil Prior to 2005: Five Rules for Survival of the Coming Collapse'. Speech presented to the New York Petrocollapse Conference, 5 October. Available at www.fromthewilderness.com/free/ww3/100405_petrocollapse_speech.shtml (accessed on 12 December 2009).
Strahan, D., 2007. 'The Real Casus Belli: Peak Oil'. *The Guardian*, 26 June, online at http://www.guardian.co.uk/commentisfree/2007/jun/26/comment. oil, accessed on 20 April 2010.
The End of Suburbia, 2004. Documentary film produced by The Electric Wallpaper Company. Belleville: Canada.
Thomas, L., Jr, 2010. 'Debt Problems Chip Away at Fortress Europe'. *New York Times*, 5 February. Available at http://www.nytimes.com/2010/02/06/business/global/08euro.html, accessed on 20 April 2010.
UKERC, 2009. 'The Global Oil Depletion Report', 8 October. Available at http://www.ukerc.ac.uk/support/tiki-index.php?page=Global+Oil+Depletion (accessed on 1 December 2009).

Vonnegut, K., 2004. 'Addicted to Oil and Violence'. *In These Times*, 13 May. Available at http://www.countercurrents.org/us-kurtvonnegurt130504.htm (accessed on 21 January 2010).

Waltz, K., 2002. 'The Continuity of International Politics'. In K. Booth and T. Dunne, eds, *Worlds in Collision: Terror and the Future of Global Order*. New York: Palgrave Macmillan, 348–53.

Wicks, M., 2009. 'Energy Security: A National Challenge in a Changing World'. Special report prepared for the British Prime Minister (August). Available at http://www.decc.gov.uk/assets/decc/What%20we%20do/Global%20climate%20change%20and%20energy/International%20energy/energy%20security/1_20090804164701_e_@@_EnergysecuritywicksreviewBISR3592EnergySecCWEB.pdf, accessed on 21 April 2010.

Zerubavel, E., 2006. *The Elephant in the Room: Secrecy and Denial in Everyday Life*. Oxford: Oxford University Press.

9
Securing Alberta's Tar Sands: Resistance and Criminalization on a New Energy Frontier

Philippe Le Billon and Angela Carter

Introduction

Unconventional oil is frequently presented as the future of petroleum-based energy resources.[1] Critics, in contrast, denounce unconventional oil as a major factor of environmental insecurity for local ecosystems, communities and the planet. In particular, they claim that unconventional hydrocarbon sources are frequently associated with deregulation of oil extraction and petroleum commodity chains, have negative environmental impacts, and increase the number and intensity of energy and environment-related conflicts.

We examine this debate about energy and environmental security through a case study of the tar sands in Alberta, Western Canada, which have been dubbed the world's second largest petroleum reserves after Saudi Arabia, and were by 2010 the largest single source of imported oil to the United States.[2] We start with a brief review of the energy and environmental security conundrum, and present two divergent views of environmental violence: violence *to* the environment and violence *for* environmental causes. We then discuss the liberalization and securitization strategies first pursued by Canadian authorities to overcome impediments to growth in the tar sands sector during the 1990s. The massive growth in tar sands exploitation which has occurred since the early 2000s has led to growing opposition, characterized by three trends: a scaling-up in alliances and actions, a move away from stalled institutionalized politics to more direct and disruptive interventions, and a growing consensus on the need for a policy readjustment that would see further developments stopped or slowed until effective environmental regulations are in place.

As opposition to tar sands exploitation has grown, Canadian authorities have responded with two strategies: a criminalization of dissent against the tar sands and a process of ecological modernization. Criminalization frames dissent (particularly on the part of environmental and aboriginal groups) as socially deviant and harmful, extending anti-terrorism legislation and rhetoric into the realm of civil disobedience. Ecological (or environmental) modernization promises to deliver both environmental and energy security through applying carbon sequestration technology to the tar sands – a process that people concerned about the environment and aboriginal people's rights generally see as a public relations exercise and major subsidy for the oil industry. From this perspective, the tar sands provide 'dirty security', likely to result in more violence *to* the environment and in violence *for* the environment, particularly as protesters seek legitimation through environmental causes.

Energy and environmental security

There is a marked tension between the demand for energy security – the need to sustain a supply of hydrocarbons to North American markets – and for environmental security, which has been threatened by the multiple and far-ranging environmental impacts of tar sands developments. This tension is evident, for example, in the international debate over tar sands. Both Canadian Prime Minister Harper and US President Obama have boasted of vast hydrocarbon reserves, bitumen and coal respectively, which could help secure energy supply for North America. Yet these projects are called into question in international debates on climate change. Both leaders have acknowledged the need to reduce their carbon footprint to ensure environmental security and are pressured to implement low-carbon legislation. As a result, reducing carbon emissions has become one of the key challenges to sustained growth in tar sands.

This tension between energy security and environmental security has also been expressed through two forms of environmental violence. The first frames environmental violence as violence perpetrated *on* the environment, and indirectly as violence perpetrated on human health and well-being through polluted environments (see Wiebe in this volume). Security is thus a matter of environmental regulation, of preventing environmental degradation through standards, regulations, monitoring, enforcement and so forth. The second perspective frames environmental violence as violence perpetrated *for* environmental motives, with 'eco-terrorism' – a catchword frequently used by the media (see Arsenault in this volume). Security, from this perspective, is thus a matter of political inclusion and policing to prevent 'radical environmental activism'.

These two narratives are closely connected, as it is often the first type of environmental violence that motivates the second.

Both narratives have been featured in the tar sands debate. The first narrative describes the violence perpetrated on ecosystems, landscapes and communities by tar sands exploitation. The environmental damage incurred by tar sands developments is most obvious in the strip-mining of over 600 square kilometres and the creation of massive toxic tailing ponds spanning over 50 square kilometres (as of 2009) of a previously undeveloped boreal forest ecosystem. This environmental violence has been vividly portrayed in advocacy campaigns against the tar sands, in magazines such as *National Geographic* (Kunzig, 2009), and in documentaries such as *Petropolies* (Mettler, 2009). The developments also result in more insidious and extensive types of pollution, including chemical leaching from the tailing ponds into groundwater and major river systems and 'acid rain' from the discharge of air pollutants and greenhouse gas (GHG) emissions, all of which in turn affect ecosystems. The scale of this pollution range from local communities to global scales, with water pollutants transported down the Athabasca river, into the fragile inland Peace-Athabasca Delta and through the Mackenzie Basin to the Arctic ocean (Kelly et al., 2009), with airborne pollutants increasing soil and lake acidification risk eastward in neighbouring Saskatchewan and Manitoba (Bytnerowicz et al., 2010; Jeffries, Semkin and Gibson, 2010), and greenhouse gas emissions contributing to global climate change (and preventing Canada from reaching emissions reduction commitments) (Charpentier, Bergerson and MacLean, 2009). It is especially at those levels that anthropogenic pollution from the tar sands exacts environmental violence upon human health and well-being (Woodford, 2007).

The second narrative focuses on the interplay of resistance and repression associated with the struggle to 'shut down' the tar sands. While the term 'eco-terrorism' is occasionally employed in the media, action taken by environmental advocates to date is primarily symbolic, such as placing hazard signs on pipes transporting waste to tailing ponds or occupying sites to prevent work. So far there has been more concern for the personal safety of demonstrators than for the target audiences as activists undertake 'spectacular' actions to stop tar sands projects or raise public awareness. This 'non-violent' approach contrasts with the rhetorical physical violence apparently wished upon activists by some anonymous commentators (VanderKlippe, 2009). There is furthermore a possibility of physical forms of violence escalating, as suggested by the firebombing of a Royal Bank of Canada (RBC) branch in Ottawa on 18 May 2010.[3] RBC had been the chief 'financial' target of tar sands activists in recent years, several groups having staged demonstrations, which included hanging banners from RBC flagpoles and buildings, as well as distributing leaflets enjoining RBC clients to quit the bank – Canada's largest financial institution and company by market capitalization[4] (Rainforest Action Network, 2008).

Promoting the tar sands

> Canada is the world's only growing producer of energy, this strategic commodity, with a secure, stable government.
>
> Canadian Prime Minister Stephen Harper (2006)[5]

Although the Albertan and Canadian governments have actively promoted tar sands exploitation for decades, major exploitation activity only began in the 1990s. Prior to that, low oil prices, the perceived difficulty of extracting the low-grade bitumen from the tar sands (which is both energy and water-intensive) and the availability of conventional oil in Alberta were disincentives for major activity. As explored next, political commitment to an integrated energy supply within North America was a key factor in the expansion of production. To stimulate tar sands development, Canadian authorities adopted two strategies: liberalization and securitization.

The first strategy, promoted largely by provincial governments (who have Constitutional responsibility for energy resources development under Canada's decentralized federalist system), is one of 'ultra-liberalization' whereby the resource was basically given out 'for free' in the 1990s. This move was in part motivated by the price crisis faced by many primary commodity producers during the late to mid-1990s, with oil reaching a bottom-price of about US$9 in 1998 (Le Billon and Cervantes, 2009). Both provincial and federal governments provided extensive financial subsidies to the industry through research and development funding as well as low taxation and royalty regimes (Plourde, 2009). Investment incentives, however, remained largely countered by low oil prices until the early 2000s. Following a meeting with the then US Vice-President Dick Cheney, Alberta Premier Ralph Klein summed up his perspective by arguing that his province 'has so much energy to burn, so to speak, and we're willing to share' (Chastko, 2004). This assistance is paired with a very welcoming fiscal environment for tar sands developers thanks to low royalty regimes and generous tax incentives like the Accelerated Capital Cost Allowance[6] (Woynillowicz, Severson-Baker and Raynolds, 2005; Hunter, 2007; Richardson, 2007).

The second strategy of Canadian authorities has been to represent these as the major source of energy security for the US in the wake of 9/11 and the Cheney National Energy Policy report which stated that 'continued development [of Canada's heavy oil sands reserves] can be a pillar of sustained North American energy and economic security' (Cheney, 2001). This association of investment incentives with US energy security has Cold War era precedents, when the US was eager to secure access to oil from Alberta (Gonick, 2007). The promotion of investments into the tar sands by Canadian provincial and federal authorities took the form of high-profile business visits, lobbying and advertisement campaigns. This energy security discourse found an echo in US interest groups such as the American Petroleum Institute (2011) – the main US oil and gas industry association – which run a campaign with the motto '[US] energy security? The answer might be closer than you think.'

While the federal and provincial governments continue encouraging the tar sands industry through a variety of financial and lobbying methods, non-governmental groups and communities have become aware of the environmental impacts of tar sands development and are opposing these projects. What is the state of opposition to the tar sands? Why is this opposition seeking to regain agency outside the narrow confines of institutionalized politics? What agendas and methods are now pursued? We elaborate these points further before discussing how government officials have responded to this opposition in the following sections.

Opposing the tar sands

Over the past decade, resistance to *status quo* environmental regulation in the tar sands has grown. Three trends are notable in this opposition and are elaborated next: a shift in scale from local to international levels of action, a shift in strategy from 'inside' and 'normal' politics to more disruptive challenges to political institutions, and the development of a consensus on alternatives or policy changes required.

Re-scaling opposition

There has been a strategic shifting of the scales at which organizing and action occur, from local to international levels. Within Alberta, aboriginal communities downstream of tar sands developments or in the path of pipelines to carry gas to the projects or to transport bitumen from them have been long-standing sources of resistance. Communities such as Fort

Chipewyan have protested the projects' environmental health impacts, their degradation of water, air and subsistence foods, as well as how the projects limit aboriginal peoples' access to traditional lands. This opposition has been joined with resistance from provincial environmental non-government organizations (ENGOs) such as the Sierra Club of Canada Prairie Chapter, Prairie Acid Rain Coalition, Alberta's Canadian Parks and Wilderness Society, and the Keepers of the Athabasca. These groups conduct or commission research on the environmental impacts of the tar sands, publicize this research through media to the public, intervene in government hearings and consultations, raise awareness through media and public education events, poll public opinion to understand the interests and concerns of Albertans and Canadians, and lobby politicians and policymakers to redress environmental policy. Simultaneously, these ENGOs and communities are supported by research from policy institutes, most notably from the provincial offices of the Pembina Institute with its 'Oil Sands Watch' research programme, and the Parkland Institute at the University of Alberta which analyses energy security and revenue issues. In addition, the provincial opposition to the tar sands includes organizations not primarily focused on environmental issues, such as Public Interest Alberta (focusing on protecting and building public services), and labour organizations like the Alberta Federation of Labour (working on reorienting Alberta's economy to 'green' development), the Communications, Energy and Paperworkers Union (lobbying to slow pipeline projects exporting raw bitumen and, therefore, jobs), and other institutions such as the Regional Municipality of Wood Buffalo and Northern Lights Health Region which object to stress the developments placed on the region's infrastructure.

As described by Hoberg and Phillips (2011), these provincial groups have been met by an unresponsive provincial government and so have shifted to lobbying simultaneously at the national level working in coalition with ENGOs such as Toronto's Environmental Defence,[7] and other NGOs such as the Polaris Institute and the Council of Canadians. Religious organizations are also involved, spearheaded by KAIROS' Ecumenical Justice Initiative, while national (and international) aboriginal organizations join provincial groups, for example, the Indigenous Environmental Network's Canadian Indigenous Tar Sands Campaign.

Resistance is also growing in Canadian sites outside of Alberta that are either impacted by pipelines fuelling the tar sands projects or transporting the product, or that are experiencing the more far-reaching environment impacts of the developments. For example, in British

Columbia (BC) there is strong opposition to pipelines and tanker traffic transporting bitumen (note the 'Tar Sands Free BC' campaign), and in the Northwest Territories, tension is building locally due to concerns about pollution and reduced volumes of water flowing north from Alberta. Meeting federal reluctance to slow or suspend tar sands developments, groups now work with American organizations such as ForestEthics while the movement continues to expand to Europe. Highly inclusive coalitions spanning environmental, social, labour, religious and Aboriginal organizations now extend from local and provincial organizers to national and international levels. Opposition in the US focuses on key political meetings and corporations. For example, Oil Change International and the Natural Resource Defence Council protested former Alberta Premier Ed Stelmach's attempts to defend and promote the tar sands during his January 2008 visit to Washington. ForestEthics joined with Toronto's Environmental Defence to protest the Albertan trade mission in the capital in April 2008 to lobby for an exclusion of the tar sands from new American EISA. Then February 2009 saw the joint launch of the obama2canada.org campaign by Canadian, American and international NGOs prior to President Obama's first visit to Canada in February 2009, when Prime Minister Harper was defending the projects and seeking to protect them against continental carbon emissions regulations. The campaign featured high-profile advertisements in major US newspapers, such as the 25 February 2009 message to Obama in *USA Today* by Mikisew Cree, Athabasca Chipewyan First Nations and ForestEthics stating, 'You'll never guess who's standing between us and our new energy economy.' The text was followed by an oil-splattered map of Canada, oozing south across the US border.

European groups are also increasingly active in opposing tar sands projects. Europe is not an export market for the tar sands but the region is a major source of investment for them, hence the rising activism, particularly in Norway and the UK, to end investments in the projects. For example, in fall 2008, the UK Social Investment Forum emphasized the environmental and long-term financial risks of Royal Dutch Shell and BP's operations in the tar sands (Crooks, 2008). UK's Co-Operative Asset Management ethical investment fund lobbied the companies to withdraw from tar sands projects. Then in spring 2009, Norwegian and Swedish banks, insurance companies and investment funds followed this lead to pressure Statoil, the Norwegian predominantly nationally owned oil company, to withdraw investments in tar sands projects. Likewise, in May 2009, the Lubicon Cree lobbied the Norwegian Government Pension Fund, Global (Oljefondet), to divest itself of investments in TransCanada.[8]

Regaining agency

Throughout this shift in scale from local to these international sites there is a second trend in opposition to the tar sands, a strategic transition from working 'inside' standard institutionalized political processes directing tar sands developments to moving 'outside' them to challenge specific companies, investors and end users directly.

Many of the organizers resisting the tar sands began by working with government and industry at the provincial and national level to manage tar sands projects via government/industry/community advisory organizations such as CEMA or through collaborative efforts such as the 2005 declaration on environmental standards and conditions for tar sands development (Canadian Parks and Wilderness Society et al., 2005). Yet as communities and organizations grow increasingly disappointed at the outcome of these processes – recommendations to manage the industry have gone unheeded while environmental impacts have become more apparent and more severe[9] – they have begun to withdraw. A key example of this was the 2007 withdrawal from the CEMA of the Athabasca Chipewyan First Nation and the Mikisew Cree First Nation in protest against the committee's lack of progress. The Pembina Institute, the Toxics Watch Society of Alberta and the Fort McMurray Environmental Association followed this lead and withdrew in 2008.

Instead of participating in the regulatory process, some communities have opened court cases against the provincial or federal governments for failure to consult and for infringements on traditional lands or treaty rights. Examples include the Chipewyan Prairie Dene First Nation's March 2008 case against the Alberta Government in relation to the Christina Lake SAGD project, the Athabasca Chipewyan First Nation's 2008 court challenge of 2006 and 2007 land tenure permits to Shell and other companies, and the Beaver Lake Cree Nation's 2009 case against the provincial and federal governments. Simultaneously aboriginal communities have vigorously protested pipeline projects running to and from the tar sands. For example, since 2007, Lubicon Lake Indian Nation, now in collaboration with local groups and Amnesty International, have opposed the installation of TransCanada Pipeline Limited's North Central Corridor project through their non-ceded territory.[10] Joint court cases are also becoming a more frequent tool of Albertan ENGOs.

Outside the courts, groups like Greenpeace have made headlines by using direct action strategies such as unfurling a banner at one of the premier's fundraising dinners in April 2008 which read, '$telmach: the best premier oil money can buy,' creating a mock tourism website of tar sands in June 2008 to satirize the province's new tourism campaign and underscore the environmental horrors of the tar sands, and erecting a sign at the mouth of one of Syncrude's tailing waste pipes in July 2008 declaring the operations to be extracting the 'world's dirtiest oil'. Groups in the US have also moved from targeting political leaders to lobbying individual companies and banks, as seen in NRDC's campaign to pressure major airlines to stop using fuel from tar sands and the Rainforest Action Network and Lubicon Lake Indian Nation's message to the Royal Bank of Canada to withdraw investment from the projects (Rainforest Action Network, 2008).[11]

Setting a 'post-oil' agenda; building issue salience

Although broadening scales and strategies, those opposed to the tar sands have also developed a general consensus on policy changes needed in the tar sands: there is widespread agreement on the need to not permit new projects until there has been a satisfactory analysis of the health and environmental impacts of tar sands projects and effective policies in place to prevent these impacts. Across most of these campaigns, there is also a common call for moving Alberta to a post-oil economy more reliant on renewable energy than fossil fuels.[12]

Formal calls for a moratorium have been made since at least the summer of 2007 and now represent a broad consensus across environmental, social, labour, religious and aboriginal organizations. Related campaigns include the Tar Sands Time Out initiative, including a petition for a 'Tar Sands Moratorium', led by the Sierra Club of Canada Prairie Chapter and the No New Approvals (NNA) for Tar Sands Development campaign which has compiled signatories of over 40 Albertan environmental NGOs, social or religious NGOs, labour organizations and research institutes, nearly 40 national and international groups of the same broad range of organizations, plus individual signatures by well-known academics, politicians, religious leaders and ENGO leaders (Désiré, 2007). Then in February 2008, aboriginal leaders representing nations from Treaties 6, 7 and 8 in Alberta unanimously passed a similar resolution to stop new approvals until there is a development plan, particularly a watershed plan, for the region. But note that a more radical faction of this opposition calls for a complete end to tar sands operations, a position captured in the campaign of organizations like Oil Sands Truth (2011) which argues that 'nothing short of a full shut down of all related projects in all corners of North America can realistically tackle climate change and environmental devastation'. Other organizations such as the Edmonton and Calgary chapters of STOP ('Stop Tar sands Operations Permanently') also forward this position through traditional

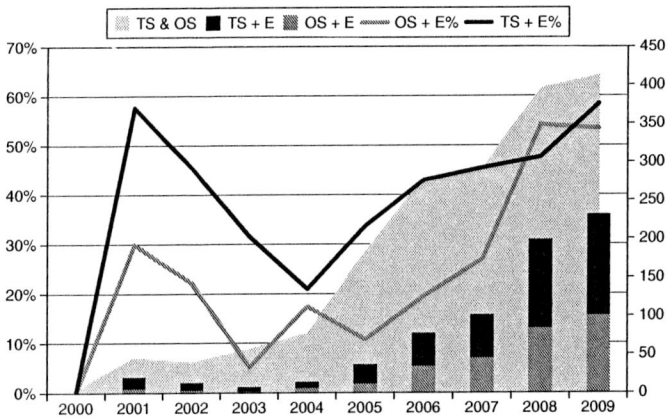

Figure 9.1 Major US and world media reports on tar sands and environmental issues[13]

letters to the editors of media and messages to election candidates but also through creative local organizing (hosting Oil Addicts Anonymous parties) and direct actions to publicly shame Albertan politicians.

Over at least the last decade, opposition to how governments have managed and supported growth of tar sands developments extended across provincial and national borders took on a more adversarial stance with government and industry, and developed clearer policy demands for the future development of the tar sands. Importantly, both levels of government have been forced to take note of this opposition given the rising media coverage of the issue over the past decade (see Figure 9.1).

Three major trends can be noted. The first is that the number of articles on the tar sands has massively increased. This not only reflects growing investments and production, but also more vivid debates. The second is that while a large proportion of the articles are in the early part of the decade, this concern sharply decreased in 2003 and 2004 before steadily rising again to reach about 50% of all reports engaging with environmental issues. This dip in environmental coverage may be explained by the emphasis placed on energy security rather than environmental concerns. The third is that while until 2006 press articles using the term 'tar sands' were twice as likely to engage with environmental issues than those using 'oil sands', the gap narrowed to a point at which environmental concerns are equally mentioned with both terms.[14] This could suggest a mainstreaming of environmental issues into debates over the tar sands. Even in media reports emphasizing the perspective of industry and government, environmental issues are noted.

In this way, the environmental impacts of tar sands developments have become an issue that cannot be ignored by officials. Part of the government's response, unfortunately, has been one that deflects attention from the environmental issues and instead calls into question the motives and strategies of those opposed to the developments. The other has been to promote carbon sequestration as the chief solution to the energy and environmental insecurity conundrum.

Criminalizing tar sands dissent

In response to the growing, coalescing opposition to the tar sands made publicly salient through extensive media coverage, the federal and provincial governments have engaged in a criminalization of dissent against the tar sands. Whereas some actions such as the 18 May RBC firebombing do fall under criminal law, this process shifts attention from the violence of environmental impacts to the violence of (radical) environmental dissent. In other words, more attention is cast on actors than on issues. This can have major impacts, including a delegitimization of environmental causes (and less radical actors) as well as delays in environmental policy reforms. Commenting in a report on the late 1990s series of bombings against gas infrastructure, the Pembina Institute – one of the main NGOs working on the oil and gas sector in Alberta – argued that

> the Alberta government and the oil and gas industry have continued to focus on a handful of violent incidents rather than addressing the underlying causes of the problem. In our view, the problems will not disappear from public discourse through the simple act of arresting a few members of the public.
> Marr-Laing and Severson-Baker (1999: 2)

The authors of this report argued that the attention of government ought to be focused on the underlying causes and grievances giving rise to violent incidents. These include the oil and gas sector's rapid expansion and increasing environmental and health footprint documented by new scientific evidence (contrary to claims made by the industry). Simultaneously, there were concerns about the weakening public and regulatory scrutiny as government environmental protection was deregulated and environmental protection agencies were downsized, resulting in 'a situation of *de facto* voluntary compliance' in the tar sands (Ibid: 1). At the same time, companies reduced environment-related expenditures due to declining prices and, therefore, thinning profit margins. Also, and perhaps most importantly, the government of Alberta's 'indifference and a seemingly unstoppable industry [caused] more and more Albertans to react with fear, frustration, and anger' (Ibid: 1).

Since this 1999 report, massive investments in oil and gas have taken place in Western Canada while environmental regulation continues to lag and public frustration continues to build (see Arsenault in this volume; also Adkin, 2012). Yet, against the expectations of government officials, there have been no reported attacks on tar sands infrastructure. Six new bombings on gas well heads and pipelines have taken place in 2008 and 2009 that were not explicitly related to tar sands issues and none of them resulted in casualties. Until 2010 direct actions against the tar sands involved only civil disobedience resulting in work stoppages. Despite this 'non-violent' character of direct actions against tar sands projects, former Alberta Premier Ed Stelmach declared that his government will use 'the full force of the law' to prosecute anti-tar sands activists, evoking in the press the idea that 'anti-terrorism' measures would be used, especially as Alberta's solicitor general declared that his office would review its 'counter-terrorism management plan' (Christian, 2009). This counter-terrorism plan, aiming among other things at protecting oil and gas infrastructures in Alberta, has been presented by Alberta's Assistant Deputy Minister of Energy as part of a way of 'Forging North American Energy Security' (Taylor, n. d.).[15]

Noting that the concept of 'eco-terrorism' is ill-defined and arguing that it limits understanding and responses to threats against the Canadian energy systems, political scientists Neville and Smythe (2009) propose a broader and less loaded concept of 'Radical Environmental Targeting' (RET). They also argue that 'it is crucial that [Canadian security] institutions adapt existing intelligence gathering and response mechanisms to deal effectively with the range of threats that RET activities pose' (Neville and Smythe, 2009). Arguably, RET is likely to increase for two main reasons. First, the public is ever more concerned that the responsible government authorities are not responding to the environmental impacts of expanding tar sands developments. Major policy reforms to control the rate of growth or tighten regulation are needed but they are not forthcoming. Second, as energy security increasingly becomes a strategic priority there is likely to be a 'hardening' of government policy – in short, heavier repression – and, in turn, a possible radicalization of dissent.

Rather than focusing on legitimate public concerns and unpacking public responses to government inaction and repression, some commentators emphasize and blame the 'radicalized' environmental activists and aboriginal people. One of the most vocal and influential of these is Tom Flanagan, a University of Calgary political scientist and Stephen Harper's former national campaign director. In a 2009 report for the Canadian Defence and Foreign Affairs Institute, Flanagan identifies five potential social groups capable of jeopardizing the security of energy supply from Alberta: individual saboteurs, eco-terrorists, mainstream environmentalists, First Nations and the Métis people.[16] Among these, individual saboteurs and First Nations are considered the most likely to carry out obstructions and violent incidents. Flanagan (2009: 9) describes a worst-case scenario of coalition 'between warrior societies and eco-terrorists', whereby

> [m]embers of warrior societies would brandish firearms and take public possession of geographical sites, while eco-terrorists would operate clandestinely, firebombing targets over a wide range of territory. The two processes could energize each other, leading in the extreme case to loss of life and a shutdown of industry over a wide area.

Flanagan (2009) argues, however, that such coalition 'has not happened in the past and seems unlikely in the future because the groups have different social characteristics and conflicting political interests'. What Flanagan (2009) sidelines here is the fact that coalitions between First Nations groups and environmentalists have the potential to forestall the type of 'eco-terrorism' he fears. Responses to the 18 May arson of the Royal Bank of Canada branch by an 'anarchic' group was instructive in this regard. The Ottawa Police Chief characterized the firebombing as 'domestic terrorism' (rather than mischief or sabotage) (CBC, 2010), and there was a general outrage at the arson with several commentators that this was 'un-Canadian'. Some anarchist media, which had echoed the importance of coalitions between First Nations and environmentalists in opposing RBC's financing of tar sands projects, recognized the counterproductive impact of the arson and looked for aboriginal voices to take a guiding position on such actions (see, for example, Kraus, 2010; Russell, 2010).

Rebranding the tar sands as environmentally secure

Alongside securitizing the tar sands issue – which sought to refocus attention from environmental issues to environmental actors – government officials have also been seeking to address rising climate change concerns in ways that do not substantially challenge the fossil fuel industry. The solution to the balance sought between energy security and environmental insecurity has been found not in policies limiting emissions but primarily through large government subsidies for carbon sequestration and rebranding exercise for the tar sands.

As the provincial and federal governments (in alliance with oil companies) have actively promoted and defended tar sands developments on both sides of the border, they have sought to redefine the 'dirty' image of the tar sands. A central message is that the tar sands are an environmentally viable solution to American energy security. Actively lobbying for tar sands has been evident in, for example, the efforts of Alberta's office in Washington and the Canadian ambassador to the US defending the tar sands from California's Low Carbon Fuel Standard and the American *Energy Independence and Security Act* (EISA). Canadian federal government representatives have also been actively supporting the industry as demonstrated most clearly in former Environment Minister Jim Prentice's pre-emptive defence of the tar sands prior to the official publication of *National Geographic*'s 1 March 2009 article comparing the developments to 'dark satanic mills' (Kunzig, 2009). Similarly, leading up to the election of President Obama, whose aide had expressed reluctance to import tar sands bitumen given its 'unacceptably high carbon emissions' (Alberts, 2008), Prime Minister Harper and key cabinet committees began a campaign to downplay environmental impacts and emphasize the importance of the tar sands to American energy security.

These statements and meetings occur alongside long-standing but far less public collaborations between Albertan, Canadian and American government representatives to increase tar sands exports to the US by five-fold and to streamline environmental regulation. The American-led North American Energy Working Group of the Security and Prosperity Partnership meets yearly to advance this agenda. Provincially there is similar support for the industry, notable in, for example, former Premier Stelmach's adamant position that his government will not 'touch the brake' on tar sands development (e.g. see McLean, 2006: A1), and the provincial government's 'rebranding' campaign to defend the industry against its growing 'dirty oil' reputation. On the environmental impact assessment side, a report prepared by Natural Resources Canada – the federal agency in charge of extractive industries – was bluntly criticized by the federal environmental agency for using a language that is 'too pro-industry, and would make the government to be perceived as biased and thus not credible or serving the public good' (Desouza, 2010).

Water pollution, land degradation and carbon emissions have been the tar sands' chief environmental concerns. Contaminated water and degraded lands have remained in the eyes of Canadian authorities mostly 'local' issues, especially as the main river – the Athabasca – flows north towards the Arctic through aboriginal peoples' settlements whose health issues are largely (if not actively) dismissed (Woodford, 2007). In contrast, carbon joins the global sink and thus more readily affects the tar sands and Canada's global image and markets. Unsurprisingly, it is on carbon that Canadian authorities and oil companies have focused. This focus on carbon emissions is relatively new and selective. The Canadian government still trails behind most G8 countries in terms of climate-related security debate, while being ironically one of the most territorially exposed within the OECD given its vastness and sub-Arctic position. This lag in a major dimension of environmental security is matched by the absence of a national energy security policy. Many critics see that the government has its hands tied with the North American Free Trade Agreement, which guarantees energy flow to the US, and that government's 'market orientation principle' means that energy policy is effectively in the hands of the energy corporations, many of which are foreign-based (Thompson, Laxer and Gibson, 2005; Laxer, 2008).

This absence of classic 'public policy' on energy does not mean a lack of focus and interest on the part of the Canadian government. On the contrary, in presenting Canada as an 'emerging energy superpower' based on its oil and gas, as well as hydropower and uranium production, Prime Minister Harper (2006) has also stressed the country's environmental responsibility:

> [H]ere in Alberta, where that energy power can almost be felt, something else must be equally appreciated. That with power comes responsibility. Given the environmental challenges that energy production presents, Alberta must also become a world leader in environmentally-responsible energy production.

Oil companies operating in the tar sands officially echoed this position a year later in a joint report arguing that carbon sequestration represented a 'Canadian environmental superpower opportunity' (ICO2N, 2007).

Barack Obama also formulated such strategy of securing energy while benefiting from 'green capitalism' opportunities. During a presidential electoral campaign speech in a 'coal state', Obama (2008) argued that the United States is 'the Saudi Arabia of coal, and the sooner we can figure out how to burn it cleanly, not only are we going to benefit but we can license that technology to countries like China and India that are putting up new coal facilities every week'. Reiterating this strategy in the context of his first visit to Canada in 2009, Obama stated:

> Oil sands creates a big carbon footprint. So the dilemma that Canada faces, the United States faces, and China and the entire world faces is

how do we obtain the energy that we need to grow our economies in a way that is not rapidly accelerating climate change ... [T]o the extent that Canada and the United States can collaborate on ways that we can sequester carbon ... that's going to be good for everybody.

(Palmer, 2009)

A high-profile review of the climate change and energy security impacts of Canadian oil sands by the US-based Council of Foreign Relations argues that 'oil sands production delivers energy security benefits and climate change damages, but that both are limited', and concludes that a 'healthy balance [between energy security and climate change] is possible' (Levi, 2009). This balance, the report claims, can be achieved by incentives cutting emissions but not discouraging increased production (Levi, 2009). One way to achieve this balance is for Canadian taxpayers to clean dirty oil to make it acceptable for the US. This, in essence, is the approach taken by the current Canadian government. Unsurprisingly, it is also the approach recommended by Shell CEO Peter Voser, who, however, sees the twin demands of greater energy and lower emissions as 'extremely tough to balance' (Voser, 2009: 3).

As the then Canadian federal minister of the environment Jim Prentice (2009) declared, 'Prime Minister [Harper] often emphasizes that, even though Canada is an emerging energy superpower, the only way to stay competitive in the global energy market is to be a clean energy superpower. Canada's Economic Action Plan includes a $1 billion Clean Energy Fund ... [that] demonstrates our Government's *balanced* approach to clean energy technologies ... including large-scale carbon capture and storage projects.'

With a budget of $30 billion for 2009, the Economic Action Plan was Canada's federal economic stimulus package after the 2008 financial market collapse. About 80% of the $1 billion Clean Energy Fund is to fund carbon capture and storage (CCS) projects.[17] Among the $200 million earmarked for non-CCS projects are notably 'new technologies to address environmental challenges in the oil sands, such as water use and tailings' (NRCan, 2009). Overall it is about $3 billion dollars that the Canadian federal and provincial governments budgeted for CCS commercial demonstration projects. The 'Clean Energy Dialogue' between Canada and the US was launched at the initiative of the Harper government in February 2009. Within this dialogue, former Federal Environment Minister Prentice argued '[o]ne of the promising areas for such cooperation involves developing and deploying clean energy technology through carbon capture and storage' (Prentice, 2009).

Yet carbon sequestration may not resolve the energy and environmental security conundrum for several reasons. At the most basic level, CCS technology is, to date, an unproven solution to carbon emissions from tar sands production. It is also only a piecemeal solution to the overall problem of carbon emissions associated with this unconventional fuel: CCS deals only with emissions associated with the extraction, upgrading and refining of bitumen but it fails to address 'tail-pipe' emissions by end users (motorists) who are the largest GHG contributors across the full life cycle of tar sands fuel. In addition, carbon emissions are only one among various and extensive forms of environmental violence associated with the tar sands (other forms are air pollution, freshwater pollution and over-withdrawal, habitat fragmentation and so on). If CCS technology manages to address the most pressing global dimension associated with this industry, it would permit increased tar sands exploitation and an expansion of these impacts. Ironically, developing CCS infrastructure may further contribute to the broader environmental impacts of industrializing Northern Alberta. Carbon sequestration is not a straightforward or complete solution to the energy and environmental security conundrum; in fact, it legitimates and facilitates the expansion of environmentally devastating oil developments.

Conclusion

Western Canada's hydrocarbon frontier has a dual front. The first consists in the advance of a 'dirty' form of energy security provided by the exploitation of unconventional fossil fuels in the face of dwindling conventional supplies. This advance is enabling Canada not only to remain a net hydrocarbon exporter, but also supposedly turning it into a new 'Energy Superpower'; however doubtful the claim is given the dearth of Canadian policy and the dominance of foreign companies. The second consists in the advance of 'technopolitical' provision of environmental security through the capture and sequestration of greenhouse gases from this exploitation. This advance, in turn, is supposedly making Canada a new 'Environmental Superpower', a position that again contrasts with its environmental policy record and absence of leadership.[18]

As bitumen production will increase in the future, few believe that carbon sequestration will deliver any major reduction in greenhouse gas emissions within the coming decade. The 'myth' of such solution, however, delays transition away from fossil fuels. By keeping the dream of cleaning domestic dirty fuels alive, this technology enables the reproduction of a hydrocarbon-based economy, and supposedly the profitability of its shareholders. The federal and provincial governments deflect attention from the continuous, far-reaching violence done *to* the environment in Northern Alberta by emphasizing violence done *for* the environment, even though the latter is infrequent and limited in scope. In reality, opposition to the tar sands – while it has spread from local to international levels, moved from working inside institutions amenable to oil interests to offering more direct challenges to industry and government, and articulated clear demands for change – is nearly exclusively non-violent. Rather than dealing with the legitimate concerns raised by those dissenting to tar sands developments and seriously considering their policy positions, both levels of government attempt to criminalize those opposed to the industry through 'eco-terrorism' framing, a position reaffirmed by the counterproductive radicalizing of dissent.

At the same time, governments promote questionable technological solutions to the most publicly salient environmental problem, carbon emissions. The apparent solution of carbon sequestration, however, re-legitimizes the industry and justifies its expansion (which will lead to further environmental impacts). It also circumvents or silences the tougher questions about the viability of this industry as a whole. Hence, the promotion of carbon sequestration as a solution to environmental impacts in the tar sands is an extension of other kinds of government support for the tar sands and it is directly in line with oil industry interests; while publicly soothing, it remains conventional thinking that sees Alberta and Canada mired in a carbon-based economy rather than transitioning into one with decreased dependence on fossil fuels. Carbon sequestration, understood in this way, is part of the problem and not the solution. In this context, genuine concerns for environmental violence perpetrated through tar sands exploitation will continue to be voiced. As the 18 May arson against a Royal Bank of Canada branch in Ottawa suggests, these concerns will also risk providing a self-legitimating narrative for more radical groups ready to use physical violence against infrastructures, symbols and potentially (even if unintentionally) people as well. Multiple forms of environmental violence will thus continue as long as environmental security takes a backseat to the promotion of highly profitable hydrocarbon-based energy security.

Notes

1. In contrast to conventional oil, which is produced using the traditional oil-well method, unconventional oil sources – which include oil shales, tar sands-based synthetic crudes and oils produced from natural gas, coal or

biomass – are more difficult to extract and/or refine, and are usually more expensive and environmentally damaging.
2. Reserves are currently estimated at 175 to 180 billion barrels. Canada's National Energy Board (NEB) predicted in 2006 that oil sands production would nearly triple over the next decade, rising from 1.1 million barrels per day (bpd) in 2005 to 3 million bpd by 2015. Exports of oil from the tar sands to the US reached 1 million bpd in 2009 and were due to surpass those of Mexico and Saudi Arabia by 2010, a prospect that made national news in Canada. See
3. A group identifying themselves as 'FFFC-Ottawa' claimed responsibility for the bombing, and claimed to be motivated by RBC's sponsoring of the 2010 Winter Olympic games which took place 'on stolen indigenous land', as well as the bank's role as 'the major financier of Alberta's tar sands, one of the largest industrial projects in human history and perhaps the most destructive' (Harp, 2010).
4. In 2007 RBC was the leading Canadian bank for fossil fuel funding, with CAN$ 15.9 billion (Rainforest Action Network, 2008).
5. Despite Harper's (2006) speech, there is no publicly available detailed policy document (similar to the US National Energy Policy reports) stating what this supposed status means in terms of energy security for Canadians and the world at large.
6. Comparisons of 'frontier oil' developments internationally show Alberta's 'take', ranging from approximately 39% to 47%, as well below that of Norway (at around 76%), Venezuela (at approximately 71%), and California, Angola and Alaska (64–7%).
7. Of course, in some cases ENGOs are influenced by the lobbying power of the tar sands industry, a point raised by those tracking of corporate donations to organizations, such as Ducks Unlimited and the Canadian Boreal Initiative (Stainsby, 2008: 647).
8. In addition to these investment protests, one financial institution in Europe is directly supporting the fight of one aboriginal community against tar sands projects: UK's Co-Operative Financial Services established a trust fund in July 2009 to support the Beaver Lake Cree Nation's lawsuit to protect their lands against tar sands projects.
9. Hoberg and Phillips (2011) describe these multi-stakeholder consultative processes as 'talk and dig' co-optation strategies used by government and industry to give the illusion of an open debate while having little impact on real policy change and defending the tar sands industry from criticism.
10. This pipeline would transport gas from north-western Alberta, and eventually from the Arctic via the Mackenzie Valley pipeline, to the tar sands projects and into Saskatchewan, potentially to fuel that province's new tar sands industry.
11. 'Opposition to the tar sands in the US is not just emanating from NGOs, challenges have also come from within political institutions such as the US Mayors with their June 2008 resolution to reduce the use of fuel from tar sands due to its high greenhouse gas intensity (US Conference of Mayors, 2008).
12. A recent example that gained national attention was the report commissioned by Greenpeace, Sierra Club Prairie Chapter and the Alberta Federation of Labour (see Thompson, 2009).

13. TS & OS: sum of reports using tar sands or oil sands (articles using both not discounted); TS + E: sum of reports mentioning 'tar sands' and 'environment(al)'; OS + E: sum of reports mentioning 'oil sands' and 'environment(al)'; other two categories idem but in % of total for tar sands or oil sands (Major US and World Publications database; Lexis-Nexis Academic, n. d.).
14. Using the term 'tar sands' is considered as evidence of a bias against their exploitation since industry and governments actors insist on the usage of 'oil sands'. This should be tampered by the fact that it is more widely used in the foreign press as opposed to the Canadian press.
15. In 2003, a presentation by the director of Alberta's Security and Information Management Unit listed as its first example of successes the identification of 'suspicious requests for maps / oil & gas lines' that could hint at sabotage plans (Pacific Northwest Economic Region, 2003).
16. For a portrait of Tom Flanagan, see McDonald (2004).
17. In the 2009 Action Plan, it states that 'at least $650 million to fund large-scale carbon capture and storage' (Government of Canada, 2009).
18. On the corporate mobilization of this concept see ICO2N (2007). On Canada's environmental policy record, see Boyd (2003), and on recent environmental performance, see Yale (2010).

References

Adkin, L., N. Krogman, and B. Miller, eds., 2012. *First World Petro-Politics: The Political Ecology and Governance of Alberta*. Toronto: University of Toronto Press.
Alberts, S., 2008. 'Obama's Oil Vow Threatens Alberta; US Democratic Presidential Hopeful Fires Shot Across Tar Sands Industry's Bow'. *Edmonton Journal*, 25 June, p. A4. Available at http://www.canada.com/edmontonjournal/news/story.html?id=4f838984-ece4-4d34-979f-e01e544f4523 (accessed on 8 February 2012).
American Petroleum Institute, 2011. *Energy Tomorrow*. Available at http://www.energytomorrow.org (accessed on 30 August 2011).
Boyd, D., 2003. *Unnatural Law: Rethinking Canadian Environmental Law and Policy*. Vancouver: University of British Columbia.
Bytnerowicz, A., W. Fraczek, S. Schilling and D. Alexander, 2010. 'Spatial and Temporal Distribution of Ambient Nitric Acid and Ammonia in the Athabasca Oil Sands Region, Alberta'.*Journal of Limnology* 69(1): 11–21.
'Canadian Parks and Wilderness Society, David Suzuki Foundation, Dogwood Initiative, Greenpeace, The Pembina Institute, Prairie Acid Rain Coalition, Sierra Club of Canada, Sage Centre, Toxics Watch Society, West Coast Environmental Law and World Wildlife Fund, 2005. *Managing Oil Sands Development for the Long Term: A Declaration by Canada's Environmental Community*. Available at www.tarsandstimeout.ca/images/press/pr_os_decl_part1.pdf (accessed on 1 August 2009).
CBC, 2010. 'RBC Firebomb Arrests Coming: Police'. Available at http://www.cbc.ca/canada/ottawa/story/2010/05/20/ottawa-rbc-firebomb-police.html (accessed on 27 May 2010).
Charpentier, A. D., J. A. Bergerson and H. L. MacLean, 2009. 'Understanding the Canadian Oil Sands Industry's Greenhouse Gas Emissions'. *Environmental Research Letters* 4(1): 1–11.
Chastko, P. A., 2004. *Developing Alberta's Oil Sands: From Karl Clark to Kyoto*. Calgary: University of Calgary Press.

Cheney, D., 2001. *National Energy Policy*, Washington DC: National Energy Policy Development Group. Available at http://www.wtrg.com/EnergyReport/National-Energy-Policy.pdf (accessed on 31 August 2011).
Christian, C., 2009. 'Greenpeace Considering Appeal after Comments by Stelmach'. *Fort McMurray Today*. Available at http://www.fortmcmurraytoday.com/ArticleDisplay.aspx?e=1975967&archive=true (accessed on 8 February 2012).
Crooks, E., 2008. 'Investors Warned of Risk to Oil Sands Plans'. *Financial Times*, 15 September. Available at http://www.ft.com/cms/s/0/eee600b0-8362-11dd-907e-000077b07658.html#axzz1Wbv4lvgX (accessed on 31 August 2011).
Désiré, O. L., 2007. 'Oil Rents and the Tenure of the Leaders in Africa'. *Economics Bulletin* 3(42): 1–12.
Desouza, M., 2010. 'Environmental Impact Study on Oilsands Slanted toward Big Oil: Federal Documents'. *Calgary Herald*, 7 January. Available at http://www.calgaryherald.com/business/Environmental%20impact%20study%20oilsands%20slanted%20toward%20federal%20documents/2417449/story.html (accessed on 8 February 2012).
Flanagan, T., 2009. 'Resource Industries and Security Issues in Northern Alberta'. Calgary: Canadian Defence and Foreign Affairs Institute.
Gonick, C., ed., 2007. *Energy Security and Climate Change. A Canadian Primer*. Halifax and Winnipeg: Fernwood.
Government of Canada, 2009. *Action Plan: Clean Energy Fund Program*. Available at http://www.actionplan.gc.ca/initiatives/eng/index.asp?initiativeID=122&mode=3 (accessed on 31 August 2011).
Harp, R., 2010. 'Activists Fire-Bomb Ottawa Bank in Name of Indigenous Rights: What Do You Think?' Poll. *Media Indigena*, 19 May. Available at http://www.mediaindigena.com/rickharp/issues-and-politics/activists-fire-bomb-ottawabank-in-name-of-indigenous-rights-what-do-you-think-poll (accessed on 30 December 2011).
Harper, S., 2006. 'Foreign Policy Speech: "Reviving Canadian Leadership in the World"'. Calgary: Office of the Prime Minister.
Hoberg, G. and J. Phillips, 2011. Playing Defence: Early Responses to Conflict Expansion in the Oil Sands Policy Subsystem. *Canadian Journal of Political Science* 44(3): 507–27.
Hudema, M., 2009. 'Greenpeace Strikes Again: Activists Occupy Shell Upgrader Expansion Site in Fort Saskatchewan'. 3 October. Available at http://www.greenpeace.org/canada/en/recent/stopstarsands3_action/ (accessed on 31 August 2011).
Hunter, W. M., 2007. *Our Fair Share: Report of the Alberta Royalty Review Panel*. Alberta Royalty Review Panel. Available at http://www.albertaroyaltyreview.ca/panel/final_report.pdf (accessed on 31 August 2011).
ICO2N, 2007. *Carbon Capture and Storage – A Canadian Environmental Superpower Opportunity, December 2007*. Integrated CO_2 network: Calgary, AB. Available at http://www.ico2n.com/ (accessed on 31 August 2011).
Jeffries, D. S., R. G. Semkin and J. J. Gibson, 2010. 'Recently Surveyed Lakes in Northern Manitoba and Saskatchewan, Canada: Characteristics and Critical Loads of Acidity'. *Journal of Limnology* 69(1): 45–55.
Kelly, E. N., J. W. Short, D. W. Schindler, P. V. Hodson, M. Ma, A. K. Kwan and B. L. Fortin, 2009. 'Oil Sands Development Contributes Polycyclic Aromatic Compounds to the Athabasca River and its Tributaries'. *Proceedings of the National Academy of Sciences of the United States of America* 106(52): 22346–22351.

Kraus, K., 2010. 'Anarchist Group Claims Responsibility for Tuesday's Bank Firebombing'. 20 May. Available at http://rabble.ca/blogs/bloggers/statica/2010/05/anarchist-group-claims-responsibility-tuesdays-bank-firebombing (accessed on 31 August 2011).

Kunzig, R., 2009. 'The Canadian Oil Boom: Scraping Bottom'. *National Geographic* 215: 3 (March). Available at http://ngm.nationalgeographic.com/2009/03/canadian-oil-sands/kunzig-text (accessed on 30 August 2011).

Laxer, G., 2008. *Freezing in the Dark: Why Canada Needs Strategic Petroleum Reserve.* Edmonton: Parkland Institute and Polaris Institute.

Le Billon, P. and A. Cervantes, 2009. 'Oil Prices, Scarcity and Geographies of War'. *Annals of the Association of American Geographers* 99(5): 836–44.

Levi, M. A., 2009. 'The Canadian Oil Sands. Energy Security Vs. Climate Change'. *Council Special Report*, 47. New York: Center for Geoeconomic Studies.

Marr-Laing, T. and C. Severson-Baker, 1999. *Beyond Eco-Terrorism: The Deeper Issues Affecting Alberta's Oilpatch.* Drayton Valley: Pembina Institute for Appropriate Development.

McCarthy, S., 2010. 'Oil Sands on Track to be Biggest Source of US Oil Imports'. *The Globe and Mail*, 19 May. Available at http://www.theglobeandmail.com/report-on-business/industry-news/energy-and-resources/oil-sands-on-track-to-be-biggest-source-of-us-oil-imports/article1574854/ (accessed on 8 February 2012).

McDonald, M., 2004. 'The Man Behind Stephen Harper'. *The Walrus*, October. Available at http://www.walrusmagazine.com/articles/the-man-behind-stephen-harper-tom-flanagan/ (accessed on 8 February 2012).

McLean, A., 2006. 'Stelmach won't "Brake" Oilsands Growth'. *Edmonton Journal*, p. A1. Available at http://www.canada.com/edmontonjournal/features/albertavotes/story.html?id=0529ba89-d54e-4f9c-a050-b57b5fd019c3&k=81516 (accessed on 8 February 2012).

Neville, K. and L. Smythe, 2009. 'Environmental Activism or National Security Threat? Policy Options for Addressing Radical Environmental Targeting'. In *CIR Working Paper No. 49*. Vancouver: Centre for International Studies.

NRCan, 2009. 'Harper Government Launches $1-Billion Clean Energy Fund, Invests in New Technology, Creates Jobs'. Press Release 2009/43, 19 May. Available at http://www.nrcan.gc.ca/media-room/news-release/43/2009-05/1684 (accessed on 15 June 2009).

Obama, B., 2008. Interview in Montana. *Flathead Beacon*, 30 May. Available at http://www.flatheadbeacon.com/articles/article/exclusive_obama_clinton_make_closing_arguments/3662 (accessed on 8 February 2012).

Oil Sands Truth, 2011. http://oilsandstruth.org/ (accessed on 30 December 2011).

Pacific Northwest Economic Region, 2003. Available at http://www.pnwer.org (accessed on 30 August 2011).

Palmer, R., 2009. 'Obama Wants to Reopen NAFTA but Keep Trade Flowing'. *Reuters*, 17 February. Available at http://www.reuters.com/article/2009/02/18/us-obama-canada-idUSTRE51G0YM20090218 (accessed on 7 February 2012).

Plourde, A., 2009. 'Oil Sands Royalties and Taxes in Alberta: An Assessment of Key Developments since the Mid-1990'. *Energy Journal* 30(1): 111–40.

Prentice, J., 2009. *Speaking Points*, Minister of the Environment Council for Clean and Reliable Energy. Ottawa, Ontario (25 October).

Rainforest Action Network, 2008. *Financing Global Warming: Canadian Banks and Fossil Fuels*. Available at http://climatefriendlybanking.com/fileadmin/materials/comms/mediacontent/reports/executive_summary.pdf (accessed on 30 August 2011).
Richardson, L., 2007. *The Oil Sands: Toward Sustainable Development*. House of Commons Standing Committee on Natural Resources. Available at http://www.parl.gc.ca/HousePublications/Publication.aspx?DocId=2614277&Language=E&Mode=1&Parl=39&Ses=1 (accessed on 31 August 2011).
Russell, J. K., 2010. 'Indigenous Voices Challenge Royal Bank Tar Sands Policies, Supported by Hundreds at Shareholder Meeting'. 4 March. Available at http://www.rabble.ca/blogs/bloggers/joshua-kahn-russell/2010/03/indigenous-voices-challenge-royal-bank-tar-sands-policies (accessed on 31 August 2011).
Stainsby, M., 2008. 'Issues – Dead Forest Standing: Greenwashing a Tar Sands Sacrifice Zone'. *Vue Weekly*, 18 September: 647. Available at http://vueweekly.com/front/story/issues_dead_forest_standing/ (accessed on 1 October 2008).
Taylor, B., n. d. 'Forging North American Security Conference'. Available at http://www.docstoc.com/docs/62138354/Forging-North-American-Energy-Security-Conference (accessed on 7 February 2012).
Thompson, D., 2009. *Green Jobs: It's Time to Build Alberta's Future*. Available at http://www.afl.org/index.php/View-document/114-Green-Jobs-It-s-time-to-build-Alberta-s-future.html (accessed on 26 May 2009).
Thompson, D., G. Laxer and D. Gibson, 2005. *Toward an Energy Security Strategy for Canada: A Discussion Paper*. Edmonton: Parkland Institute.
US Conference of Mayors, 2008. *Adopted Resolutions: High-Carbon Fuels* (20–4 June). Available at usmayors.org/resolutions/76th_conference/energy_05.asp (accessed on 4 January 2010).
VanderKlippe, N., 2009. 'Protests in Oil Sands Raise Anxieties'. *The Globe and Mail*, 12 October. Available at http://mediamonitoring.dvn.com/apps/mmc/Lists/Posts/Post.aspx?ID=1318 (accessed on 8 February 2012).
Voser, P., 2009. 'Energy Security and Climate Change – a Tough Balance'. *World Business Forum, New York*. Available at http://www-static.shell.com/static/media/downloads/speeches/voser_world_business_forum_07102009.pdf (accessed on 8 February 2012).
Woodford, P., 2007. *Health Canada Muzzles Oilsands Whistleblower*. Available at http://www.nationalreviewofmedicine.com/issue/2007/03_30/4_policy_politics1_6.html (accessed on 8 February 2012).
Woynillowicz, D., C. Severson-Baker and M. Raynolds, 2005. *Oil Sands Fever: The Environmental Implications of Canada's Oil Sands Rush*. Pembina Institute. Available at www.pubs.pembina.org/reports/OilSands72.pdf (accessed on 13 November 2006).
Yaffe, B., 2008. 'In fact, Every Canadian has a Stake in this; Alberta Oilsands Industry Fights a Public Relations War in Advance of a New Energy Policy in the US'. *Vancouver Sun*, 25 November, p. B2. Available at http://www.canada.com/vancouversun/story.html?id=b6061d6d-1dfb-44b2-ab55-216c37dc19d2 (accessed on 8 February 2012).
Yale, 2010. *Environmental Performance Index* (EPI). Available at http://epi.yale.edu/ (accessed on 8 February 2012).

10
The State-Corporate Nexus: Trading Social Benefits for Environmental Costs and Localized Vulnerability

Chris Arsenault

Introduction

The road to the Volz farm winds though the rolling foothills of British Columbia's (BC's) Peace River region, dotted by cattle farms, bails of hay and oil-pump jacks. The Volz family has grown hay and raised cattle on the picturesque 2000 acre spread for the last 35 years. June Volz taught grade school while her husband Lynn ran a backhoe business, providing services to petroleum companies. In 1983, companies drilled the first oil well on their property. 'At first, things went quite well,' said Lynn Volz over iced tea in the family's modest farmhouse. The family used rents from oil revenue to send their daughters to university. In the early days of extraction, the family had few problems in its relations with companies, and negotiations over payment rates and nuisance issues, such as noise or dust, generally went well. 'It was almost kind of fun, they'd make an offer and you'd go back and forth. And it was always with respect. It was fine and always got sorted out,' said Volz (interview, 2009; also, see Arsenault, 2009a). The general tone of negotiations and the attitudes of petroleum companies have shifted since legislative changes helped fuel a boom in unconventional oil extraction beginning in the late 1990s and taking off after 2002. Companies now show 'a great degree of arrogance', said Volz, and consistently threaten farmers and other land users with legal action if they complain about extraction activities or company practices (Harvey, 1999).

When visiting the Volz farm in summer 2009, the region was buzzing with talk about sabotage, police harassment and major reward money. Saboteur(s) attacked six gas installations in the area between October 2008 and July 2009 causing a small amount of property damage and igniting major debates about the actions of gas companies, the future of the area's economy and the nature of regulations upon industry. EnCana, North America's largest gas company and the biggest player in BC's gas extraction, is the exclusive target of sabotage. The company is offering a $1 million bounty for information leading to the saboteur's conviction, equal to the largest reward ever offered in Canadian history. BC's gas is concentrated in a 194,000 square kilometre region above the Western Canada Sedimentary Basin in the province's north-east. In 2001, a newly elected BC Premier Gordon Campbell (2001) told industry officials 'the road ahead for us in oil and gas is a multi-lane highway'. In 2008, BC's oil and gas industry provided the single largest source of resource revenue to the provincial government, $4.09 billion dollars (Government of British Columbia, n. d.), up from about $75 million in 1992 and $1 billion in 2001 (CERI and R. McManus Consulting, 2004: 21). The share of oil and gas investment (as a proportion of total investment in the province) has risen from about 5% in the early 1990s to 14% in 2001 (CERI and R. McManus Consulting, 2004: 8). BC averaged exports of 641 million cubic metres of natural gas per month in the 1990s and 952 million between 2000 and 2006 (BC Progress Board, 2009). Between 1993 and 2003, drilling activity increased 320% and total revenues from oil and gas licences, permits, leases and royalties grew 634% (Howard et al., 2005: 9).

As of 2009, BC through its Department of Mines and Energy (MEPR) administered more than 14,600 oil and gas agreements covering 23.5 million acres (Government of British Columbia, n. d.). The 'multi-lane highway' is, to carry forward the Premier's analogy, missing adequate guard-rails, signage and other safety features. A report commissioned by the provincial government notes that '[r]apid growth of the oil and gas industry within the province of BC has outpaced the development of health and safety policies' (Meed, n. d.: 1). As of 11 February 2010, there were '20,400 oil and gas well sites in the province, with the vast majority of activity taking place in northeast British Columbia' (Auditor General of British Columbia, 2010: 5).

Stating a common view among long-term residents of BC's northeast, Eric Kuenzl, a landowner from Tomslake who met with EnCana in June 2008 about concerns such as road traffic, noise and possible health effects from sour gas, told a local newspaper: 'I feel like the company [EnCana] is the bully on the block, and I'm the kid who's trying not to have my lunchbox stolen' (Cunningham, 2008). Kuenzl, whose family has lived on the same property since 1939, said he is ready to leave because he's scared of the long-term health effects of flaring pollutants and hydrogen sulphide, or sour gas. As Canada becomes an 'energy superpower', in the words of Prime Minister Stephen Harper (2008), debates about the nature of regulation and conflicts in the oil patch will only grow more intense.[1] This chapter analyses sabotage against EnCana in British Columbia in the context of broader conflicts between gas companies and other land users, specifically, farmers, rural residents and environmentalists. Social conflicts stemming from environmental grievances have become a major field of study for academics (Mathews, 1989; Dyer, 2008; Graeger, 1996; Deudney and Matthew, 1999; Homer-Dixon, 1999). Battles between farmers and oil companies are traditionally framed as conflicts stemming from property relations.[2] In contrast, this chapter argues that property relations, where individual owners control the above-ground area but not subsoil resources, are *not* the driving force inspiring conflict. Rather, the underlying cause of conflict in northeastern BC stems from captive regulatory agencies – regulators who favour petroleum companies and increased extraction at the expense of other land users.

This capture arises from growing government dependence on petroleum revenues (Nikiforuk, 2008) along with power imbalances between oil companies and other land users (Evans and Garvin, 2009).[3] The main reasons why regulations are flawed or improperly enforced, argues environmental law expert David Boyd (2003: 251), are 'short term economic considerations such as profits, competitiveness and jobs'. In a commentary, the Canadian Association of Petroleum Producers concurs with the notion that pro-industry provincial regulatory regimes are a prime reason for the exponential increase in extraction:

> Through its policies, BC has established the conditions to ensure it has positioned its natural gas resource to be competitive in the North American market place. In particular, *targeted regulatory and fiscal measures* have been very successful in attracting investment that would not otherwise occur.
>
> Collyer (2009; italics added)

In order to properly analyse recent sabotage in BC, this chapter will briefly review some of the literature on sabotage and environmental conflict to ascertain how pipeline sabotage fits with other emerging trends in the discourse (e.g. Kaplan, 1994, 2009; Marr-Laing and Severson-Baker, 1999; Fedorowicz, 2007; Ross, 2008; Steinhäusler et al., 2008). Secondly, it will analyse debates around property rights. This section will place conflicts in the context of evolving legislation for extraction and within the historical realities of rapidly increasing petroleum exploitation in north-eastern BC. Until legislation governing petroleum exploitation is seen as even handed, sabotage is likely to increase as demand for petroleum rises and new areas are opened to extraction. Tom Flanagan (2009: 5), for example, concurs that sabotage and general opposition to petroleum development is likely to increase with the 'rapid expansion of natural resource industries' (see Le Billon and Carter, this volume). EnCana's comparative advantage in its North American holdings comes not from the resource itself, which is unconventional and harder to access than typical petroleum deposits (Youngquist and Duncan, 2003), but from Canadian political stability. The desire to exploit stable deposits as fast as possible in BC, is, ironically, creating instability.

The threat of political instability is the main cause for aggressive state (250 highly trained officers sent to the region) and corporate (a $1 million bounty) responses to sabotage in north-eastern BC. 'Capital is a coward and it runs away from risk,' notes the CEO of TransCanada Corp, another major pipeline company (VanderKlippe, 2010). This question of capital is crucial. The oil and gas industry contributes less than 1.5% of the province's GDP. However, it accounts for over 40% of non-residential construction investment (14% of total investment) in British Columbia (these figures are for 2001 in CERI and R. McManus Consulting, 2004: 24). Thus, investment capital is a prime beneficiary of the boom. This kind of capital is disproportionately affected by political risk: apartment buildings in Vancouver cannot pick up and move. Oil capitalists fear that sabotage will create risks, leading investment to flow to other resource patches.

The lack of risk was supposed to be the key feature of Canada's political landscape – the jurisdiction's comparative advantage over other regions. The bomber is undermining that stability and thus causing consternation for elites. The final section of the chapter presents a case study from a well explosion at an EnCana facility to dispel the idea that oil capitalists, police and politicians are using aggressive measures against sabotage due to concern for public safety. In making its case, this study utilizes interviews and original research from communities where sabotage has taken place, a series of freedom of information requests to relevant government departments, including the Royal Canadian Mounted Police, the Department of Fisheries and Oceans and the Canadian Security Intelligence Services (CSIS) and a review of secondary literature. Before going any deeper into an analytical framework, the chapter will provide a brief summary of recent sabotage.

Synopsis of the sabotage

On 12 October 2008, a hunter in north-eastern BC stumbled across a six-foot crater at the base of a natural gas pipeline (RCMP, 2008a). The crater, some 50 km from the town of Dawson Creek, was caused by a deliberate explosion. Police guess the act of sabotage took place on the night of Saturday, 11 October. On 10 October, *Coffee Talk Express*, a small-town publication in Chetwynd near the sabotaged site, along with EnCana energy, the operators of the attacked pipeline, received handwritten letters referring to oil and gas companies as 'terrorists ... endangering our families with crazy expansion of deadly gas wells' (Stueck and Hume, 2008; CSIS, 2009). The area is in the midst of a major unconventional gas boom.

The pipeline targeted in the first blast carried dangerous hydrogen sulphide, or sour gas, to EnCana's Steeprock gas plant (Nikiforuk, 2009). The US Agency for Toxic Substances and Disease Registry calls hydrogen sulphide an 'extremely rapidly acting, highly toxic gas ... Just a few breaths of air containing high levels of hydrogen sulfide', it reports, 'can cause death' (Nikiforuk, 2009).[4] Another blast occurred in the morning of 16 October 2008 (Stueck and Hume, 2008). In late October, presumably around midnight on the 30th, the bomber struck for a third time, with an explosion causing a pipeline rupture, releasing a limited amount of sour gas near the community of Tomslake (CSIS, 2009. Police described the attacks as 'violent' and asked for the public's help, but stopped short of calling the sabotage 'terrorism' (RCMP, 2008b)).[5] The Integrated National Security Enforcement Team (INSET), a mix of top law enforcement officials, sent some 250 officers to the region (Hume, 2009). This shows how seriously the state views minor attacks on energy infrastructure.

By late October 2008, the name Wiebo Ludwig began surfacing in media reports. Ludwig, an evangelical preacher whose actions will be discussed in greater depth later in the chapter, was sentenced to prison in 2000 for orchestrating a similar sabotage campaign against gas infrastructure in Alberta during the late 1990s (Brooke, 2000). In November, police made it clear that Ludwig was not a suspect in the BC attacks. Freedom of Information requests to the Canadian Security Intelligence Service for internal documents on 'sabotage against Canadian oil infrastructure from 1990 to 2009' show that 'more than 160 incidents of sabotage' against Alberta's resource industries (oil, gas, hydro and forestry) took place between 1997 and 1999 causing 'millions of dollars in damages' (CSIS, 2009). Ludwig's campaign alone is estimated to have cost the Alberta Energy Company, one of the two companies that merged to create EnCana in 2002, $10 million (Nikiforuk, 2001). The heavily censored CSIS documents did not provide any figures for acts of sabotage in the twenty-first century (CSIS, 2009).[6]

In December 2008, police and EnCana conducted a joint press conference, asking for the public's help in catching the bomber. On 3 January 2009, EnCana employees discovered the forth blast, which damaged a storage shed and well head located 250 metres from the nearest residence (RCMP, 2009). In a news release, police denied persistent rumours that the bombings are linked to the theft of dynamite from a facility near Chetwynd in the summer of 2008. On 13 January 2009, EnCana announced a $500,000 reward for information leading to the convention of the saboteur. The front page of Vancouver's tabloid *The Province* featured a Wild West-style poster with a 'wanted' sign when EnCana offered the bounty.

After a lull of several months, another blast hit on Canada Day. EnCana staff discovered a fifth blast on 1 July 2009 at a well head near Pouce Coupe. The bomber struck for a sixth time on 4 July, attacking another site near Pouce Coupe. In July, police changed their analysis of the attacks, calling them 'domestic terrorism' for the first time (Mercer, 2009). On 15 July 2009, the *Dawson Creek Daily News* received a second letter, this time being handwritten and two pages long. The letter writer gave EnCana a three-month ultimatum to

> [c]ease all your activities and remove all your installations. Return the land to what it was before you came, every last bit of it, including your fancy gas plant at Kelly Lake before things get a lot worse for you and your terrorist pals in the oil and gas business.[7]

The letter writer said that attacks would be discontinued during a three-month period, 'so we can all take a summer vacation'. The purpose of the attacks, according to the bomber's letter was 'to let you [EnCana and the rest of the gas industry] know that you are indeed vulnerable, [and] can be rendered helpless despite your megafunds, your political influence, craftiness, and deceit'.

Wiebo Ludwig re-entered the story in September 2009 when he wrote an open letter to the pipeline bomber. 'You need to know that you have already set a lot of good things in motion,' wrote Ludwig, saying, 'You've truly woken a lot of people up and stimulated some very valuable discussion.' The decision to limit sabotage to remote infrastructure showed 'thoughtful restraint', according to Ludwig, who urged the bomber to end the campaign in favour of peaceful means (Cormier, 2009). The reasoning behind Ludwig's letter is contested; police arrested him on 8 January 2010 and initially planned to charge him with extortion related to the BC bombings. The warrant to search Ludwig's farm included the desire to find specific objects such as red and blue pens to match the bomber's letter, a specific type of postage stamp and boots to match a tread print found at one of the bombed sites (CTV W5, 2010).

After a day of interrogations and an extended search of his property, Ludwig was released without charges (Arsenault, 2010). During the search of Ludwig's property, a police spokesperson, Tim Shields, told reporters, 'obviously we have to take this seriously, it is not minor, it is not controlled, it is domestic terrorism' (CTV W5, 2010). While Ludwig's role in the BC sabotage campaign remains unclear, there is little debate that rapid energy development in the area coupled with a climate of distrust between many farmers and the industry represent the political backdrop underpinning broader debates on sabotage. *The Vancouver Sun*'s headline 'First Came the Energy Boom, Now the Bombs' describes the situation in its rightful context (McMartin, 2009).

Sabotage and environmental conflict

There is little debate that the global environment is facing increased stress from human activities, including petroleum extraction. And there is an emerging consensus across the political spectrum that environmental sustainability and political security are fundamentally linked (Ronnfeldt, 1997). Thus, environmental stresses or insecurities can and often do precipitate, exacerbate or contribute to political unrest and violence (Neefjes, 1999; Barnett, 2001). In the case of Western Canada, environmental stresses from petroleum exploitation include loss and disturbance of living spaces, landscape fragmentation, wildlife disturbance, oil spills; aquifer depletion and pollution; health and ecological effects from the flaring of sour gas; and greenhouse gas emissions (Timoney and Lee, 2001). The private broadcaster CTV's flagship investigative program W5 states the bombings have put a spotlight on the underlying struggle of 'energy versus the environment' (CTV W5, 2010). Freedom of Information documents from the Integrated Threat Assessment Centre (ITAC) marked 'secret' explain the state's interpretation of what is inspiring sabotage in north-eastern BC:

> The Western Canadian oil industry (two lines blanked out) encounters many opponents. Pollution, the use of lands owned or claimed

by native communities, the employment of people living in the area and the distribution of contracts are examples of the issues that create tension between companies and interest groups.

CSIS (2009)

Thus, state security analysts concur that environmental grievances, in this case 'pollution', are possible causes of recent sabotage. Environmental conflict includes a wide variety of actions and concerns; in terms of the broader literature, the BC attacks are likely best classified as 'disputes arising directly from local environmental degradation' (Homer-Dixon, 1999: 5). The local nature of the bomber's concerns is witnessed by the fact that he or she only sent letters to small media outlets in north-eastern BC, rather than aiming for the broader reach of *The Globe and Mail, Calgary Herald* or *The Vancouver Sun*.

Traditional historical studies of attacks against oil infrastructure usually focus on 'non-democratic' countries where grievance mechanisms are not established and the rule of law is tenuous: as in Iraq, Nigeria, Saudi Arabia and Colombia (Ross, 1999; Feng, 2001; Klare, 2004). Canadian companies operating outside the state's borders have been attacked in such regions. On 15 September 2006, fighters in Yemen used car bombs to attack the Ash Shihr terminal on the Arabian Seat owned by the Canadian firm Nexen.[8] Historical scholarship on oil sabotage also focuses on inequality in wealth distribution and ethnic exclusion as prime motivators for those who take violent action against oil interests (Jenkins and Schock, 1992; Farrell, Zerriffi and Dowlatabadi, 2004; also, see Arthur in this volume). These aspects of the literature are not supposed to apply to a country such as Canada, which is ostensibly governed by the rule of law and a political psychology of 'democratic pluralism' (Nesbitt-Larking, 2004).

Regardless of how pluralism and legalized grievance procedures are interpreted and enacted, new literature on pipeline sabotage, especially work coming directly from military researchers, emphasizes that '[a]ttacks on oil and gas installations have become the weapon of choice' for a variety of organizations and will likely increase 'irrespective of the political system and social-financial boundary conditions of the society under attack' (Steinhäusler et al., 2008). The BC case seems to fit within this and other aspects of the new pipeline securitization literature. Likewise, saboteurs 'typically are member of the surrounding communities' near oil infrastructure (Steinhäusler et al., 2008). A police media spokesperson believes the saboteur/s is/are local 'because of their familiarity with the community as well as knowledge of the oil and gas industry' (Canwest, 2008).

Overview of the property rights debate

As a former adviser to Canadian Prime Minister Stephen Harper and an analyst on petroleum infrastructure security for the influential Canadian Defense and Foreign Affairs Institute, Tom Flanagan's opinions hold considerable sway. The University of Calgary academic is likely familiar with the work of Niccolò Machiavelli (2003: 59) who argues in *The Prince* that the 'majority of men live content' when 'neither their property nor their honor is touched'. Petroleum companies in Western Canada have a history of touching both of these things (Pearse, 1988: 307–20). Tom Flanagan argues that

> the underlying cause of sabotage is the peculiar structure of property rights; the fact that the Crown owns the mineral resource and individuals own the surface rights. If you go back to Ludwig, he owned the surface rights and not the mineral rights. Individual landowners aren't happy to see oil and gas companies on their land; it's not just the drilling but the roads, the land that has to be cleared for the drilling pad, and the noise. Maybe part of the answer would be to amend the legislation for companies to pay greater compensation to surface rights owners.
>
> Interview, summer 2009; also see Arsenault (2009b) for details

Small farmers around North America have a history of considering individual property rights as the 'basis for freedom and independence' (Hahn, 2006: 253). Moreover, conventional wisdom maintains that these independent farmers and other rural residents do not want oil company representatives demanding space for pipelines or compressor stations on their land.

Despite the politics of Machiavelli, through John Locke, Thomas Jefferson and twenty-first century progenitors of the property relations thesis such as Flanagan, questions surrounding property rights are not the fundamental driver of conflicts in north-eastern BC. Conflicts around property relations are certainly important, but captive regulatory agencies are in fact the driving force inspiring sabotage. The Western Canadian country singer and cattle rancher Corb Lund offers a rebuttal to Flanagan's property rights interpretation. After lambasting the environmental effects of oil drilling in his song 'This is My Prairie' – 'The water is poison, my calves are all dead / The children are sick and the aquifer is bled' – Lund opts instead for an analysis of conflict rooted in regulatory captive theory:

> I don't got the money that lawyers can buy
> I don't got my own government's laws on my side
> But I got this old rifle that my granddaddy owned
> This is my prairie and this is my home.[9]

Farmers, and other residents who have a connection to the land where petroleum extraction is happening, say rules governing extraction favour corporate land access above health, safety, the environment and basic dignity for other land users. In essence, petroleum companies have 'captured' government regulatory bureaucracies for their own benefit.

Regulation in BC

In 1998, the BC government announced an overhaul of petroleum regulations with the creation of the *Oil and Gas Commission Act* (OGCA). Prior to this legislation, created by the BC New Democratic Party and the Canadian Association of Petroleum Producers (Vancouver Sun Editorial Board, 2005), extraction was covered by a range of bureaucracies, including Ministry of Energy and Mines, the Ministry of Environment, Lands and Parks (now Ministry of Water Land and Air Protection or WLAP) and the Ministry of Forests (Ministry of Employment and Investment, 1997). The heart of the OGCA was to transfer power of approvals for pipelines, surface tenure and gas wells to the Oil and Gas Commissioner, powers previously held by the aforementioned ministries (Rankin et al., 2000–1, 152).

The provisions of the OGCA were first established by a Memorandum of Understanding between the provincial government and the Canadian Association of Petroleum Producers signed in February 1998 aimed at making BC 'one of the most attractive places in North America for oil and gas investment' (Rankin et al., 2000–1: 146). The reason for the new Oil and Gas Commission was to create a 'single window' regulator who could grant approvals for new projects. This design was fundamentally linked with petropolitics or government dependence on resource revenues. As a group of legal scholars note, 'very simply, in the oil and gas industry, the government saw the potential for substantially increased production and industrial activity in the province with a corresponding boost in government revenue' (Rankin et al., 2000–1: 145).

The then Minister of Mines and Energy Dan Miller signed *The Oil and Gas Commission Act* into law on 21 July 1998. Part of the reason for creating a formal single window regulator was that 'both government and industry wanted to avoid ... procedural trappings such as oral hearings and legal representation' (Rankin et al., 2000–1: 147). In other words, the Act was designed to limit the abilities of citizens to resist industry incursions. Prior to the OGCA, the 1996 *Petroleum and Natural Gas Act* set forth the processes by which a gas company could access private land, along with other regulatory issues. The Mediation and Arbitration Board, a quasi-judicial body tasked with settling disputes between gas companies and surface holders, was established by the 1996 Act. While the 1998 OGC Act changed the *Petroleum and Natural Gas Act*, along with a host of other legislation, the Mediation and Arbitration Board (MAB) continues to operate alongside the Oil and Gas Commission (OGC).

The MAB is responsible for mediating disputes between surface holders and oil companies on an individual basis and is responsible for granting right of entry deals to oil companies when negotiations with landowners fail; it can impose settlements on opposing parties (Ministry of Mines and Energy, n. d.). The OGC is tasked with macro regulatory oversight, including 'balancing a broad range of environmental, economic and social considerations' and specifically ensuring 'public safety, conservation of petroleum resources, fostering a healthy environment, and equitable participation in production' (Ministry of Mines and Energy, n. d.). In north-east BC, some 95% of gas wells are drilled on crown land, with just 5% on private land, although the latter number will likely rise as industry searches for new frontiers (Amos, 2009). Still, this fact means that the OGC is the more important of the two regulators because the MAB only deals with disputes involving private landowners.

When the two regulatory authorities signed a memorandum of understanding on 10 March 2008, both agencies admitted that farmers and other landowners have been confused and irritated by the regulatory process. 'Both organizations understand there can be confusion over which organization is best suited to address issues facing landowners and oil and gas companies,' said the then OGC commissioner Alex Ferguson (OGC, 2008). Since that time, landowners and oil companies can run simultaneous cases through both agencies. Since the BC government initiative, a major overhaul of the province's environmental regulations in 2002, both regulators are seen as captive. The *Dawson Creek Daily News* reports that many landowners 'believe both of these groups are in the pocket of oil and gas companies and have little faith in their ability or desire to take their issues seriously' (Bergland, 2009).

The Oil and Gas Commission and the BC Liberals

During the NDP's tenure, which ended when the Gordon Campbell Liberals were sworn into office in June 2001, the OGC was described as 'neutral' by one environmental watchdog (Westcoast Environmental Law Association, 2005: 25). While other environmentalists and some scholars may question if the OGC was ever neutral, it is clear that the Liberals changed the organization, along with other regulatory bodies in the interests of industry. After their 2001 election, the Liberals promised to double gas production by 2011 (Westcoast Environmental Law Association, 2005: 24). The year 2002 is arguably the most important single point for assessing when regulatory bodies in BC became captive to the interests of industry.

The Campbell government amended the *Oil and Gas Commission Act* as part of a far-reaching energy strategy, placing the OGC Commission under the direct control of the Minister of Mines and Energy, the same body tasked with expanding the gas industry (Howard et al., 2005). This move eliminated notions of the OGC as a neutral regulator. The Liberals also changed the province's Environmental Assessment Act 'replacing one of the country's most progressive provincial EA laws with one of the weakest' according to David Richard Boyd (2003).

Some of these repercussions can be seen in the high number of spills, accidents and other problems. In its 2002/03 annual report, the Oil and Gas Commission stated that compliance with regulations is 'the responsibility of the oil and gas industry ... This can be achieved through the implementation of self-imposed guidelines' (OGC, 2002/2003: 18). Allowing industry to 'self-impose' is not a sensible way to enforce environmental laws. *The Vancouver Sun* obtained statistics from the commission indicating that when inspectors did check in on gas operations the vast majority was breaking the law. From 3305 field inspections performed in 2004, 64% were out of compliance – resulting in a total of 5734 infractions – compared with just 36% of gas operations who extracted according to the rules. The total number of operations found out of compliance in 2004 increased 14% from 1862 operations in 2003, and the number of violations jumped 26% from 4535 (Plynn, 2005: A1).

At the height of the anti-EnCana sabotage campaign, the situation with compliance had not improved in many respects. In an 11 February

2010 report, BC's Auditor General found that the Oil and Gas Commission was not making significant progress in cleaning up contaminated sites. 'I had expected more progress because this is not our first audit dealing with contaminated sites in British Columbia,' said the auditor, referencing a 2002/03 report on provincial contaminated sites. 'The oil and gas industry in BC has seen significant growth over the last decade, which has the benefit of increased revenues for the province, but also carries greater risks of contamination,' the auditor's report said. Among the report's findings, companies are not doing enough to restore exhausted drilling sites, placing undue pressure on the province's orphan well fund.

Mediation and Arbitration Board (MAB)

Upon becoming chair of the Mediation and Arbitration Board in 2007, Cheryl Vickers admitted that the board was 'a mess' and had 'no credibility' (McMartin, 2009). Normally, the words of bureaucrats should be taken with a grain of salt, but when someone admits their own organization is dysfunctional, that is a pretty good sign that it is. Vickers was not the first MAB official to criticize the organization. 'From my experience in the past I do not believe that government really wants a Mediation and Arbitration Board to be a help to the landowners or anyone else that wants to bring a case before the board,' said former board member Thor Skafte in 2006 (Friedrich, 2006a). Gas companies were (and are) using the MAB to gain access to private land without disclosing the locations of wells and pipelines. Essentially, companies were filing arbitration orders before explaining their plans to farmers, leading Vickers to admit that the MAB was 'all sort of ass backwards' (McMartin, 2009).

When asked by a newspaper reporter about moving the MAB outside of the Department of Mines and Energy, the organization responsible for bringing resource investment to the province, Vickers said: 'There's this perennial debate about whether that's appropriate or whether they should all be housed under the Ministry of Attorney General' (Gousseau, 2007). Regulatory reform advocates believe the Attorney General's office would be a fairer location for the board. To understand how MAB rulings work in practice, the experience of Ken and Loretta Vause provide a useful case study in captive theory. 'It's like the Wild West out here,' said Ken Vause, a farmer living in Farmington about 20 minutes from sabotaged sites who also works part-time in the gas industry (Arsenault, 2009a). 'A land agent came here for an hour, he didn't show us any plans for where the new pipeline would go (Arsenault, 2009a),' said Vause, who blames government's unwillingness to properly regulate the industry on his present standoff with the company who wants to put a sour gas line through one of his canola fields. In BC, land agents, the people who represent gas companies in negotiations with farmers, do not have to be licensed, unlike neighbouring Alberta (Friedrich, 2006b). This, according to farmers, allows land agents to act like bullies without repercussions. EnCana, however, has its own code of conduct for land agents which is the same in Alberta and BC (Arsenault, 2009a). In the past, Vause had always negotiated deals with gas companies, but recent negotiations, especially since the gas boom began in 2000 leading to increased government dependence on petroleum revenue, have been far worse. He calls the MAB a 'kangaroo court'.

After the land agent's initial visit, Vause hired a lawyer and drove to Grand Prairie Alberta to be in the lawyer's office for a conference call with representatives from the MAB and the gas company (Spectra Energy). He recounts how captive theory plays out on the ground:

> On the conference call, everyone identifies themselves. When Spectra's representative introduced himself, the mediator [from the MAB] said, 'Oh, how are you Brian? Haven't talked to you in a while.' The mediator knew him personally. You don't stand a chance. This pipeline they put here, I am stuck with the liability forever. I never signed a paper or anything for it, but I am still liable. If I drive over it and damage it, I am responsible.
>
> Arsenault (2009a)

Vause received $19,000 dollars from Spectra as compensation for the land disturbance, which didn't even cover half their legal bills. In Alberta, companies have to pay the legal bills during disputes with landowners. This isn't the case in BC, leading Vause to assert that the rules are unfair (McMartin, 2009). Companies in BC can use what legal experts colloquially call 'scorched earth': marshalling superior financial resources to bankrupt your opponent and force them to concede defeat.

Dual identities

At the height of Wiebo Ludwig's sabotage campaign against EnCana's predecessor in the late 1990s, *The Wall Street Journal* headlined a story: 'Oil-Well Sabotage in Canada Reflects Tension with Farmers' (Carlisle, 1998: 17). The headline is a little misleading. In north-eastern BC identities between 'farmer' versus 'oil worker' are not uniform. Certainly, there were and are tensions between oil companies and farmers. However, the two groups are not necessarily stagnant categories. Most farmers near Dawson Creek have, at some point, worked in the oil industry. Many farmers disputing present extraction policies, including the Volzs and Vauses, continue to work as subcontractors for gas companies.

The dual identities of opponents to current extraction policies are important for the analysis of this chapter. Few in north-east BC uniformly oppose gas extraction, in fact most farmers who have connections to the industry support a form of property rights where surface owners are not subsurface owners. 'I can understand that the oil doesn't belong to us and I have no problem with that,' said June Volz, stressing, 'Society needs the oil, there are no ifs, ands or buts. But at night I have to get up sometimes and close the windows because a flare had been blown out, so we had all this pollution' (Arsenault, 2009a). Thus, opponents are not angry about extraction *per se*, but they are upset with how it is being carried out. If regulations were less friendly to the industry in the short-term and gave residents more power to shape the nature of development and to oppose specific incursions, there would be significantly less conflict in north-eastern BC.

Blowouts and a conclusion

Since the sabotage campaign began in the fall of 2008, police, government officials and EnCana have claimed that protecting public safety is the reason for a harsh state security response and a $1 million bounty on the saboteur. 'We take the bombings of our facilities very seriously. The safety of our workers and the people who live in the communities where we operate is of paramount importance. That's why we are putting up this reward to help stop these bombings and end the threat that they pose to people in the Dawson Creek area,' said EnCana spokesman Mike Graham (Nguyen, 2009). However, when recent history is scrutinized, these statements seem disingenuous. On 22 November 2009, an EnCana pipeline near Tomslake burst, releasing 30,000 cubic metres of toxic sour gas into the community (OGC, 2010: 5). 'This is a very serious event,' said Oil and Gas Commission spokesman Steve Simon. 'This shouldn't have happened' (Kleiss, 2010).

In its assessment of the 22 November 2009 leak, the OGC reported a resident first smelled gas at 2:30 a.m. The company's emergency shut-off valve failed (OGC, 2010: 8). The first call came into the emergency telephone line 911 at 8:36 a.m., after a resident drove through a cloud of poisonous gas (OGC, 2010: 7). The community self-organized an evacuation with a flurry of phone calls. EnCana didn't tell residents about the danger until 10:16 a.m., several hours after the pipeline burst. The company didn't stop the leak until 10:45 a.m. (OGC, 2010: 11). 'Clearly, procedures were not followed,' EnCana vice-president Mike McAllister told reporters at a Calgary press conference, where he issued an apology (Kleiss, 2010). No one was arrested or criminally charged as a result of the incident; in fact, Encana did not even have to pay a fine (Kuhl, 2010). 'This leak probably released thousands of times more gas than what has been released by the bombings,' said Tim Ewert, one of the dozens of people who had to self-evacuate (Arsenault, 2010).

If safety was the over-riding concern, EnCana would have had to do more than issue an apology. And while the 'captive' OGC regulator did issue a thorough report and strong statements on the leak, there was no concrete action. This incident, and the responses to it, provides clear evidence that public safety is not the factor motivating state responses to sabotage. Thus, it seems as though providing security for capital investment, partially as a means to bolster government petroleum revenues, is the over-riding public policy concern for the police, EnCana and the BC government. Unlike the seemingly intractable problem of property relations, these grievances can be dealt with primarily through legal changes. Thus captive regulators, not issues with property rights are the main cause of conflict and sabotage in north-eastern BC.

Notes

1. For key information on Canada's emerging importance as an energy exporter and some of the ensuing conflicts around environmental sustainability see also Chastko (2003), Marsden (2007), Clark (2008) and Nikiforuk (2008).
2. Interview with Tom Flanagan by phone, summer 2009. For quotes from the interview, see Arsenault (2009b). See also Flanagan (2009) for his broader work on resource securitization and conflicts in the oil patch includes. The idea that 'lost property rights' incite conflict in oil extracting areas can also be seen in: Michael L. Ross, 'Blood Barrels: Why Oil Wealth Fuels Conflict,' Foreign Affairs, 87:3 (May/June 2008): 2-9; Anthony Scott, The Evolution of Resource Property Rights (New York and Oxford: Oxford University Press, 2008), 340.
3. Nikiforuk's work places theories of Thomas Friedman (2006) into a Canadian context. Friedman makes a sweeping and in some cases unfounded argument

that the price of oil and the pace of freedom move in opposite directions in petroleum-rich states. Nikiforuk uses the idea of petropolitics arguing that government dependence on resource revenue rather than tax payments from individuals leads governments to serve the petroleum companies which finance them, rather than voters who elect them. In BC, gas revenue is the largest source of resource revenue for the provincial government.
4. For a literature review on the effects of hydrogen sulphide exposure see Meed (n. d.) (while the Meed Report isn't formally dated, it was written in 2005/06).
5. For an analysis of the term 'terrorism' in the case of the EnCana bombings see Neville and Smythe (2010).
6. The figure of 160 incidents is likely misleading. The package of information from CSIS contained articles by Andrew Nikiforuk, which likely means CSIS is relying on the veteran environmental journalist for some of their information. For his part, Nikiforuk (2009) believes that '[i]n the space of two years [during the 1990s, the period covered by the CSIS requests] there were more than 600 acts of vandalism and industrial sabotage'. Thus, the ongoing campaign in BC is not without precedent.
7. See Letter to the Editor (2009).
8. Document: Integrated Treat Assessment Centre 'Top Secret' 06/68, 'Yemen: Canadian Company Targeted in Attack'.
9. Corb Lund, 'This is My Prairie' released on the album *Losin' Lately Gambler*, New West Records, 2009. It is worth noting that Lund's music video for the song 'the roughest neck around' won an award in 2004 for historical preservation from the Petroleum History Society. Such awards are normally given to academics and the award should dispel any notions that hard-drinking country musicians aren't appropriate source material for an academic paper (see http://www.petroleumhistory.ca/history/awards.html). Accessed on 13 December 2008.

References

Amos, G., 2009. 'Lekstrom Announces Oil and Gas Initiatives; Aim is to Reduce Conflict between Land Owners and Oil and Gas Industry'. *Dawson Creek Daily News*, Accessed on 26 January 2010.

Arsenault, C., 2009a. 'BC Pipeline Bombings'. *Vue Magazine*, 17 September. Available at http://www.vueweekly.com/article.php?id=13116. Accessed on 1 November 2009.

Arsenault, C., 2009b. 'It's like the Wild West Out Here'. *Inter Press Service*, 30 August. Available at http://ipsnews.net/news.asp?idnews=48269. Accessed on 7 September 2009.

Arsenault, C., 2010. 'Hunt for Oil Patch Bomber takes New Twist'. *Inter Press Service*, 18 January. Available at http://www.ipsnews.net/news.asp?idnews=50025. Accessed on 25 January 2010.

Auditor General of British Columbia, 2010. News Release: 'Improved Oversight Needed to Manage Contamination Risk at BC Oil and Gas Sites'. 11 February. Available at www.bcauditor.com/pubs/2010/report8/oil-and-gas-site-contamination-risks-improved-oversight-n. Accessed on 1 March 2010.

BC Progress Board, 2009. 'Export Detail: Topic Box from the 2009 Ninth Annual Benchmark Report'. Available at http://www.bcprogressboard.com/archives/aTB09ExportDetail.html. Accessed on 1 February 2010.

Barnett, J., 2001. *The Meaning of Environmental Security: Ecological Politics and Policy in the New Security Era*. London and New York: Zed Books.
Bergland, A., 2009. 'Land Disputes Tossed Around'. *Dawson Creek Daily News*, 25 September. Accessed at archives on March 5, 2010.
Boyd, D. R., 2003. *Unnatural Law: Rethinking Canadian Environmental Law and Policy*. Vancouver: UBC press.
Brooke, J., 2000. 'Radical Environmentalist Convicted of Gas Well Blast in Canada'. *The New York Times*, 20 April. Available at http://www.nytimes.com/2000/04/20/world/radical-environmentalist-convicted-of-gas-well-blast-in-canada.html. Accessed on 1 February 2008.
Campbell, G., 2001. Address to the BC Oil and Gas Development Conference, 6 December. Available at http://www.gov.bc.ca/premier/media_gallery/speeches/2001/dec/address_to_the_bc_oil_and_gas_development_conference_2001_12_06_96548_o_1.html. Accessed on 5 October 2008.
Canadian Energy Research Institute (CERI) and R. McManus Consulting, 2004. *Economic Impacts of the Oil and Gas Industry in British Columbia*. Calgary, AB: CERI for British Columbia Mines and Energy (November).
Canadian Security Intelligence Service (CSIS), 2009. FOI (Freedom of Information) 117-2009-54 sent to CSIS, received 8 September 2009. Document Integrated Treat Assessment Centre 08/145, 'A Third Small-Scale Explosion Targets EnCana Pipeline on 2008 10 30'.
Canwest, 2008. 'BC Pipeline Bombings may not be Eco-Terrorism: Expert'. *The Vancouver Sun*, 3 November. Available at http://www.canada.com/ottawacitizen/news/story.html?id=90884d4d-d582-4d5d-9be8-ba6c9ab9cc97. Accessed on 1 December 2008.
Carlisle, T., 1998. 'Oil-Well Sabotage in Canada Reflects Tension With Farmers'. *The Wall Street Journal* (Eastern Edition) New York, N.Y.: October 30, p. A17. Accessed via Lexus-Nexus on September 22, 2008.
Chastko, P., 2003. *Developing Alberta's Oil Sands*. Calgary: University of Calgary Press.
Clark, T., 2008. *Tar Sands Showdown: Canada and the New Politics of Oil in an Age of Climate Change*. Toronto: James Lorimer & Company.
Collyer, D., 2009. 'Maintaining Momentum in BC's Oil and Gas Sector'. Statement made by the president of Canadian Association of Petroleum Producers, 7 May. Available at http://www.capp.ca/aboutUs/mediaCentre/CAPPCommentary/Pages/MaintainingMomentuminBCsOilandGasSector.aspx#dBJ5MZpZBMVS. Accessed on 1 March 2010.
Cormier, R., 2009. 'Wiebo Ludwig Writes Open Letter to EnCana Pipeline Bomber'. *Edmonton Journal*, 12 September. Available at http://www.edmontonjournal.com/news/Wiebo+Ludwig+writes+open+letter+EnCana+pipeline+bomber/1988515/story.html. Accessed on 1 October 2009.
CTV W5, 2010. 'Behind the Pipeline Bombings in Northern BC'. 23 January. Available at www.ctv.ca/servlet/ArticleNews/story/CTVNews/20100122/w5_tomslake_100123/20100123?s_name=W5. Accessed on 22 February 2010.
Cunningham, T., 2008. 'Tomslake Homeowners Request Buyout from EnCana'. *Dawson Creek Daily News*, 25 June, sec. A1. Accessed on 7 September 2009.
Deudney, D. H. and R. A. Matthew, eds, 1999. *Contested Grounds: Security and Conflict in the New Environmental Politics*. New York: SUNY Press.
Dyer, G., 2008. *Climate Wars*, 2nd edition. Toronto: Random House.

Evans, J. and T. Garvin, 2009. '"You're in Oil Country": Moral Tales of Citizen Action against Petroleum Development in Alberta, Canada'. *Ethics, Place and Environment* 12(1). (March) 49–69.
Farrell, A. E., H. Zerriffi and H. Dowlatabadi, 2004. 'Energy Infrastructure and Security'. *Annual Review of Environment and Resources* 29 (August) 421–69.
Fedorowicz, J. K., 2007. 'The Ten Thousand Mile Target: Energy Infrastructure and Terrorism Today'. *Critical Energy Infrastructure Protection Policy Research Series*. Ottawa: Canadian Centre of Intelligence and Security Studies (CCISS) and The Norman Patterson School of International Affairs (March).
Feng, Y., 2001. 'Political Freedom, Political Instability, and Policy Uncertainty: A Study of Political Institutions and Private Investment in Developing Countries'. *International Studies Quarterly* 45(2): 271–94.
Flanagan, T., 2009. *Resource Industries and Security in Northern Alberta*. Prepared for the Canadian Defense and Foreign Affairs Institute (June).
Friedman, T., 2006. 'The First Law of Petropolitics'. *Foreign Policy* (May/June). Available at http://www.foreignpolicy.com/story/cms.php?story_id=3426&print=1. Accessed on 3 October 2008.
Friedrich, H., 2006a. 'Former Member Slams Mediation Board'. *Alaska Highway News*, 14 December. Accessed from archives on February 3, 2010.
Friedrich, H., 2006b. 'Province Might License Land Agents'. *Alaska Highways News*, 21 December. Accessed from archives on February 3, 2010.
Gousseau, K., 2007. 'Resolution Process for Oil and Gas will Improve says Chair'. *Dawson Creek Daily News*, 26 November. Accessed from archives on February 3, 2010.
Government of British Columbia, n. d., *What your BC Government is doing for Oil and Gas*. http://www.gov.bc.ca/yourbc/oil_gas/og_workers.html?src=/workers/og_workers.html. Accessed on 26 March 2009.
Graeger, N., 1996. 'Environmental Security?' *Journal of Peace Research* 33: 109–16.
Hahn, S., 2006. *The Roots of Southern Populism*. New York: Oxford University Press.
Harper, S., 2008. 'Prime Minister Harper Addresses the Canada-U.K. Chamber of Commerce in London', 29 May. Available at http://pm.gc.ca/eng/media.asp?category=2&id=2131 (accessed on 1 March 2009).
Harvey, D., 1999. 'Considerations of Environmental Justice'. In N. Low, ed., *Global Ethics and Environment*. New York: Routledge, 109–131.
Homer-Dixon, T., 1999. *Environment, Scarcity and Violence*. Princeton, NJ: Princeton University Press.
Howard, T., B. Parfitt, J. King and J. Milligan, 2005. *This Land is Their Land: An Audit of Regulation of the Oil and Gas Industry in BC*. Vancouver: Sierra Legal Defense (June).
Hume, M., 2009. 'Hunt for Pipeline Bomber Draws Harassment Complaints'. *The Globe and Mail*, 10 July. Accessed on 12 August 2009.
Jenkins, C. and K. Schock, 1992. 'Global Structures and Political Processes in the Study of Domestic Political Conflict'. *Annual Review of Sociology* 18 (August) 161–85.
Kaplan, R. D., 1994. 'The Coming Anarchy'. *The Atlantic Monthly*, February. Available at http://www.theatlantic.com/magazine/archive/1994/02/the-coming-anarchy/4670/. Accessed on 1 November 2008.

Kaplan, R. D., 2009. 'Pakistan's Fatal Shore'. *The Atlantic Monthly*, May. Available at http://www.theatlantic.com/magazine/archive/2009/05/pakistan-8217-s-fatal-shore/7385/. Accessed on 1 November 2008.

Klare, M. T., 2004. *Blood and Oil*. New York: Metropolitan Books.

Kleiss, K., 2010. 'EnCana Apologizes after BC Watchdog Finds Fault'. *Edmonton Journal*, 5 February. Available at http://www.edmontonjournal.com/entertainment/music/EnCana+failed+during+leak+watchdog/2522549/story.html. Accessed on 22 February 2010.

Kuhl, N., 2010. 'November Gas Leak Raises Questions'. *The Daily Herald-Tribune*, February. Available at http://www.dailyheraldtribune.com/ArticleDisplay.aspx?archive=true&e=2439979. Accessed on 1 March 2010.

Letter to the Editor, 2009. Sent to the *Dawson Creek Daily News*, received by the paper 15 July 2009, released by the RCMP 16 July 2009. Available at www.scribd.com/doc/17419555/Letter-to-the-editor, accessed on 31 July 2009 or www.bc.rcmp.ca/digitalAssets/16/16791_Encana_Letter.pdf. Accessed on 31 July 2009.

Lund, C., 2009. 'This is My Prairie', released on the album *Losin' Lately Gambler*, New West Records.

Machiavelli, N., 2003. *The Prince*. New York and London: Bantam classics.

Marr-Laing, T. and C. Severson-Baker, 1999. *Beyond Eco-Terrorism: Deeper Issues Affecting Alberta's Oilpatch*. Drayton Valley, AB: Pembina Institute, February.

Marsden, W., 2007. *Stupid to the Last Drop*. Toronto: Knopf Canada.

Mathews, J. T., 1989. 'Redefining Security'. *Foreign Affairs* 68: 162–77.

McMartin, P., 2009. 'First Came the Energy Boom, Now the Bombs'. *The Vancouver Sun*, 1 August. Available at http://www.vancouversun.com/story_print.html?id=1853127&sponsor=. Accessed on 30 August 2009.

Meed, L. M., n. d., *Population Health and Oil and Gas Activities: A Preliminary Assessment of the Situation in Northeastern BC, A Report from the Medical Health Officer to the Board of Northern Health*. http://www.northernhealth.ca/Portals/0/About/NH_Reports/documents/OilandGasreport.pdf. Accessed on 1 December 2008.

Mercer, K., 2009. 'RCMP Investigating Sixth Bombing of EnCana Pipeline since October'. *The Province*, 4 July. Accessed on 1 August 2009.

Ministry of Employment and Investment, 1997. *British Columbia Oil and Gas Handbook*. Vancouver: MEI.

Ministry of Mines and Energy, n. d., 'Q & A Companion Document, Standard Surface Lease Agreement'. Available at www.empr.gov.bc.ca/MACR/communities/Neemac/Documents/BC%20Standard %20Surface%20Lease%20Agreement%20-%20web%20version.pdf. Accessed on 31 January 2010.

Neefjes, K., 1999. 'Ecological Degradation: A Cause for Conflict a Concern for Survival'. In A. Dobson, ed., *Fairness and Futurity: Essays on Environmental Sustainability and Social Justice*. New York: Oxford University Press, 249–78.

Nesbitt-Larking, P., 2004. 'Political Psychology in Canada'. *Political Psychology* 25 (January) 97–114.

Neville, K. J. and L. Smythe, 2010. *Ecotage and Eco-Terrorism: A Problem with Labels Policy Responses to Radical Environmental Targeting*, Working Paper. Vancouver: Liu Institute for Global Issues and Department of Political Science, University of British Columbia (17 February).

Nguyen, L., 2009. 'EnCana Offers BC Pipeline Bombing Reward'. *The National Post*, 13 January. Available at http://www.nationalpost.com/news/canada/story.html?id=1172106. Accessed on 23 February 2009.

Nikiforuk, A., 2001. *Saboteurs: Wiebo Ludwig's War Against Big Oil*. Toronto: Macfarlane Walter & Ross.
Nikiforuk, A., 2008. *Tar Sands: Dirty Oil and the Future of a Continent*. Vancouver: Greystone books.
Nikiforuk, A., 2009. 'Industrial Sabotage: Under Attack'. *Canadian Business*, 17 August. Available at http://www.canadianbusiness.com/markets/commodities/article. jsp?content=20090817_10006_10006. Accessed on 1 October 2009.
Oil and Gas Commission (OGC) of British Columbia, 2002/2003. *Annual Report, 2002/2003*. Available at http://www.ogc.gov.bc.ca/documents/annualreports/0203annualreport.pdf. Accessed on 31 January 2010.
Oil and Gas Commission (OGC), 2008. 'Oil and Gas Commission and Mediation and Arbitration Board Sign Coordination Agreement'. Press release, 10 March. Available at www.surfacerightsboard.bc.ca/Documents/.../coordination.pdf (accessed on 1 February 2009).
Oil and Gas Commission (OGC) of British Columbia, 2010. Failure Investigation Report: 22 November 2009; Failure of Piping at EnCana Swan Wellsite A5-7-77-14 L W6M, 4 February. Available at http://www.ogc.gov.bc.ca/documents/annualreports/OGC%20Investigation%20Report%2004.02.10.pdf. Accessed on 2 March 2010.
Pearse, P. H., 1988. 'Rights and the Development of Natural Resource Policies in Canada'. *Canadian Public Policy/Analyse de politiques* 14(3): 307–20.
Plynn, L., 2005. 'Oil, Gas Industry Violating Rules: Audit'. *The Vancouver Sun*, 12 May. Accessed on 11 January 2009.
Rankin, M., S. Carpenter, P. Burchmore and C. Jones, 2000–1. 'Regulatory Reform in the British Columbia Petroleum Industry: The Oil and Gas Commission'. *The Alberta Law Review* 38(144): 143–68.
Ronnfeldt, C. F., 1997. 'Three Generations of Environment and Security Research'. *Journal of Peace Research* 34(4): 473–82.
Ross, M. L., 1999. 'The Political Economy of the Resource Curse. *World Politics* 51, 297–322.
Ross, M. L., 2008. 'Blood Barrels: Why Oil Wealth Fuels Conflict'. *Foreign Affairs* 87(3) (May/June): 2–9.
Royal Canadian Mounted Police (RCMP), 2008a. 'Explosion on Natural Gas Pipeline'. 14 October. Available at www.bc.rcmp.ca/ViewPage.action?siteNodeId=38&languageId=1&contentId=6652&q=dawson%20creek. Accessed on 3 November 2008.
Royal Canadian Mounted Police (RCMP), 2008b. 'Third Explosion on Natural Gas Infrastructure'. 1 November. Available at www.bc.rcmp.ca/ViewPage. action?siteNodeId=38&languageId=1&contentId=6893&q=dawson%20creek. (For an analysis of the term 'terrorism' in the case of the EnCana bombings.) Accessed on 1 December 2008.
Royal Canadian Mounted Police (RCMP), 2009. Available at www.bc.rcmp.ca/ViewPage.action?siteNodeId=531&languageId=4&contentId=7730. Accessed on 1 December 2009.
Steinhäusler, F., P. Furthner, W. Heidegger, S. Rydell and L. Zaitseva, 2008. 'Security Risks to the Oil and Gas Industry: Terrorist Capabilities'. *Strategic Insights* VII(1) February 1–44.
Stueck, W. and M. Hume, 2008. 'Second Pipeline Explosion Bears Marks of Sabotage, RCMP say'. *The Globe and Mail*, 16 October. Available at

http://www.theglobeandmail.com/news/national/article716402.ece. Accessed on 1 December 2008.

Timoney, K. and P. Lee, 2001. 'Environmental Management in Resource Rich Alberta, Canada: First World Jurisdiction, Third World Analogue?' *Journal of Environmental Management* 63: 387–405.

Vancouver Sun Editorial Board, 2005. 'Watch Dogs over the Oil and Gas Industry Need More Clout. *The Vancouver Sun*, 16 May. Accessed Lexus-Nexus December 1, 2009.

VanderKlippe, N., 2010. 'The Art of Defusing the Green Protests'. *The Globe and Mail*, 25 February. Available at www.theglobeandmail.com/.../the-art-of-defusing-the-green-protests/article1481763. Accessed on 20 March 2010.

Westcoast Environmental Law Association, 2005. *Cutting Up the Safety Net: Environmental Deregulation in British Columbia*. Vancouver: Westcoast Environmental Law Association.

Youngquist, W. and R. C. Duncan, 2003. 'North American Natural Gas: Data Show Supply Problems'. *Natural Resources Research* 12(4) December 229–40.

11
Bodies on the Line: The In/Security of Everyday Life in Aamjiwnaang

Sarah Marie Wiebe

Introduction

When you walk onto the Aamjiwnaang First Nations reserve, residents tell you to pay attention to your body.[1] Your lips might tingle, your body temperature may rise, a rash may appear, you may get a headache; you will smell the stench of pollution in the air. Smokestacks on the horizon dominate the landscape. Your heart may race as fear and anxiety about the unknown health effects set in. Psychosomatic affect becomes a real, embodied experience. Community members express anger, laugh off the experiences through black humour, or turn inward and deny their circumstances (Luginaah, Smith and Lockridge, 2010). These are common emotions of normalization, for those living amidst uncertainty 'on the volcano of civilization' at the 'contours of a risk society' (Beck, 1986). This chapter is about the location of risk and insecurities of everyday life, where some bodies are emplaced in vulnerable environments, bearing the burden of modern civilization more so than others.

In the kind of risk society Ulrich Beck describes, advanced modernities, which are part of globalized economies, come at a cost. In this respect, wealth couples risk (Beck, 1986; Giddens, 1990). As a consequence, some individuals live a more 'at risk' life, where the potential to be exposed to toxins in the environment is heightened. In such environments – which can be seen from the Achuar in Peru, to the Q'eqchi' in Guatemala to aboriginal[2] peoples in Canada – uncertainty reframes health circumstance, being and citizenship (Beck, 1986; Giddens, 1990; Petryna, 2006; Rose, 2007). In our globalized world, some risks take precedence over others. With the creeping influence of transnational security threats, in societies increasingly defined by risk, new problems call for new solutions. In this context, risks appear somewhere 'out there' necessitating security, and simultaneously 'attached' to some specific site as potentially everywhere. For some communities, transnational threats are not all that 'new'. In one such risky environment, on the Aamjiwnaang reserve, surrounded by a high concentration of noxious chemical, sewage treatment and landfill facilities, in Canada's 'Chemical Valley', changes happen to the body at an unknown pace. Consequently, I argue that those living in Aamjiwnaang – a downstream community from this Chemical Valley – live with their bodies on the line. The line I refer to is the space in between security and insecurity; it is a place of liminality, where scenes of everyday life are politicized.

Rather than thinking about security issues as inherently tied to the state, or to a conventional scale of government, I contend that we can understand practices and processes of security in, upon, and internal to the body. I am writing neither about a site that registers as part of 'Canada's foreign policy agenda', nor about a site that 'should be' securitized. Instead, I am particularly interested in the experience of those at the intersection between local/global harm, where conventional boundaries dissipate, and new borders can be found. I contend that the body is a site where demarcations between the local/global, national/international, secure/insecure, internal/external breakdown. It is the ultimate translocal site, where power relations are enacted, contested and resisted (see, for example, Muller, 2004; Bigo, 2006; Aradau, 2007; Aradau and Munster, 2007; Broeders, 2007; Amoore and De Goede, 2008).[3]

The body becomes a site for multiple boundaries. Following critical political geographer Louise Amoore, bodies become the carriers of borders as they are inscribed with multiple encoded boundaries of access (Amoore, 2006). To this, I add that they internalize borders, as toxic environments affect body-borders from within. While security scholars have discussed the (in)security of bodies as the focus of targeted border management practices, I contend that the body is equally rendered (in)secure through more informal practices of seemingly latent environmental harm.[4] In this respect, global security threats seep through traditional scales or levels of government to the body, where processes of accumulation, crisis and risk management manifest. In particular, I suggest that environmental violence or harm occurs within and upon the bodies of those living in precarious space. This space is not a dead or passive space; rather, the spaces of liminality I discuss produce meanings and experiences that are revealing about the state of politics in Canada at the local/global interface. The Canadian First Nations reserve is a place that often finds itself at this nexus.

All spaces have histories. Some histories are visible, others invisible.[5] I discuss place as a variable shaping the materiality and corporeality of bodies through subtle, yet harmful environmentally uncertain, insecure practices.[6] The central concern of this chapter is a move towards a place-informed, locally situated understanding of (in)security as it manifests on and within the human body. In toxic environments, at the nexus of security and insecurity, borders become de-territorialized; yet, the body internalizes territories through the infiltration of invisible harm in the form of chemical exposure. To demonstrate this empirically, I present this discussion in three sections: (i) the body-place relationship drawing from the Aamjiwnaang First Nation experience, (ii) a reading of how environmentally violent places form toxic bodies from within and (iii) an examination of how toxic bodies are formed in and through (non)places, in places between places, liminal spaces or 'third spaces' (Foucault, 1986; Soja, 1996). This provides a lens through which theorists, security experts and policymakers alike can reconceptualize global ecology through a place-based understanding of at-risk bodies.

Situating the body at the global/local interface

The Aamjiwnaang First Nation Reserve, home to about 850 Aanishnaabek peoples, is just across the Canada-US border from Port Huron, Michigan, approximately seven kilometres south of Sarnia, Ontario. For nearly half a century, their land has been almost completely surrounded by Canada and the United States' largest concentration of petrochemical manufacturing. Much of their original reserve, founded in 1827, was sold to industry through suspect land deals in the 1960s, and is now occupied by pipelines, factories and dozens of petroleum storage tanks. The location of this community in Canada's Chemical Valley profoundly affects the local residents.

Continuously waking up to the shrill of chemical plant warning sirens caused Ada Lockridge, member of the Aamjiwnaang First Nation, to wonder about the effects of neighbouring chemical plants on her community's health. Consider the following:

> On a recent autumn day, Lockridge stood in the Aamjiwnaang band's cemetery. The burial ground occupies a gently sloping patch of ground sandwiched between a petroleum storage tank farm and a low cinderblock building with half a dozen pipelines running through it.
>
> CTV News (2005)

This imagery juxtaposes the reserve with neighbouring industrial development, both in Canada and the United States, encircling Aamjiwnaang. In an article published in *Environmental Health Perspectives*, Lockridge and her team of researchers made a shocking discovery: two girls are born in her small community for every boy (Mackenzie, Lockridge and Keith, 2005). It is hard to dispute that this sex ratio indicates serious environmental contamination by an unknown mixture of toxic chemicals in the air, soil and water.

The area has come to be dominated by its surrounding industry, and is now commonly referred to as Canada's 'Chemical Valley' by residents and the media. Tension between industrial development and environmental protection remains strong in the Valley. According to a report by non-governmental organization Ecojustice (formerly the Sierra Legal Defence Fund), titled *Exposing Canada's Chemical Valley*, there are 62 large industrial facilities, literally in their backyards (Ecojustice, 2007). The report states that Canada's Chemical Valley contains many of the toxins listed in *Canada's Environmental Protection Act*; yet, economic productivity as a beneficial component of community living remains a strong priority. In fact, many companies express an interest in partnering with the Indigenous community to provide employment for members of the Aamjiwnaang First Nation. For example, the *Chippewas of Sarnia Business Park* is a group organized to promote local employment of the members of the First Nations community. Consequently, industrial development and conceptions of progress come into tension with questions of ecological responsibility and environmental health.

The unbalanced sex ratio appears as vivid evidence that the environment plays an adverse role affecting reproduction on the reserve. Scientists have used the sex ratio as a very sensitive indicator demonstrating the effects as a result of exposure to chemicals disrupting the endocrine system and reproductive health. A 2008 Canadian Broadcasting Corporation (CBC) documentary indicated that pollutants known as 'endocrine disruptors' interfered with hormones that determine whether a baby boy or girl will be born (CBC, 2008). Furthermore, statistics collected by Lockridge and her team indicate that one in four Aamjiwnaang children have a behavioural or learning disability. Children suffer from asthma at nearly three times the national rate, and four of ten women on the reserve have had at least one miscarriage or stillbirth.[7] There are few cases of such a disproportionate gender imbalance in the world as on the Aamjiwnaang reserve, let alone the other health-related harms facing this community.

As synthetic organic chemicals begin to interfere with natural hormones, several scientists and members of the Aamjiwnaang community believe that these hormone-mimicking endocrine disrupters are to blame. Because hormones are so important to the development and healthy performance of the body's organs, endocrine disrupters have the potential to cause a wide range of effects, from damage to the brain and sex organs, to decreased sperm production and immune suppression in adults (CBC, 2007, 2008). Furthermore, some biologists argue that endocrine disruptors could influence sexual behaviour and violence. Biologist Theo Colborn hypothesizes that endocrine disrupters may be responsible for physical, mental and behavioural disruption in humans, which could affect fertility, learning ability and aggression (Colborn, 2009; Colborn, Dumanoski and Peter Myers, 1997). In addition, endocrine disrupters may be responsible for rising rates of testicular and breast cancer, a higher frequency of reproductive tract abnormalities, declining sperm counts and increases in learning disabilities. While much of the science remains 'unknown', the Aamjiwnaang community lives with these unknowns on a daily basis, waiting for the security of the known.

For low-level exposures, the effects of endocrine disrupting chemicals are subtle and harder to document. Research is less clear on the effects of low-level exposures. According to Marc Weisskopf, a research associate at the Harvard School of Public Health, there are a lot of unknowns. In a 2003 study, he and several colleagues found that mothers who consumed large amounts of PCB-contaminated fish from the Great Lakes were more likely to have girls (Weisskopf, Anderson and Hanrahan, 2003). It is difficult to say how exactly the effects of endocrine disrupters are impacting the general population;[8] however, there is little doubt that endocrine-disrupting pollutants are affecting the sexual development of wildlife next to the Aamjiwnaang reserve.

In Lake St Clair, about 30 miles from their reserve, fish have both male and female gonads. The condition, known as intersex, is caused when a young fish that is genetically male is exposed to chemicals such as the fertilizer atrazine, which causes female gonads to develop by acting like the hormone oestrogen (Kavanagh et al., 2004). Research has identified increased reproductive abnormalities for women who consume the fish. Weisskopf's findings suggest that maternal exposure to polychlorinated biphenyls may decrease the sex ratio of offspring (Mackenzie, Lockridge and Keith, 2005). The phenomenon has been documented all over the southern Great Lakes, not just in fish, but also in birds and amphibians (Mackenzie, Lockridge and Keith, 2005). It is significant that the environment here appears to affect both wildlife and human health.[9]

While the science is revealing about the impact of toxins in wildlife, the human health impacts remain unproven. Members of Aamjiwnaang are increasingly worried about the pollution of their reserve. While it seems clear that the environment has a physical, organic impact on health, there are also considerable cultural and emotional effects. Community members express a growing sense of fear – fear of the sirens, fear of the outdoors, fear of the air, fear of the water A report by Ecojustice (2007) suggests that:

> These chemicals and related incidents have significant impacts on their cultural life, including hunting, fishing, medicine, gathering and ceremonial activities. Health impacts include asthma, reproductive effects, learning disabilities and cancer. The most common reported impact was fear. People on the reserve feared the outdoors, the warning sirens and unreported incidences.

According to Aamjiwnaang environmental community activist and father Ron Plain, members of their community worry about what is wrong with every child that is born (Crenson, 2005). Unlike adults, children cannot excrete or store contaminants and are more vulnerable to toxins. Toxins are generally stored in fat, and during pregnancy and lactation, women's fat is metabolized and exposes foetuses and newborns at vulnerable stages of development to these chemicals (Smith, 2005). Toxic endocrine disruptors mimic natural hormone production, consequently disrupting reproduction and foetal development. As such toxins are found in food and wildlife sources, avoidance becomes impossible and exposure an everyday reality.

In response, the Aamjiwnaang have engaged in a variety of tactics to raise awareness about the severity of the situation. Tactics include blockades, body mapping, biomonitoring and bucket brigades to resist the bodily and psychological harms (Scott, 2008). At the current time, the band does not have sufficient resources to fund large-scale environmental monitoring or enforcement initiatives. Lockridge currently partners with community health officials, academic researchers and NGOs to lobby government and industry for change. In a *Sarnia Observer* article, scientist Dr Schetter states: 'We know enough now about the exposures. Reducing exposures is the prime objective' (Poirier, 2008). Research continues; however, little government or industry action is taking place.

The Aamjiwnaang environment committee is frustrated by the lack of government and industry intervention. Band member, activist, mother and self-declared 'victim of the Chemical Valley' Ada Lockridge is lobbying for more stringent government regulations on industrial emissions.[10] The *Sarnia Observer* illuminates her frustration: 'How much studying do we have to do to get the government to toughen emission standards?' (Poirier, 2008). Some progress – albeit at a snail's pace – is being made. At the very least, the community is the only First Nation to be provided an air monitoring station from Ontario's Ministry of the Environment (MOE). Subsequent air monitoring by Aamjiwnaang's environmental committee found elevated levels of the carcinogen benzene in the area, and the province is looking into establishing a standard (Ecojustice Press Release, 2008). Unsatisfied with the progress to date, the Aamjiwnaang community is pressing for further government action. Lockridge teamed up with the NGO Ecojustice to request a provincial environmental review and to create environmental legislation. On 30 January 2009, Ecojustice filed a formal application with the Environmental Commissioner of Ontario calling on the Ministry of the Environment to fill serious gaps in Ontario's pollution laws that currently put the health of Ontario residents at risk in highly polluted areas of the province (Ecojustice, 2009). On 7 April 2009, Ontario Minister John Gerretsen introduced Bill 167, the *Toxics Reduction Act* (Legislative Assembly of Ontario, 2009) with the aim of (a) preventing pollution and protect human health and the environment by reducing the use and creation of toxic substances, and (b) informing Ontarians about toxic substances. Within the legislation, enforcement remains voluntary.

The current Canadian regulatory environment fails to address the issue of chronic exposure. Part of the problem is the challenge of accepting the reality that chronic pollution and low-dose exposures characterize life in the industrialized world. The Canadian government continues to attribute the declining birth rate to *choices* such as smoking rates, nutrition, obesity and addiction (Scott, 2008). The lifestyle choice model does little to address the Aamjiwnaang concerns. Following Scott (2008), an individualistic interpretation of health policy coincides with the dominant epidemiological paradigm, which is a 'set of practices and beliefs embedded within science' where government and official understandings emphasize individual behaviour factors rather than environmental or social factors as keys to disease prevention. Legal structures further undermine support for meaningful interventions. Environmental health harms appear as 'incidental' to industrial production, making it legally challenging to comprehend the fusion between a polluting environment with an economically productive one (Scott, 2008). Only high-profile spills and leaks warrant government intervention.

In addition, the international policymaking regime fails to recognize an environmental health approach to the issue of possible endocrine disruptors in humans caused by chemical pollution. As the Public Health Agency of Canada (PHAC) takes much of its regulatory direction from the World Health Organization (WHO), we might turn to this organization to see what it has to say about this issue. Take, for example, the International Programme on Chemical Safety (IPCS), which is a collaboration between three United Nations (UN) bodies, the WHO, the International Labour Organization (ILO) and the United Nations Environment Programme. An IPCS report discussed the evidence that endocrine-active chemicals adversely affect human health. The report's first chapter stated that analysis of the human data by itself, while generating some concerns, has so far failed to provide firm evidence of direct causal associations between low-level (i.e. levels measured in the general population) exposure to chemicals with EDCs and adverse health outcomes (Damstra et al., 2002). Chapter five stated there is limited evidence to suggest that changes in the sex ratio may represent a general trend in society as a consequence of exposure to EDCs (Damstra et al., 2002). The report did, however, note the *potential* effects of endocrine disruptors, and highlighted the need for further research. According the the epidemiological model governing much of the ongoing health research, 'general population trends' are required to generate scientifically-proven, evidenced-based results. In the meantime, communities 'on the ground' with smaller population sizes await recognition of their health concerns. Consequently, small communities like Aamjiwnaang face slow, latent crises.

There appears to be a disconnect between such meta-analyses and what lived-body experience tells us about the impacts of the environment on our bodies. It is clear that environmental exposure involves an unpredictable, unknown mix of chemicals with a wide variance and duration, making epidemiological, population-based health strategies challenging. Evidently this unknown space creates problems for policymakers. In the meantime, while policymakers wait for the science, something is happening to the body in this environment, as the external environment affects the body from the inside. In this context, it is difficult to know where the body ends and environment begins, blurring the strict demarcation – the 'body-border' – between bodies and environments.

Toxins at the body-boundary

Our bodies are becoming environments, and environments are becoming bodies. As Steve Kroll-Smith and Joshua Kelley (2008) argue, environments form the body from within. Many of these processes seem invisible, as they operate in the realm of the unknown and the uncertain. There is often 'more than meets the eye' (or nose) in environmental stories (Parr, 2006). Sensory perception, affect and emotion become mobilized; the body – embedded within material and discursive contexts – takes form through a process of emplacement. This process of becoming in place – emplacement – is a two-way flow: not only is the body *in* place – the *place* forms the body from within.

Bodies are shaped by *space* from within the body. The location of the Indigenous reserve is a unique space – a geographical site – which produces certain meanings. These meanings reveal place. Health geography literature distinguishes between space and place to suggest that space refers to a physical location, while place refers to the symbolic and interpretive meanings that emanate from individual and collective relationships to a space (Gattrell and Elliot, 2008). Both are of interest here. The space of the reserve contains multiple meanings – discursive constructions – which accompany the toxins as they infiltrate the body in Aamjiwnaang. Interpretations of these meanings about environments, or spaces, produce understandings of place.

Residents of Aamjiwnaang interpret their experience differently than do many policymakers. In response to the health circumstances in Aamjiwnaang, government officials frequently blame the unfortunate health scene on individuals themselves as a result of their irresponsible lifestyle practices (smoking, drinking, poor diet, lack of exercise, obesity, diabetes) (Scott, 2008). Governments, however, fail to take responsibility for the systemic harm produced in the Chemical Valley. In the documentary *Toxic Trespass*, Dr Davis bluntly states: 'you can say "no" to drugs, sex and alcohol, but you cannot say "no" to breathing' (Cohen, 2007). Along similar lines, Winona LaDuke (2005) argues:

> Our health conditions are a result of the environment and the economic, political, legal situations that we're in. They're not caused by our genetic, biological makeup. We are not dying from our physical inheritance. We are dying from the environments that we live in, and the conditions that we have to survive in.

The relationship between bodies and land takes on particular meaning in an Indigenous context. This relationship is made tenuous due to the presence of precarious, toxic environments.

Speaking about Indigenous Communities in Canada cannot be excluded from the legacy of colonialism. Moreover, colonialism has specific gendered effects on First Nations women living in close proximity to heavy industrial environments. As Cherokee scholar Andrea Smith discusses, Indigenous lands and territories have become marked as violable culminating in a simultaneous violation of Indigenous women's bodies (Smith, 2005). Consequently, attacks on nature are concurrent attacks on Native women's bodies. Smith states: 'Through rape of the earth, Native women's bodies are raped once again.' Smith raises serious questions about the legacy of colonialism and its impact on environmental racism, which has specific effects on marginalized people, particularly women. She discusses environmental racism in the context of uranium production, which have also been attributed to high cancer, miscarriage and birth defect rates.[11] A closer examination of the experiences of women on the Aamjiwnaang First Nation reserve reveals these synchronous colonial, paternalistic and oppressive practices.

Place as a concept plays an active role in identity formation, as individuals take on meanings about their personhood in relation to their environment. Borrowing insights from the literature on intersectionality, I suggest that bodies and places are not devoid of identity, social formation or attachments; they are simultaneously classed, raced and gendered (see, for example, Crenshaw, 1991; Morrow et al., 2007; Monture-Angus, 1995; Smith, 2005; Hankivsky and Christofferson, 2008; Kelm, 1998; Maracle, 1996; LaDuke, 1999). The birth experience is not devoid of meaning in such precarious places. As Leanne Simpson (2006) discusses, before colonial contact, Indigenous peoples lived in a healthier time, women were valued for their roles and responsibilities as life-givers. The birth experience, the physical and symbolic power to transform, create and recreate was central to being an Indigenous woman. Full-time mothering was recognized for its importance in growing and maintaining healthy nations. With the arrival of colonialism, this important role within many Indigenous cultures changed. Colonialism changed the birthing process. By targeting the power of Indigenous women as life-givers, colonizers were able to disintegrate communities and move people towards genocide (Simpson, 2006). In Aamjiwnaang, the legacy of colonization is manifest through the transformation of bodies exposed to a multitude of chemicals and disruption of the endocrine system, culminating in an array of reproductive health harms, including a skewed sex ratio and high rates of miscarriage (Mackenzie, Lockridge and Keith, 2005; Ecojustice, 2007). Through the transformation of bodies and the birth experience, colonization and gender intersect in a precarious, toxic place, revealing environmental violence from within the body. Resisting and challenging one's own body becomes an almost insurmountable feat. Locating injuries in precarious spaces goes beyond physical geography. Some geography literature refers to the importance of locating health clusters of harm and illness in order for environmental health concerns to garner the attention of policymakers (Gatrell and Elliott, 2008). Recognition of the racialized and gendered body in Aamjiwnaang, embedded within the historical legacy of colonialism, adds a few more dimensions to the already complicated health cluster story. For example, the Aamjiwnaang reserve sits next door to the first rubber polymer plant in Canada, which was erected during the Second World War. Today, a plaque marks the site of the former plant. The plaque indicates that in 1966, residents were moved away from the nearby community of 'Blue Water', which no longer exists, due to 'health and safety concerns'. Aamjiwnaang, Indian Sarnia Band 45, remained. Identifying harm clusters is not enough to garner a sufficient policy response; precarious place continues to creep onto the body in Aamjiwnaang.

Places form the body from within. Following environmental sociologists Kroll-Smith and Kelley (2008),

> [t]inker with a place – change its ambient air, its flora, its fauna, or the quality of its water, for example – and the body responds by making physiological, organic, and perhaps at times, psychical changes. The retina contracts smartly when exposed to bright light; a sinus detects cat dander and as a defence releases millions of histamines; far more troubling, reduce the ozone in the atmosphere and ultraviolet radiation creates metastizing skin cells. And the dance goes on.

Bodies react to environments and they react to places. The 'imaginative fixture' of considering 'environments *in* bodies' proves a vexing problem for medical professionals and individual bodies resisting such impositions (Kroll-Smith and Kelley, 2008). Resisting against the invasive nature of modern places is no simple feat. Bodies react, but resistance remains allusive: ideal in theory, difficult in practice. For many citizens living in precarious, toxic places, this challenge is more provocative. As 'anthropoid molecules find their way into bodies', residing in the bloodstream, tissue, nerve centres and bones, we must confront the realities of how industrial environments enter our corporeal bodies, literally becoming part of us (Kroll-Smith and Kelley, 2008).

In Aamjiwnaang, place affects the materiality and symbolism of the body; bodies are simultaneously infiltrated with toxins and discursive meanings. The intense proximity of the Aamjiwnaang reserve to pollution – surrounded by the highest concentration of chemical facilities in North America – reveals the racialized nature of pollution. Residents tell stories of the days when it was 'normal' for industry employees to dump toxic waste right onto the reserve, already commonly considered to be a junkyard or wasteland.[12] Today, landfills and sewage treatment facilities litter the Chemical Valley, which add to the landscape's toxic pollution burden. The distribution of environmental health harms in Aamjiwnaang reveals the importance of locating bodies in a particular geographic context, and moreover, locating these contexts in bodies.

Environments can place bodies in danger. As Kroll-Smith and Kelley (2008) articulate, 'bodies and environments are in a relentless embrace, a dance of sorts that never ends'. Such dances are material and symbolic. This precarious dance between the body and environment makes it difficult to determine where the body begins and the environment ends, and vice versa. These boundaries are fluid, porous and in continuous reproduction. The toxins are continuously flowing, advancing and infiltrating; however, bodies in these environments remain somewhat static, trapped in place, accumulating harm from within. As environments impose themselves on bodies, policymakers will have to develop the tools to respond to these health threats.

The effects of industrial harm can be understood through location. Some individuals bear the burden of environmental harm more than others. Authors have discussed the inverted or disproportionate burden that many of lower socio-economic status face in this respect (see, for example, Luke, 2000; Beck, 1986; Harvey, 1996; Brown, 2007; Kroll-Smith, Brown and Gunter, 2000; Bullard, 1993). In Aamjiwnaang, not only do the Indigenous peoples live 'more downstream than others', they also live 'across the tracks', and are sandwiched between heavy industry. Talfourd Creek, once a site of pleasure and play, now gathers pollution and runs through the reserve to Lake St Clair. The Aamjiwnaang burial site is encircled by chemical facilities, with the closest edge being the location of a waste disposal site for one of the plants. Individuals leading funeral prayers describe the startling and unsettling effect alert sirens have on ceremony participants. It is often only the sound of the weekly test siren, and ceremonies can resume.[13] This raises another concern that the indicated burial site is not necessarily representative of the ancestral burial ground; many bodies remain unmarked beneath the chemical plants. Obfuscating this scene, the current Canadian health and environment policy framework makes claims based upon tangible harm elusive. As Scott suggests:

> No one mother could ever prove that she specifically was harmed; that she specifically should have conceived a boy. No child has been harmed. But it is difficult to fathom that there is no harm being done. It is clear that there is wounding to be accounted for.
>
> Scott (2009)

Harm is legally permitted through an ad hoc provincial certificate permit and legal tort system. In this environment, harm is an invisible cost of state-sanctioned acts of productive economic activity. Generally speaking, the Provincial governing statute contains a general discharge prohibition on 'contaminants' in combination with the issuance of 'permits' for emissions in accordance with a certificate issued by the relevant authority Ontario Environmental Protection Act (OEPA). The certificate is a legally binding licence that sets out the conditions under which a facility can operate, including, often, the maximum permissible contaminant emission levels (Scott, 2009). Harm caused by legally sanctioned, permitted pollution is considered to be a by-product or an accidental side effect of the economic activity. It remains 'unintentional'. And yet, pollution is a 'fixed feature' of modern economies (Luke, 2000). Furthermore, the current Canadian environmental regulatory context remains largely voluntary (Agyeman et al., 2009).

While the provincial government shares a responsibility for environmental issues with the federal government, the province does not have formal a role in on-reserve health issues. The federal-provincial division of powers produces a zone where environmental health issues become 'lost in a limbo of inter-jurisdiction or layered jurisdiction' (Agyeman et al., 2009). The location of the reserve as a federal responsibility adds another layer to this complex array of responsibilities. Consequently, the reserve becomes lost in jurisdictional battles over who has to foot the bill for those wounded in this space.

Liminality, (in)security and places-in-between

The bodies in Aamjiwnaang are located on reserve. The reserve can be understood as a place between spaces, and simultaneously as a place through space. It is a place at the nexus of security and insecurity, as individuals on this reserve live with the everyday reality of unknown harm. In Foucauldian terms, it is a 'place without a place' (Foucault, 1986). In Canada, it is a space outside the federal, provincial or municipal concentrations of power. It is not a neutral space; it is a *place*, with many stories, narratives, interpretations and meanings. I maintain that the reserve is a paradoxical space: it places bodies on reserve, as a mode of preservation; however, this preservation of a 'traditional way of life' is delineated by the boundaries set by the Canadian government (Indian and Northern Affairs Canada), and produces a structured, pre-modern, colonized way of life. On the one hand, members of this community are free to live a traditional life; on the other hand, any way of living is being squeezed out through the continuous creep of heavy industrialization beside their land, challenging their very existence. As their ponds, creeks, rivers, homes, burial sites and bodies become sedimented with toxicity, their ability to 'be' bears the mark of a colonial creep in the form of a body burden. At once, the Aamjiwnaang are trapped in the past, and trapped by the future as 'progress' through economic materialism shapes the physical becoming of the body in this space.

The reserve is a space of juxtapositions: the reserve sets Indigenous peoples 'free' to practice their way of life in a pre-contact time, associated with a mythic ideal of the hunter-gatherer inherently connected to nature and able to live off the land. Simultaneously, the space, or literally the land provided, is often toxic, unusable land. This is especially salient with in the Aamjiwnaang community. Individuals who swore they would never leave this place are leaving. Mothers who have left the reserve to give birth are not returning. As community member and activist Ron Plain articulates: 'Our culture is dying. We have nowhere to *be*.'[14] Play and outdoor activity is highly restricted in this toxic space.

Parks are erected over closed landfills. Limitations to play and outdoor enjoyment have harmful psychological impacts on this resilient community, who appear to be 'living in a bubble' (Luginaah, Smith and Lockridge, 2010). The chemical alert sirens go off weekly, the community is frequently ordered to maintain a 'shelter-in-place'; one never knows if it is a test or a real spill. Regardless, Aamjiwnaang residents are expected to remain indoors, and wait until the potential harm clears and security of life resumes. So they wait.

The reserve is a space that keeps people in *place*. As Razack (2002) discusses, the marginalized body appears almost transparent, forgotten, left behind as a part of earthy debris.[15] The Indigenous body as part of the natural landscape is perceived as an obstruction to industrial progress. This raises important questions: How are people kept in place? What contested meanings are derived from this space? Colonization and empire building are inextricably linked to space. During the initial years of settler contact, many colonial explorers thought of space as an empty concept, something to be filled. As a result of the colonial perpetuation of the notion of *terra nullius* – empty land – Indigenous peoples are not seen as civilized masters of the land (Alfred, 2009). Consequently, they are reduced by the White settler society as natural savages to be controlled and contained through confinement in the reserve system. This (mis)conception of land as an empty space has permitted, and continues to permit its colonization (Taussig, 1987). *Terra nullius* produces an 'empty zone' or space to be fortified through state boundaries. The pre-contact notion of *terra nullius* historically justified European settlement and movement of Indigenous peoples onto reserves cut off from necessary resources (Razack, 2002). Today it justifies filling these spaces with toxic waste.

Meanings derived in space reveal power relations. It is a powerful act to name, claim and blame in (non)spaces. Foucault articulates how power relations are revealed across space, as subjects are produced (Crampton and Eldon, 2007). Space is fundamental to the exercise of power. Bodies, individuals, citizens – delineated as abject or well – become ranked, classed and segregated across space. As discussed in the documentary *Toxic Trespass*, location is perhaps the 'greatest carcinogen' infiltrating the body (Cohen, 2007). Foucault explored the physical segregation of marginal populations in spaces: asylums, prisons and clinics. His institutional work in this respect provides evidence of the exclusionary practices embedded within the modern liberal state. Later work on biopolitics and biopower reveal how power no longer takes shape by the hand of a sovereign state authority; rather, control and surveillance takes form at the individual level of the body, thorough micro-practices of responsibilization and self-governance (Rabinow and Rose, 2003; Orsini, 2007; Rose, 2007). Limited agency, freedom and mobility ensue.

Time, progress and movement have different meanings on reserves across Canada. Reserves – spaces – are highly demarcated, delineated and structured, each with their own particular colonial history. As Razack (2002) argues, the marginalized space, a liminal space, is the border between 'civilized' (i.e. the city) and 'primitive' (i.e. the reserve) space. The civilized only appear in these chaotic zones to assist the vulnerable towards modernity, justifying a 'moral topography' of chaos, where the privileged White people come in to justify their own policies (or lack thereof) (Taussig, 1987).

The way in which knowledge about modernity is constructed in this liminal zone is of central concern. A complex historical mapping of bodies and their relationship to space is necessary for a rigorous interrogation of how to understand bodies that have travelled across time. Any mobility, freedom or agency is highly demarcated by the colonial delineations of the reserve. Mobility and freedom of the body is not the same in a liminal zone as it is in a privileged space. Following Razack, this case reveals the ways in which freedom of mobility is associated with privilege. Individuals situated on reserve often lack the resources, means or desire to leave. Rather, they must form resistances to their environment through an appropriation of responsible self-monitoring practices. While the movement and mobility of capitalism and market possibilities in the chemical valley require endless expansion, this possibility continuously drips with the threat of toxicity and fatality.[16] Modern discourse creates the 'need' for development, expansion and movement, while simultaneously trapping communities like Aamjiwnaang in place.

Conclusion: Fleshing out a politics of place

Politics occurs in and on the flesh. The flesh in this story has symbolic meaning, as the site for which invisible, unknown harm manifests. Moreover, the symbolic space of the Aamjiwnaang First Nation reserve has been filled with physical and discursive meaning. As a White middle-class female, my location in this symbolic reproduction is an essential one to demarcate and challenge. It is my anticipation that by questioning how spaces came to be, and tracing what meanings they produce and what produces those meanings, I will contribute to the discursive project of creating possibilities for difference, identity and voice, as a means to unsettle problematic everyday risk experiences facing communities such as the Aamjiwnaang First Nation, which is revealing of the ways in which some Canadians are rendered more insecure than others.

Through a situated, place-based analysis of the (in)security of everyday life, this discussion underscores the importance of engaging in conversations about politics at the local/global interface. In this chapter, I have argued that bodies operate at the local/global interface, as an ultimate site of (in)security. By discussing bodies at this interface of the local/global, where the body-boundaries become increasingly blurry, and where environments form corporeality from within, I sought to demonstrate how some bodies are rendered more vulnerable than others through the persistence of a kind of toxic colonialism.

Bodies, I suggest are 'on the line' at the nexus between the local and global, the secure and insecure. While some bodies are on the frontlines, sooner or later the risks associated with this social positioning catches up with the producers and immediate beneficiaries of industrial production. Risks in this respect, display a kind of 'boomerang effect' through their diffusion (Beck, 1986). These seemingly latent, dormant externalities of production and extraction render even the most secure bodies insecure through the creep of environmental illnesses, of which many etiologies remain unknown, unscientific and unproven. Consequently, we must begin to reimagine the ways in which our bodies relate to environments. Future discussion of environmental violence, security and harm will benefit from a rigorous examination of global political ecology, which takes into consideration the multifaceted ways in which the lines between bodies and environments increasingly coalesce (Patterson, 1996; Peet, Robbins and Watts, 2011). A critical global political ecology approach to studies of (in)security turns away from an overemphasis on the role of the nation state to look at broader human-nature connections across a variety of political scales. The site of utmost importance in this context is the human body; increasingly, all of our bodies are on the line.

Notes

1. This chapter is a work-in-progress, based upon research assistance and field-work for Dr Dayna Scott, who is conducting an SSHRC-funded project titled *Constructions of Risk and Cause at the Local/Global Interface: Environmental Justice for the Aamjiwnaang*. These sentiments from the community are also expressed in a variety of documentaries and news articles. See, for example, M. Peterson (2009), *Men's Health Magazine*. http://www.menshealth.com/men/health/other-diseases-ailments/industrial-pollution-health-hazards/article/442a7febcb6c4210vgnvcm10000030281eac (accessed on 28 January 2010).
2. Following from the language in the 1982 Constitution of Canada, I use the term 'aboriginal' to refer to peoples of 'Indian', First Nations, Inuit and Métis descent. I also use the term 'Indigenous' to refer to First Nations, Metis and Inuit peoples of Canada, in line with the language used by Indigenous scholars Jeff Corntassel and Taiaike Alfred. When quoting an author, or speaking about a specific community, we will make attempt to use the term appropriate to that community.
3. Thanks to Jenny Vermilyea for sharing her reflections on 'translocal' sites of security.
4. See, for example, Amoore (2006) and Muller (2004) for an extensive discussion of biometrics and bodies at the border.

5. The concept of place has garnered considerable interest in environmental justice and health geography literature. See, for example, Fischer and Hajer (1999), Harvey (1996), Torgerson (1999), Kroll-Smith, Brown and Gunter (2000), MacIntyre, Ellaway and Cummins (2002), Cresswell (2004), Brown (2007), Gattrell and Elliott (2008) and Agyeman et al. (2009). Much of the environmental (in)justice literature seeks to understand the societal effects of environmental racism, equity and justice, in terms of institutional rules, regulations and policies that result in the disproportionate exposure of toxic and hazardous waste (e.g. Bryant et al., 1995). Where these injustices occur have particular locations, which produce meanings of place. Specifically, the concept of place seeks to explore differential health impacts of physical (spatial) environments as a social, or 'environmental (in)justice' issue, as a determinant of health (see editorial, *Health & Place*, 2007).
6. Drawing from Elizabeth Grosz, I understand this concept to refer to the experience of the body as a continuous process of knowledge production, emanating from the very real, tangible physicality of the body. This *includes* emotional – psychosomatic – and organic or physical health experiences (see Grosz, 1994).
7. In response to the 2005 article in *Environmental Health Perspectives*, the Aamjiwnaang First Nation conducted a Community Health Study with the assistance of the Occupational Health Clinic for Ontario Workers, in Sarnia. These results were published by the 2007 Ecojustice report, *Exposing Canada's Chemical Valley*.
8. This presents the significant challenge of proving 'general population-based trends' through epidemiological research vis-à-vis local embodied knowledge and experience.
9. It is important to recall that humans are animals as well. In addition, many Indigenous cultures value the relationship between human and animal health as inherently linked (see Smith, 2005).
10. Interview with Ada Lockridge for Dr Dayna Scott, 20 January 2010.
11. An intersectional analysis of gender, development and the environmental impacts of uranium production on Indigenous communities has also been discussed by John O'Neil, Elias and Yassi (1998) in *Situating Resistance in Fields of Resistance: Aboriginal Women and Environmentalism*. This article looks at the conflicting interpretations of the residents of Wollaston Lake in Northern Saskatchewan and the proximity of uranium development.
12. Interviews with Ron Plain, 18 January 2001 and Ada Lockridge, 20 January 2010 for Dr Dayna Scott.
13. Interviews with Ron Plain, 18 January 2010 and Ada Lockridge, 20 January 2010 for Dr Dayna Scott.
14. Interviews with Ron Plain, 18 January 2010 and Ada Lockridge, 20 January 2010 for Dr Dayna Scott.
15. Making this image strikingly clear, one simply has to tour the perimeter of the Aamjiwnaang First Nation reserve in order to see landfills, disposal sites and sewage treatment facilities, in addition to the numerous chemical facilities surrounding the small space this First Nation is left with from their initial treaty agreements. In fact, conversations with residents reveal the history of repeated dumping of toxic waste on land that was already 'wasted' through Indigenous occupation. Field notes from 20 January 2010 for Dr Dayna Scott.

16. Thanks to Jen Bagelman for this notion of 'dripping with fatality' (26 January 2010).

References

Agyeman. J., P. Cole, R. Haluza-Delay and P. O'Riley, eds, 2009. *Speaking for Ourselves: Environmental Justice in Canada*. Vancouver: UBC Press.
Alfred, T., 2009. *Peace, Power, Righteousness: An Indigenous Manifesto*. Oxford University Press.
Amoore, L., 2006. 'Biometric Borders: Governing Mobilities in the War on Terror'. *Political Geography* 25, 336–51.
Amoore, L., & de Goede, M. (2008). Transactions After 9/11: The Banal Face of the Preemptive Strike. *Transactions of the Institute of British Geographers*, 33 (2), 173–185.
Aradau, C. (2007). Law transformed: Guantanamo and the 'other' exception. *Third World Quarterly*, 28 (3), 489–501.
Aradau, C., & van Munster, R. (2007). Governing terrorism through risk: Taking precautions, (un)knowing the future. *European Journal of International Relations*, 13 (1), 89–115.
Beck, U., 1986. *Risk Society*. London: Sage.
Bigo, D. (2006). Security, Exception, Ban and Surveillance. In D. Lyon, *Theorizing Surveillance, the Panopticon and Beyond* (pp. 46–68). Kingston: Willan Publishing.
Broeders, D. (2007). The new digital borders of Europe. EU databases and the surveillance of irregular migrants. *International Sociology*, 22 (1), 71–92.
Brown, P. (2007). *Toxic Exposures: Contested Illnesses and the Environmental Health Movement*. New York: Columbia University Press.
Bryant, B. (1995). *Environmental Justice: Issues, Policies, Solutions*. Washington: Island University Press.
Bullard, R. (1993). *Confronting Environmental Racism: Voices from the Grassroots*. Boston: South End Press.
CBC, 2007. *Toxic Trespass*. Ottawa: National Film Board of Canada.
CBC, 2008. *The Disappearing Male*. Available at http://www.cbc.ca/documentaries/doczone/2008/disappearingmale/. (accessed on 14 February 2010).
Colborn, T., D. Dumsanoski and J. Peterson Myers, 1997. *Our Stolen Future*. New York: Dutton. Available at http://www.ourstolenfuture.org/ (accessed on 9 March 2009).
Cohen, B. (Director). (2007). *Toxic Trespass* [Motion Picture]. National Film Board of Canada.
Colborn, T. (2009, April 27). EPA's New Pesticide Testing is Outdated. *Scientific American*.
Colborn, T., Dumanoski, D., & Peter Myers, J. (1997). *Our Stolen Future: Are We Threatening Our Fertility?* New York: Dutton.
Crampton, J. W. and S. Eldon, eds, 2007. *Space, Knowledge and Power: Foucault and Geography*. Burlington: Ashgate.
Crenson, M., 2005. 'Canadian Natives Blame Toxins for Fewer Sons'. *The Associated Press*. 19 December 2005. Available at http://www.msnbc.msn.com/id/10531498/from/RS.1/ (accessed on 11 February 2010).

Crenshaw, K. (1991). Mapping the Margins: Intersectionality, Identity Politics and Violence Against Women of Colour. *Stanford Law Review,* 43 (6), 1241–1299.
Cresswell, T. (2004). *Place: A Short Introduction.* Oxford: Wiley-Blackwell.
CTV News, 2005. 'Pollution on Native Reservation is Probed, 18 December. Available at http://www.ctv.ca/servlet/ArticleNews/story/CTVNews/20051218/reserve_pollution_051218. (accessed on 8 January 2012).
Damstra, T., S. Barlow, A. Bergman, R. Kavlock and G. Van Der Kraak, 2002. *Global Assessment of the State-of-the-Science of Endocrine Disruptors.* International Programme on Chemical Safety. WHO/PCS/EDC/02.2. Geneva, Switzerland: World Health Organisation. Available at http://www.who.int/ipcs/publications/endocrine_disruptors/en/japan_workshop_report.pdf. (accessed on 10 February 2010).
Ecojustice, 2007. *Exposing Canada's Chemical Valley,* Toronto: Ecojustice. Available at http://www.ecojustice.ca/publications/reports/report-exposing-canadas-chemical-valley/attachment. (accessed on 10 February 2010).
Ecojustice, 2009. 'Chemical Valley Residents Demand New Law for Ontario's Pollution Hot Spots'. Available at http://www.ecojustice.ca/media-centre/press-releases/chemical-valley-residents-demand-new-law-for-ontarios-pollution-hot-spots?searchterm=hotspots. (accessed on 18 January 2010).
Ecojustice Press Release, 2008. 'Aamjiwnaang Bucket Brigade Discovers Alarming Levels of Toxic Chemicals in Sarnia'. Available at http://www.Ecojustice.ca/media-centre/press-releases/aamjiwnaang-bucket-brigade-discovers-alarming-levels-of-toxic-chemicals-in-sarnia. (accessed on 20 February 2010).
Foucault, M. (trans. J. Miskoweic), 1986. 'Of Other Spaces'. *Diacritics* 16(1): 22–7.
Fischer, F., & Hajer, M. A. (1999). *Living With Nature: Environmental Politics as Cultural Discourse.* Oxford: Oxford University Press.
Gattrell, A. C. and S. J. Elliot, 2008. *Geographies of Health: An Introduction.* Oxford: Blackwell.
Giddens, A., 1990. *The Consequences of Modernity.* Cambridge: Polity Press.
Grosz, E. (1994). *Volatile Bodies: Toward a Corporeal Feminism.* Bloomington: Indiana University Press.
Hankivsky, O., & Christofferson, A. (2008). Intersectionality and the Determinants of Health: A Canadian Perspective. *Critical Public Health ,* 8 (3), 271–283.
Harvey, D. (1996). *Justice, Nature and the Geography of Difference.* Malden: Blackwell Publishers Ltd.
Kavanagh, R. J., G. C. Balch, J. Kiparissis, A. J. Niimi, J. Sherry, C. Tinson and C. D. Metcalfe, 2004. 'Endocrine Disruption and Altered Gonadal Development in White Perch (*Morone Americana*) from the Lower Great Lakes Region'. *Environmental Health Perspectives* 112(8): 898–902.
Kelm, M.-E. (1998). *Colonizing Bodies: Aboriginal Health and Healing in British Columbia 1900–1950.* Vancouver: UBC Press.
Kroll-Smith, S. and J. Kelley, 2008. 'Environments, Bodies and the Cultural Imaginary: Imagining Ecological Impairment'. In P. Moss and K. Teghtsoonian, eds, *Contesting Illness: Processes and Practices.* Toronto: University of Toronto Press, 304–22.
Kroll-Smith, S., Brown, P., & Gunter, V. J. (2000). *Illness and the Environment: A Reader in Contested Medicine.* New York: New York University Press.

LaDuke, W. (1999). *All Our Relations: Native Struggles for Land and Life*. Cambridge, MA: South End Press.
LaDuke, W. (2005). *Recovering the Sacred: The Power of Naming and Claiming*. Cambridge, MA: South End Press.
LaDuke, W. (2002). *The Winona LaDuke Reader: A Collection of Essential Readings*. Penticton, BC, Canada: Theytus Books.
Legislative Assembly of Ontario, 2009. Bill 167 *Toxics Reduction Act*. Available at http://www.ontla.on.ca/web/bills/bills_detail.do?locale=en&BillID=2168. (accessed on 14 January 2011).
Luginaah, I., K. Smith, A. Lockridge, 2010. 'Surrounded by Chemical Valley and "Living in a Bubble": The Case of the Aamjiwnaang First Nation, Ontario'. *Journal of Environmental Planning and Management* 53(3): 353–70.
Luginaah, I., Smith, K., & Lockridge, A. (2010). Surrounded by Chemical Valley and "Living in a Bubble": The Case of the Aamjiwnaang First Nation, Ontario. *Journal of Environmental Planning and Management, 53* (3), 353–370.
Luke, T., 2000. 'Rethinking Technoscience in Risk Society: Toxicity as Textuality'. In R. Hofrichter, ed., *Reclaiming the Environmental Debate: The Policies of Health in a Toxic Culture*. Cambridge, MA: The MIT Press, 239–56.
Mackenzie, C. A., A. Lockridge and M. Keith, 2005. 'Declining Sex Ratio in a First Nations Community'. *Environmental Health Perspectives* 113(10): 1295–1298.
MacIntyre, S., Ellaway, A., & Cummins, S. (2002). Place effects on health: how can we conceptualise, operationalise and measure them? *Social Science & Medicine, 55*, 125–139.
Maracle, L. (1996). *I am Woman. A Native Perspective on Sociology and Feminism,* . Vancouver: Press Gang Publishers.
Monture-Angus, P. (1995). *Thunder in my Soul: A Mohawk Woman Speaks*. Halifax: Fernwood Publishing.
Morrow, M., Hankivsky, O., & Varcoe, C. (2007). *Women's Health in Canada: Critical Perspectives on Theory and Policy*. Toronto: University of Toronto Press.
Muller, B. (2004). (Dis)Qualified Bodies: Securitization, Citizenship and 'Identity Management. *Citizenship Studies, 8* (3), 279–294.
O'Neil, J., Elias, B. D., & Yassi, A. (1998). Situating Resistance in Fields of Resistance: Aboriginal Women and Environmentalism. In M. Lock, & P. Kaufert, *Pragmatic Women and Body Politics* (pp. 260–286). Cambridge: Cambridge University Press.
Orsini, M. (2007). Discourses in Distress: From 'Health Promotion' to 'Population Health' to 'You are Responsible for Your Own Health''. In M. O. Smith, *Critical Policy Studies* (pp. 347–363). Vancouver: UBC Press.
Parr, J., 2006. 'Smells Like? Sources of Uncertainty in the History of the Great Lakes Environment'. *Environmental History* 11(2): 269–99.
Patterson, M., 1996. 'Green Politics'. In S. Burchill & A. Linklater, eds, *Theories of International Relations*, 2nd Edition. New York: Palgrave Macmillan, 277–307.
Petryna, A., 2006. *A Life Exposed: Biological Citizens After Chernobyl*. Princeton: Princeton University Press.
Peet, R., Robbins, P & Watts, M.J., eds. (2011) *Global Political Ecology*. London and New York: Routledge.
Petersen, M. (2009). *Men's Health Magazine (Online)*. Retrieved January 28, 2010, from http://www.menshealth.com/men/health/other-diseases-ailments/

industrial-pollution-health-hazards/article/442a7febcb6c4210vgnvcm100000 30281eac

Poirier, J., 2008. 'Push for Stronger Emission Controls: Leading Scientists Gather at Local Health Symposium to Discuss Impact of Pollution on Aamjiwnaang Residents'. *Sarnia Observer.* 27 March 2008. Available at http://www.theobserver.ca/ArticleDisplay.aspx?e=960350&archive=true. (accessed on 8 January 2012).

Rabinow, P., & Rose, N. (2003). *The Essential Foucault.* New York: The New Press.

Razack, S., 2002. *Race, Space and the Law.* Toronto: Between the Lines.

Rose, N., 2007. *The Politics of Life Itself.* Princeton: Princeton University Press.

Scott, D., 2008. 'Confronting Chronic Pollution: A Socio-Legal Analysis of Risk and Precaution'. *Osgoode Hall Law Journal* 46(2): 293–343.

Scott, D., 2009. 'Gender-Benders: Sex and Law in the Constitution of Polluted Bodies'. *Feminist Legal Studies* 18(1): 241–65.

Simpson, L., 2006. 'Birthing as an Indigenous Resurgence: Decolonizing our Pregnancy and Birthing Ceremonies'. In M. D. Levell-Harvard, ed., *Until Our Hearts are on the Ground: Aboriginal Mothering, Oppression, Resistance and Rebirth.* Toronto: Demeter Press, 25–33.

Smith, A., 2005. *Conquest: Sexual Violence and the American Indian Genocide.* Cambridge: South End Press.

Soja, E., 1996. *Thirdspace: Journeys to Los Angeles and Other Real and Imagined Places.* Cambridge: Blackwell.

Taussig, M., 1987. *Shamanism, Colonialism and the Wild Man: A Study in Terror and Healing.* Chicago: Chicago University Press.

Torgerson, D. (1999). *The Promise of Green Politics.* Durham: Duke University Press.

Weisskopf, M. G., H. A. Anderson and L. P. Hanrahan, 2003. 'Decreased Sex Ratio Following Maternal Exposure to Polychlorinated Biphenyls from Contaminated Great Lakes Sport-Caught Fish: A Retrospective Cohort Study'. *Environmental Health: A Global Access Source.* 2(2) (March): 1–14. Available at http://www.ehjournal.net/content/2/1/2 (accessed on 8 January 2012).

Afterword: Ecoviolence, Security, Geopolitics

Simon Dalby

Invoking security is easy; dealing with the finer points of what it means, who is insecure why and where is much more difficult. As the chapters in this volume suggest it is even more so when notions of environment are linked to matters of security, conflict and violence. In the face of repeated invocations of environmental dangers, and the potential for conflict over water, food and, most recently, climate, these matters deserve careful attention from scholars. Careful attention requires wariness of both media enthusiasms for hot topics, as well as state agendas for both security and development.

The most obvious category of all, that of environment, turns out to be at least as tricky as security. All of which is compounded by the vagaries of communication in contemporary culture. In short as these chapters attest in various ways, scholars face a series of complicated puzzles when addressing the topic of environmental security. As climate change accelerates, all these will become more pressing issues; clarifying which claims make sense in all this is clearly a useful analytical exercise. Careful critique is going to be a very important part of the intellectual response to events in the coming decades. But that alone now is not enough – communicating clearly to policymakers and the public matters too, although neither task will be easy in the coming decades.

In particular all the chapters in this volume pose the question of how this discussion should be appropriately contextualized. 'Environment' is a contextual term, one that refers to things that surround the entity that is 'environed'. But quite what the entity that is in need of securing against potential threats is is not at all clear in much of the debate about environmental security. Sometimes it is environment understood as a natural entity that needs to be protected against the depredations of human activity. But 'natural' environments and the marginal peoples who live in them outside the Northern metropoles are also frequently understood as the security threat that needs attention. In turn those who would protect environments may be understood as the threat if their activities challenge the prerogatives of the industry that provides all the products that now make metropolitan life liveable. Now, most recently, climate is that which needs to be secured in this latest twist on a now very persistent discourse of environmental danger.

Peter Stoett offers some useful clarifications in his chapter (Chapter 2) not least pointing to just how highly contested notions of justice and violence are, and hence how important it is to bring some analytical rigour to matters of violence attributed to environmental change. His normative focus on what is important in terms of justice rather than security is a useful corrective to much of the literature that invokes 'security' as the ultimate desideratum without the necessary reflection on who invokes the term in what circumstances and to what effect. Likewise his concern to distance serious scholarship from Malthusian prejudices is also important in focusing attention on the specifics of who suffers where and when, and in the process undercutting the easy invocations of a naturally violent world as an excuse for inaction in the face of avoidable harm.

At the very biggest scale the links between war and environment have been reinvented of late in the discussion of climate security. As Chris Russill (Chapter 3) makes clear, the discussions of tipping points and the fears of abrupt climate change have infused the debate with both urgency and the frisson of imminent apocalyptic disruptions. All of which garners attention, but given the huge uncertainties makes policy decisions difficult. His emphasis on the roots of all this discourse in 'big science' and the congruence of geophysical concerns with the global managerial aspirations of security agencies is a useful corrective to simple assumptions that any of this has much to do with environmentalism as traditionally understood. This literally is geopolitics, the politics of geology, of planet management and the making of possible futures for particular human configurations. If the US military is charged with maintaining some notion of political order as climate change accelerates, then the possibilities of violence mount, but not as a result of marginal peoples threatening civilization, but as an attempt to reimpose the order that caused the instabilities in the first place.

What kind of stability might be imposed, and how the security assumptions of Northern or developed states shape the policy discourse is Wilfrid Greaves' concern (Chapter 4). The discussion of human security is shaped by assumptions of what a normal state is and a uniform norm of population behaviour is implicitly assumed. But within Northern states there are numerous injustices and marginal peoples who are insecure in many ways. This matters not just within Northern states but also when such notions of human security are used as the template for judgement in justifying international 'interventions' under the rubric of the responsibility to protect or similar formulations where sovereignty is rendered contingent upon certain externally defined norms of political behaviour. It is not a lengthy extension of the argument to use environmental concerns to justify interventions in the South too. When linked to dubious arguments that Darfur among other cases are climate wars or that massive migrations of vulnerable peoples are a security threat to Northern states such formulations themselves may be the danger!

Larry Swatuk (Chapter 5) invokes Peter Stoett's focus on justice to remind readers that postcolonial states, despite their invocations of national self-determination or promises of development, may not be any guarantee against depredations on the part of elites. Injustice is in part a legacy of the colonial encounter undoubtedly, but invoking national security has frequently, in the African case, been a matter of ensuring the well-being of political elites in these states, rather than the general welfare of the population. A key point here is that the colonial heritage is one of extraction of resources, both agricultural as well as mineral, fuel and forest products, in a commercial economy that is frequently disconnected from the lived economic realities of subsistence that support the rural poor. Getting this political economy clearly in focus would help greatly in much of the discussion of Africa and adaptation to climate change. Not least this would help focus attention on more than the modernization of the commercial economy. Focusing on how property relations work with regard to subsistence patterns, paying attention to the gendered divisions of production and how monocultures are frequently more of a problem than a solution in the face of environmental change will give much greater analytical purchase on matters that make people rather than state elites insecure.

Violence and failures of governance are part of the problem too. As Shelley Whitman makes painfully clear in her analysis of the Democratic Republic of the Congo (Chapter 7) and the prevalence of sexual violence in the war zone in its eastern provinces, human insecurity is a problem on the large scale there. But the struggles to control the revenue from coltan are not about environmental change or Malthusian scarcities. They are much more about struggles over valuable minerals and the interconnections between metropolitan consumption and peripheral sources of resources. She concludes her chapter with policy implications that suggest controlling trade, and in particular the illegal trade in resources, rather than simply adding to the violence by military interventions. Once again the solution to violence isn't more violence, but political measures designed to undercut the economic forces that drive the conflict.

Shane Mulligan's contribution to this volume (Chapter 8) picks up the theme of resources but does so with a discussion of another one of the major potential security threats to the future: that of peak oil. The assumptions that petroleum production will peak in the near future, or perhaps already has in fact reached its peak, drive a discussion of resource shortages and the potential that this will have for future conflict. The dominant tropes of this discussion replay the realist assumptions of inevitable rivalry among great powers, and the possibilities of conflict as states struggle for access to fuel needed to run their societies. But Mulligan's concern is with the failure of states to pay attention to the looming dangers of fuel shortages. In this his concerns ironically match those of the scientists and security analysts concerned to raise the alarm concerning potentially dangerous tipping points in the climate system. Ironic, because if peak oil had in fact arrived back in the 1970s when the OPEC crisis led to alarms about fuel shortages, and economies had responded by building an energy infrastructure much less dependent fossil fuels, we would probably not be discussing climate security now at all.

A further irony follows in Peter Arthur's contribution (Chapter 6) that is once again concerned with the matter of resource wars. Peak oil drives up petroleum prices and that in turn encourages further exploration and development in regions where petroleum is either difficult to access or where the political circumstances make reliable exploration and development difficult. The possibilities of further development in Ghana are the particular focus in this contribution but the larger pattern of African petroleum production suggests that policies to improve governance are essential if the violence and political problems related to resources exploitation are to be avoided in the future. Once again the question of who precisely is insecure and what modes of security are being invoked to protect what kind of political order are unavoidable. One of the consistent findings in the literature on conflict and environment has been that governance is key to the whole issue. Once again this is a matter of the political economy of petroleum much more than it is something environmental, at least in the traditional sense of rural matters, wildlife protection and pollution control. While concerns over future climate change frequently point to vulnerable populations in Africa as potential causes of violence, it seems that the industrial infrastructure that causes climate change is more immediately threatening to many across the continent.

In a useful corrective to the normal geographical specification of environmental violence as something that originates in the underdeveloped parts of the world, Philippe Le Billon and Angela Carter turn their attention to the politics of Canadian tar sands (Chapter 9). Here the Canadian state follows the pattern of supporting the industry, and making the security of this mode of industrial development the top priority. Opponents of the exploitation of these bitumen deposits are then seen as the security problem, political deviants or criminals who can be dealt with harshly when understood as a security threat. As Le Billon and Carter make clear, the discussion of the Canadian tar sands brings to a head the contradictions between energy security and environmental security. This especially dirty and energy-intensive production of petroleum uses huge quantities of gas and water to turn bitumen into the very fuel that is making climate change a problem. In thermodynamic terms it makes no sense to use relatively clean burning natural gas to turn rocks into gasoline. But market logics tied into the infrastructure of the oil industry in North America produce this destruction on a massive scale. What then is being secured? Despite the relentless public relations campaigns to reassure everyone that the petroleum companies are in fact environmentally responsible, it seems that conventional notions of environment are most definitely not what is being secured in this case.

In the face of such political power working to enhance environmental insecurity in many ways, Chris Arsenault (Chapter 10) poses the question of the politics of resistance and the possibilities of such actions as sabotage of facilities that are both clearly an environmental hazard and ones that defy local political opinion. The politics of who decides what happens in particular places once again poses the question of what kind of security and what kind of human being is being secured in all this. It also, as Arsenault so bluntly puts, confronts the issue of Canada supposedly not being a risky investment location vulnerable to either resource wars or political instabilities. Hence the large effort on the part of the British Columbia provincial apparatus to prevent sabotage of oil infrastructure despite the apparently cavalier approach the industry has to hydrogen sulphide and other hazards. Does local democracy count in resource-rich environments? As pressure mounts in the period of peak oil, such confrontations can be expected to increase and in the process the questions Peter Stoett raises about justice and violence will emerge repeatedly.

But these are not, as Sarah Wiebe (Chapter 11) reminds us, a new matter of environmental politics. Dirty industrial facilities have frequently been placed where political opposition and real estate prices are lowest. There is a geography to environmental insecurities that has a long and particularly painful history on aboriginal lands and among poor and marginal populations whose places are most vulnerable to encroachment by industries and resources extractions. But the significance of her engagement with First Nations peoples in the Canadian context adds an important historical dimension to the discussion of environmental violence. Much of the story of what is being secured and how this happens is tied into the history of the expansion of European power in the processes of empire building and conquest. These are all about providing new resources for the expanding metropolitan economies. Canada's history is of displacement and conquest related to the extraction of resources. Resistance to these processes has a long history too, and the struggles of contemporary First Nations against the despoliation of their places has to be understood in the longer-term trajectory of economic expansion, a process that is now encapsulated in the term 'globalization'.

The violent processes of development are about the transformation of environments and about the displacements of people in the way. That these peoples resist isn't surprising, although whether they are labelled as criminals, poachers, deviants or security threats may matter very considerably in terms of the specific processes states use to deal with them. These processes are now ubiquitous, and recognizing that struggles over many environments are not new is made easier by reading the chapters in this volume. But how these are framed matters in the politics of the coming decades. What kind of security is invoked and who is portrayed as a threat will be crucial to how politics plays out in the near future.

How these discussions play out in Canada will be particularly interesting, and relevant to the larger global patterns that are unfolding. Canada is both a metropolitan power and a resource periphery. It is both a consumer of fossil fuels on a large scale and a producer too. The uneven geographies of this are clear in the contributions to this volume. Climate change matters greatly in the Canadian north and here too resource companies are salivating over the possibilities that may open up as the ice recedes in the Arctic. Who decides how development is done and how the local peoples adapt are key to the future of Canada. What gets secured matters greatly.

The environmental transformations of the planet at the largest scale loom over all this discussion, and once again Canada is at the forefront because of its enthusiastic investment in the tar sands and the steadfast refusal to get serious about policies to reduce greenhouse gas emissions. What is being secured here is the mode of economy dependent on resource extraction, not one designed to work towards keeping the atmospheric composition within the range that made human civilization possible in the first place. The implications of all this are quite startling, and for those who value the kind of political order promised by liberal democracies, worrisome indeed. Not least because as the chapters in this volume make clear, the hidden consequences of the consumption practices of the current versions of these democracies have so many environmental consequences.

What is at stake is nothing less than what kind of planet should be secured. Will security be, as Russill's chilling discussion of the geophysical premises of climate security discussions suggests, an attempt to use force to perpetuate the political order that has, through its fossil fuel use, set climate change in motion? Or will security be an attempt, as Stoett hopes, to engage in a much larger conversation about justice, and the obligations of the present generation to other peoples and future generations to live in ways that keep political and environmental options open for the future? Nothing less is at stake in these discussions. Much new thinking is needed urgently, about how we understand security and environment as well as how we organize politically to change the economic systems that make our lives possible precisely by changing environments, both 'ours' directly and 'theirs' indirectly.

Index

Aamjiwnaang First Nations, 215ff
Aboriginal, 70
  in Nunavut, 73
  and domestic violence, 76
  health, 215ff
Africa, 83, 239
  kingdoms in, 93
  water issues in, 84
  poverty, 86
agriculture, 91–2
Anthropocene, 3
apartheid, 1
Arctic, 73, 242
Athabasca River, 172
Atta Mills, John, 120

Ban Ki-Moon, 144
Barnett, Jon, 5
Beck, Ulrich, 215
bioapartheid, 25
biopolitics, 229
Blair, Tony, 45–6
bombing, 172, 180, 181, 197, 207
Booth, Ken, 3
borders, 216
boundaries, 216
British Columbia, 176
  oil and gas industry in, 194, 196

Campbell, Gordon, 194, 204
Canada, 20, 194ff, 242
carbon sequestration, 186
China, 94, 112, 143, 184
clean energy dialogue, 185
climate change, 40, 241
  and African agriculture, 92
  and catastrophy, 40
  and epistemological hierarchy, 41
  and peak oil, 156
  as a public health issue, 40
climate justice, 25

climate security, 33
  discourse, 33, 54
  and IPCC, 55
  and war (*see also*, war), 33–4
  tipping points, 35, 54
Colombia, 200
colonialism, 223, 229, 239
  gendered effects of, 224
Comer, Gary, 49
conflict, 83
  and sexual violence, 135–7
  discourses of, 84
  environmental, 23, 27
  in the DRC, 129–33
  social, 195
  violent, 20, 26
  water wars (*see also*, war), 85
  youth bulge and, 83
consumption, 239
counter-terrorism (*see also*, terrorism), 181
Cox, Robert, 20
critical environmental security (*see also* environmental security), 5–6

Dalby, Simon, 3
Darfur, 239
Democratic Republic of Congo (DRC), 10, 128ff
democracy, 122, 241, 243
  and democratic governance, 122–4
  in the DRC, 128
deregulation, 180
discourse, 230, 238
domestic terrorism (*see also*, terrorism), 198
Dutch disease, 115

ecological limits, 165
eco-terrorism (*see also*, terrorism), 182, 187
eco-violence, 17, 224–5, 231

endochrine disruption, 218–19
EnCana, 194ff
energy security, 160, 180, 181, 183, 241
environment, 3
  and war (see also, war), 238
  as a security issue, 3
  environmental change, 2
  and violent conflict, 2
environmental injustice, 22
  definition of, 22
  normative platform for, 26
environmental justice, 5, 10
  and race, 71–2
  and structural violence, 84
  and water, 101
  definition of, 22, 23
  global, 25
environmental non-governmental organizations (ENGOs), 175, 221
environmental security, 1, 3, 5, 8, 16, 171
  and energy, 185
  and political power, 241
  and violent conflict, 1
  as state security, 8
  geography of insecurity and, 241
  levels of analysis problem, 8
environmental stress, 199
environmental violence, 187
Extractive Industries Transparency Initiative, 115–17
ExxonMobil, 112

Flanagan, Tom, 201
food insecurity, 91
Foucault, Michel, 228

Galtung, Johan, 20, 21
gas
  companies, 194, 205–7
  greenhouse emissions, 199
  industry, 194
  installations, 193
  pipeline, 197
  sour, 194, 197, 207
genocide, 138
geopolitics, 238
Ghana, 108ff, 240

Ghana Petroleum Regulatory Authority (GPRA), 119
Global South, 11
governance (see also, democracy), 240
Greenpeace, 177

Harper, Stephen, 173, 183, 184, 195
hazards, 72
Homer-Dixon, Thomas, 2
humanitarianism, 27
human rights, 24
  and water, 86
human security, 2, 3, 4, 25, 26
  and state capacity, 165
  and state centrism, 64
  theory of, 64–70
hydraulic mission, 86
  and empire, 94
hydropolitics, 85

identity, 67, 207
  and post-colonial history, 71
  and security, 68
India, 143, 184
industrial development, 75
inequality, 200
insecurity (see also, security), 5, 74, 230
  and environment, 5
  multiple forms of, 74
  physical, 76–7
  societal, 77
integrated water resources management (IWRM), 89
International Criminal Court (ICC), 144
International Energy Agency, 156
Intergovernmental Panel on Climate Change (IPCC), 35
intersubjectivity, 67
  and aboriginal cultures, 77–8
Iraq, 200

justice (see also, environmental justice), 17

land grab, 93
livelihoods, 9
Lund, Corb, 201–2

Machiavelli, Niccolo, 201
Malthusian (*see also*, neo-Malthusian), 238, 239
marginalization, 238
   and insecurity, 230, 239
Merkel, Angela, 51
modernization, 90, 94, 171
   environmental, 171
moral agency, 17

Namibia, 6
neo-Malthusian (*see also*, Malthusian), 17
Nigeria, 200
Nile Basin Initiative (NBI), 99–100
Nile River, 95
   agreement, 98
   and infrastructure development, 99
non-compliance, 202
non-dominance, 68
   in Canada, 70
   and aboriginal people, 71
Non-Governmental Organizations (NGOs), 175
North American Free Trade Agreement (NAFTA), 184
Norway, 113–14

Obama, Barack, 183, 184
oil (*see also*, peak oil), 108
   and economic development, 112–13
   and Ghana, 108
   and MNCs in Africa, 112, 176
   and Norway, 113–14
   and rent-seeking, 124–5
oil sands, 179

Peace River, 193
peak oil, 9, 152, 240
   and climate change, 156
   and global production, 152
   definition of, 153–4
persistent organic pollutants (POPs), 77
petrochemical manufacturing, 217
   and aboriginal health, 218–19
physical harm, 228

place, 225–6, 227–8
   and mobility, 230
political ecology, 2
   definition of, 23
pollution, 220
   chemical, 220
   racialized nature of, 226
   water, 183
privatization, 117
property rights, 201–2, 208, 239

radical environmental targeting (*see also*, terrorism), 181
rape, 137
   in South Kivu, 139
regulation, 221
   international, 222
rent-seeking, 124–5
resource abundance, 2
resource capture, 92
resource curse, 11, 129
   definition of, 109–10
resource dependence, 22
resource wars (*see also*, war), 240
risk, 216
Russia, 143

Sabotage, 197
   and environmental conflict, 199
   and inequality, 200
   of gas installations, 193
Saudi Arabia, 200
Schellnhuber, John, 51–3
securitization, 3, 11, 173
   pipeline, 200
security, 4, 171
   aboriginal health, 215ff
   and development, 95, 237
   and globalization, 242
   dominant discourse of, 10
   economic, 74–5
   energy, 159, 180, 181, 182, 241
   environmental, 1,3, 5, 8, 171, 186, 241
   human, 2, 3, 4, 25, 26, 64–70, 165
   military, 4
   gendered nature of, 66
   state, 4, 10, 231

Index 247

sexual violence, 135–7
SinoHydro, 99
South Kivu, 139
sovereignty, 6
space, 227–8
   marginalized people and, 229
structural violence, 12, 87

tantalum, 10
tar sands (*see also*, oil sands), 155, 170, 243
   aboriginal groups and, 174–5, 177
   and environmental degradation, 183
   opposition to, 172
   securitization of, 182
terra nullius, 229
terrorism,
   counter-, 181
   domestic, 198
   radical environmental targeting and, 181
The End of Suburbia, 161
tipping points, 35, 240
Toxic Trespass, 223, 229
tragedy of the commons, 6
transboundary waters, 88–9

UNCED, 1
UN Security Council, 47, 147
urbanization, 87
   and water security, 102

in Africa, 87
in the Nile Basin, 98
violence, 15
   and environmental stress, 199
   collective, 20
   definition of, 18–19
   eco-, 17, 19, 224–5, 231
   gender-based, 20
   sexual, 135–7
   structural, 12, 87
Vonnegut, Kurt, 152
vulnerability, 22

war
   and environment, 238
   climate security and, 34
   resource, 240
   in Iraq, 159, 163
   water, 85
water
   access to, 90
   agricultural, 90–1
   and conflict, 85–6
   and human rights, 86
   pollution, 183
   scarcity, 85
   security, 9
   wars, 85
World Health Organization (WHO), 18
Wiebo, Ludwig, 198–9, 206

Yemen, 200